# J. ROBERT OPPENHEIMER

PETER GOODCHILD

# J. ROBERT OPPENHEIMER
## Shatterer of Worlds

1981   HOUGHTON MIFFLIN COMPANY BOSTON

To my wife and to Abigail and Hannah for their patience
and understanding, and to my constant companion Katie

First American Edition 1981

Copyright © 1980 by Peter Goodchild

*Library of Congress Cataloging in Publication Data*

Goodchild, Peter.
  J. Robert Oppenheimer : Shatterer of Worlds.
  Published in conjunction with the BBC/WGBH
television series Oppenheimer, produced by Peter
Goodchild and written by Peter Prince.
  Bibliography: p.
  Includes index.
  1. Oppenheimer, J. Robert, 1904-1967. 2. Physicists
—United States—Biography.     I. Title.
QC16.O62G66   1981        530'.092'4   [B]   81-1331
ISBN 0-395-30530-6                      AACR2

Printed in the United States of America

V 10 9 8 7 6 5 4 3 2 1

This book is published in conjunction with the BBC/WGBH television
series *Oppenheimer,* produced by Peter Goodchild; the television
scripts were written by Peter Prince.

Diagrams by Quill

# CONTENTS

# SANTA FE NEW MEXICAN

*The Oldest Newspaper in the Southwest, Founded in 1849*

Vol. 96, No. 213 | MEMBER AUDIT BUREAU OF CIRCULATIONS | SANTA FE, NEW MEXICO, MONDAY, AUGUST 6, 1945 | ASSOCIATED PRESS UNITED PRESS | Price 5c


# Los Alamos Secret Disclosed by Truman

# ATOMIC BOMBS DROP ON JAPAN

By WILL HARRISON

Last week's "Big I" handout from the Governor's office was today still reverberating in educational and legislative circles.

Governor Dempsey was quoted in the news handout as saying:

**"During the 1943 Legislature I sponsored a bill which transferred all of the mineral leasing act funds, except that portion used for free textbooks and the Bureau of Mines, to the school equalization fund."**

The act, in two years, has produced $1,165,173 for the school equalization fund.

Comes today a letter from Sen. J. H. Mullis of Roswell:

**"Before the 1943 Legislature I conferred with J. D. Shinkle, superintendent of the Roswell schools, Col. E. L. Lusk of the New Mexico Military Institute, and Clarence E. Hinkle, president of the Roswell board of education, regarding legislation which would increase the teachers' salaries. We decided on three bills:**

**"1.—To transfer to the school fund, to be used to increase the teachers' salaries, the balance of the Mineral Leasing Act fund, mentioned by Governor Dempsey;**

**"2.—Reducing from 5 per cent to 3 per cent the amount allowed the Bureau of Revenue for collecting the sales tax;**

**"3.—Limiting the Commissioner of Public Lands to $100,000 per year.**

**"I had these bills prepared before the Legislature convened and Governor Dempsey had nothing to do with the preparation of these bills. It is my recollection that Governor Dempsey was opposed to the mineral funds bill because it took that amount from the general fund.**

**"I introduced the bills and with the help of the New Mexico Educational Association secured the passage of the first but the Governor had the other two killed."**

As noted in this space Saturday, the teachers act which the Governor said "I sponsored" was permitted to pass only after the school lobby consented to support a Dempsey measure permitting the transfer of certain surplus administrative funds to the state general fund.

**And after the "I sponsored bill" became law the administration even then tried to grab part of the mineral leasing money for other than school support. Nov. 20, 1943, state records show, Governor Dempsey's State Board of Finance ordered $85,612.16 of mineral leasing money transferred to the general fund. Educational groups put up a fight and on Nov. 29, 1943, the amount was returned on the authority of an Attorney General's opinion**

Although the schools received during the past two years $1,165,173 as a result of the "I sponsored bill" a complete and truthful statement would show that funds almost equalling that amount were taken from the schools by Dempsey sponsored bills in the same Legislature that enacted the mineral leasing funds law.

The transfer law, for which Dempsey traded with the school lobby, in the past two years has taken $357,593.64 for the general fund that would otherwise have gone to schools. ($163,106.71 from surplus in emergency school tax administrative fund in 1945, and $95,000 in 1944; $89,486.93 from surplus in income tax administration fund in 1945, and $30,000 in 1944.)

A total of $514,000 from the Casual Indebtedness fund was transferred to the general fund when no deficit existed. This money, under administrations prior to Dempsey, would have been transferred to the schools as witnessed June 30, 1942, when Gov. John Miles transferred to the schools $145,761.24 of casual deficit funds which were not needed to meet actual deficits.

The transfers under Dempsey of casual deficit money to the state general fund were $262,000 in 1944 and $252,000 in 1945.

**Net Gain $283,580**

The sum of these losses to school funds is $871,593.64, leaving a net gain through the mineral easing funds law of $283,580.

And that gain may be credited to Sen. J. H. Mullis of Roswell and the New Mexico Educational Association who first fought the administration and then traded out with the Governor for the increased revenue.

**$700 STOLEN**

Mrs. Ida M. Glynn, living in one of La Posada's cabins, reported to city police that $700 was stolen from a purse which she had hidden under a pillow in one of her rooms. The money included a $500 bill, police said.

## Deadliest Weapons in World's History Made In Santa Fe Vicinity

Santa Fe learned officially today of a city of 6,000 in its own front yard.

The reverberating announcement of the Los Alamos bomb, with 2,000 times the power of the great Grand-Slammers dropped on Germany, also lifted the secret of the community on the Pajarito Plateau, whose presence Santa Fe has ignored, except in whispers, for more than two years.

Decision to locate the Atomic Bomb Project Laboratory on mesa an hour's drive from Santa Fe, meant that it was necessary for the Army Engineers to construct an entirely new town to house the workers and their families. Primary reason for selection of the isolated site was security.

**Ranch School Site**

When the Army took over the property early in 1943 there were a few buildings which had been occupied by the Los Alamos Ranch School. New buildings began going up at once. Today there are 37 in the main technical area and about 200 others on the property used for the project itself. Three hundred buildings containing 620 family units, also were constructed, as well as military barracks, hospital buildings and structures for administrative offices.

Dr. J. R. Oppenheimer, one of the foremost physicists in the coun-

**REVOLUTIONARY**

**News of the development at Las Alamos of an atomic bomb immediately raised conjecture regarding the potential industrial uses of the energy.**

**The power of the atomic force harnessed by scientists in the secret projects is almost beyond comprehension—one bomb packing the wallop of the bomb loads of 2,000 Superforts. Talk was at once heard of the possibility of the newly controlled energy replacing coal, electricity, gasoline, water as a source of power.**

**That the study of the subject will continue was assured by the appointment by the Secretary of War of a committee to carry on investigation of atomic energy.**

**Spokesmen for the Las Alamos project said they had not been informed if this meant post-war continuation of the mountain project.**

try and director of the laboratory, came to the site during early stages of construction. Other scientists and technical workers followed soon after.

Scientific groups which had been working on the project elsewhere in the country moved in rapidly, bringing their equipment with them. The Harvard cyclotron was in operation six weeks after it had reached the site.

**Tortuous Route**

Nearest railroad facilities are at Albuquerque and Santa Fe. This made it necessary to truck everything from those cities, at least. The road from Santa Fe is a tortuous one, and in the beginning, the last 18 miles were not paved. This was bad enough for passenger cars, and presented a particularly tough problem in hauling heavy loads.

Today the community has more than 6,000 residents. Slightly less than two-thirds are civilian men, women and children and the remainder military personnel. The post commandant is Col. Gerald R. Tyler.

First need of arriving personnel in mess halls, or in a large cafeteria. was housing. Various types were constructed, to meet different needs. There are three-room prefabricated, individual houses; three-room apartments, eight to a building, and four- and five-room apartments, four in a two-story unit. There are some hutments, Quonset-type huts and government and personally-owned trailers.

**Bachelor Dorms**

Dormitories have been constructed for unmarried personnel, or persons who do not have their families with them. Rents, for family groups, are based on earnings. Apartments are unfurnished and family groups ordinarily bring their furniture with them, although some items of government furniture have been available.

Housewives shop for food for daily meals at an army commissary where ration points are as important as elsewhere. A "trading post" offers items needed in everyday life and there are the usual post exchange stores.

Personnel living in dormitories eat There is also a dining room with waitress service.

**City Dads, Too**

A "town council" of eight elected members serves in an advisory capacity, meeting with representatives of the project and of the commanding officer. There is a school board, appointed by Colonel Tyler and Doctor Oppenheimer, which oversees operation of an accredited elementary school and high school. There

(Continued on Back Page)

## Hi Johnson Dies at 79

WASHINGTON, Aug. 6 (AP)—Sen. Hiram W. Johnson of California, militant opponent of the League of Nations and the San Francisco Charter for a United Nations organization, died today.

The veteran Republican senator succumbed at Naval Hospital, where he had been confined for 2½ weeks. His physician, Capt. Robert E. Duncan, USH, said he died from a thrombosis of a cerebral artery.

The 79-year-old Californian died at 6:45 a. m., after having been in ill health for some time.

His political activities extended over a third of a century covering some of the most stirring events in the nations history.

A striking figure in the Senate since first elected to Congress in 1916, he played a leading part in defeating President Wilson's League of Nations Covenant and later in opposing United States' adherence to the World Court.

His wife, whom he referred to as "the boss," was with him at the time of his death.

Senator McKellar (D.-Tenn.), President of the Senate, today will appoint a committee to attend the funeral of the silver-haired veteran.

**TERRITORIAL CHANGES OF WORLD WAR II—Black areas on map are those parts of Germany which the Big Three proposes will come under Polish rule. Shaded area is territory which Russia has taken control over since the start of hostilities on the continent. Northern East Prussia, proposed as Russian by the Big Three, is the newest addition to Soviet territory. There still remains some question as to final disposition of the port of Stettin. Note the large section of Baltic coastline of the proposed new Poland.**

## *4 More Nippon Cities Now Smoldering Ruins*

By The Associated Press

American airmen said they turned four more forewarned Japanese cities to ashes today as 750 Superforts and Mustang fighters reportedly swept the enemy's sacred islands with fire bombs, rockets and parachuted mines.

B-29 crewmen returning to their Marianas Island bases told of setting fires visible for 150 miles at sea. Some ran into intense antiaircraft fire and strong interception including rocket planes as they raided cities Tokyo described as "defenseless".

Waves of B-29s from the Marianas Islands and Mustang fighters from Iwo Jima struck as American commanders announced 70 Nipponese ships and small craft and 61 locomotives were destroyed or damaged in previous aerial blows, reaching over 4,500 miles from Paramushiro to Singapore.

Terror-ridden China carried the brunt of ground actions. Elsewhere land armies hunted for Japanese generals in the northern Philippines, drove toward trapping the largest Japanese force remaining in New Guinea and counted 13,000 Nipponese dead in recent fighting in monsoon-swept south Burma.

Superforts warned 12 more cities Sunday morning they were on their fire list. A formation of 580 followed up today by lighting towering fires in four of the 31 forewarned cities.

Today's targets include Nishinomiya, noted in prewar days for producing Japan's best sake, favorite alcoholic beverage of Nippon. The other industrial targets were Maebishi, 80 miles from Tokyo, saga on northern Honshu Island, and Imbari, on the southern island of Honshu. One B-29 unit hammered the Ube coal liquefaction plant with high explosives.

Japanese also reported Mustangs from Iwo raked the capital with rockets, bombs and machinegun bullets in daylight for the third time in four days.

For consolation, Japanese propagandists reported: Americans "lead a starvation life;" Nipponese raiders caught U. S. planes lined up wing to wing on two Okinawa air fields; a U. S. submarine was sunk off the coast of Japan; Nipponese subs sank two Allied vessels in the central Pacific.

Chinese reports told of new terror in China. Once-beautiful Kweilin, former southeast China air base city, was left thoroughly sacked. Fifty-thousand Chinese were killed or missing from Kanhsien in east central China. A thousand civilians were reported killed by forced poisonous injections at Ichang, enemy-held central China river port.

Americans and Filipinos eliminated an ambushing Japanese company and beat back two desperate counterattacks on northern Luzon island, running last week's toll in the Philippines to 4,740 Japanese killed and 444 taken prisoner. U. S. losses for the week were 27 killed, ti wounded.

Maj. Gen. William Gill offered a 45-day furlough to any member of the 32d Division who captures an enemy general alive. Chief prize is Gen. Tomoyuki Yamashita, onetime "Tiger of Malaya" variously reported cornered, killed or flown from northern Luzon mountains.

## 'Utter Destruction,' Promised in Potsdam Ultimatum, Unleashed; Power Equals 2,000 Superforts

**WASHINGTON, Aug. 6 (AP)—The U. S. Army Air Force has released on the Japanese an atomic bomb containing more power than 20,000 tons of TNT.**

**It produces more than 2,000 times the blast of the largest bomb ever used before.**

**The announcement of the development was made in a statement by President Truman released by the White House today.**

**The bomb was dropped 16 hours ago on Hiroshima, an important Japanese army base.**

The President said that the bomb has "added a new and revolutionary increase in destruction" on the Japanese.

Mr. Truman added:

"It is an atomic bomb. It is a harnessing of the basic power of the universe. The force from which the sun draws its power has been loosed against those who brought war to the Far East."

The base that was hit is a major quartermaster depot and has large ordnance, machine tool and aircraft plants.

The raid on Hiroshima, located on Honshu Island on the shores of the Inland sea, had not been disclosed

**MADE IN SANTA FE**

**WASHINGTON, Aug. 6 (AP)—The atomic bomb disclosed by President Truman today was developed at factories in Tennessee, Washington and New Mexico.**

**Mr. Truman said that from 65,000 to 125,000 workers were employed on the project at Oak Ridge near Knoxville, Tenn., at Richland near Pasco, Wash., and at an unnamed installation near Santa Fe, New Mexico.**

**He said the work was so secret that most of the employes did not know the character of it.**

previously although the 20th Air Force on Guam announced that 580 Superforts raided four Japanese cities at about the same time.

The city of 318,000 also contains a principal port.

**2 Billion Gamble**

The President disclosed that the Germans "worked feverishly" in search of a way to use atomic energy in their war effort but failed. Meantime American and British scientists studied the problem and developed two principal plants and some lesser factories for the production of atomic power.

The President disclosed that more

**WILL SHORTEN WAR**

**WASHINGTON, Aug. 6 (AP) — Secretary timson predicted today that the atomic bomb will "prove a tremendous aid" in shortening the war with Japan.**

**The war secretary made his statement as the Army reported that an "impenetrable cloud of dust and smoke" cloaked Hiroshima after it was hit by the new weapon from the air.**

**An accurate assessment of the damage inflicted by the bomb is not yet available, however, the War Department said. As soon as details of its effectiveness are learned, the department added, they will be released.**

than 65,000 persons now are working in great secrecy in these plants, adding:

"We have spent $2,000,000,000 on the greatest scientific gamble in history — and won."

"We are now prepared to obliterate more rapidly and completely every productive enterprise the Japanese have above ground in any city. We shall completely destroy Japan's power to make war."

The President noted that the Big Three ultimatum issued July 26 at Potsdam was intended "to spare the Japanese people from utter destruction" and the Japanese leaders rejected it. The atomic bomb now is

**PUNCH CATASTROPHIC**

**WASHINGTON, Aug. 6 (AP) — The atomic bomb announced by President Truman today packs a punch equivalent to that normally delivered by 2,000 B-29s.**

**The President said the missile has an explosive force equal to 20,000 tons—40,000,000 pounds—of TNT. Assuming a B-29 carries a bomb load of 10 tons of TNT, four 500-plane raids by the world's biggest bombers would be necessary to equal in destructive power the exploding fury of one atomic bomb.**

**The atomic bomb dwarfs by 2,000 times the blast power of the British "grand-slam" bomb, which weighed approximately 11 tons.**

the answer to that rejection and the President said "they may expect a rain of ruin from the air, the like of which has never been seen on this earth."

**Process Secret**

Mr. Truman forecast that sea and land forces will follow up this air attack in such numbers and power as the Japanese never have witnessed.

The President said that this discovery may open the war for an

**LONDON, Aug. 6 (AP)—Germany possessed some atomic power secrets, Winston Churchill said tonight, but "by God's mercy, British and American science outpaced all German efforts."**

entirely new concept of force and power. The actual harnessing of atomic energy may in the future supply the power that now comes from coal, oil and the great dams, he said.

"It has never been the habit of the scientists of this country or the policy of this government to withhold from the world scientific knowledge," Mr. Truman said. "Normally therefore everything about the work with atomic energy would be made public." That will have to wait, however, he said, until the war emergency is over.

## May Be Tool To End Wars; New Era Seen

Mankind's successful transition to a new age, the Atomic Age, was ushered in July 16, 1945, before the eyes of a tense group of renowned scientists and military men gathered in the desertlands of New Mexico to witness the first hand results of their $2,000,000,000 effort. Here in a remote section of the Alamogordo Air Base 120 miles southeast of Albuquerque the first man-made atomic explosion, the outstanding achievement of nuclear science, was achieved at 5:30 a. m. of that day.

Mounted on a steel tower, a revolutionary weapon destined to change war as it has been known, or which may even be the instrumentality to end all wars, was set off with an impact which signalized man's entrance into a new physical world. Success was greater than the most ambitious estimates. A small amount of matter, the product of a chain of huge specially constructed industrial plants, was made to release the energy of the universe locked up within the atom from the beginning of time.

**Credit J. R. Oppenheimer**

This phase of the Atomic Bomb Project, which is headed by Maj. Gen. Leslie R. Groves, was under the direction of Dr. J. R. Oppenheimer, theoretical physicist of the University of California. He is to be credited with achieving the implementation of atomic energy for military purposes.

Tension before the actual detonation was at a tremendous pitch. Failure was an ever-present possibility. Too great a success, envisioned by some of those present, might have meant an uncontrollable, unusable weapon.

Final assembly of the atomic bomb began on the night of July 12 in an old ranch house. As various component assembles arrived from distant points, tension among the scientists rose to an increasing pitch. Coolest of all was the man charged with the actual assembly of the vital core, Dr. R. F. Bacher, in normal times a professor at Cornell University.

**Lightning Threatens**

On Saturday, July 14, the unit which was to determine the success or failure of the entire project was elevated to the top of the steel tower.

The ominous weather which had dogged the assembly of the bomb had a very sobering effect on the assembled experts whose work was accomplished amid lightning flashes and peals of thunder.

Nearest observation point was set up 10,000 yards south of the tower where in a timber and earth shelter the controls for the tests were located. At a point 17,000 yards from the tower at a point which would give the best observation the key figures in the atomic bomb project took their posts. These included General Groves, Dr. Vannevar Bush, head of the Office of Scientific Research and Development, and Dr. James B. Conant, president of Harvard University.

**Lie Face Down**

Actual detonation was in charge of Dr. K. T. Bainbridge of Massachusetts Institute of Technology. He and Lieutenant Bush, in charge of the Military Police Detachment, were the last men to inspect the tower with its cosmic bomb.

At the Base Camp, all present were ordered to lie on the ground, face downward, heads away from the blast direction.

Tension reached a tremendous pitch in the control room as the deadline approached. The several observation points in the area were tied in to the control room by radio and with 20 minutes to go, Dr. S. K. Allison of Chicago University took

(Continued on Back Page)

## Tomato Juice Off Rationing

WASHINGTON, Aug. 6 (AP)—Grocers scratched point values today from canned tomato juice, mixed vegetable juice and grapefruit-orange juice blends.

OPA's action in making those products ration-free yesterday followed a recommendation from Secretary of Agriculture Anderson based on lowered military demands.

Anderson also announced that civilian store shelves will get 10,000,000 more cases of canned vegetables from this year's pack than had been expected.

Despite the 10 per cent increase, however, the Agriculture Department said the total still will be less than last year's.

**SENTENCED**

Pat Chavez, 333 Urioste Street, faced a 100-day jail sentence and $100 fine today on conviction before Peace Justice A. E. P. Robinson of assault and battery on a woman taxi driver. The court reported the case Saturday as involving a Pat Lopez and called attention today to the correct name of the defendant.

## *Now They Can Be Told Aloud, Those Stoories of 'the Hill'*

By WILLIAM McNULTY

The secret of Los Alamos is out and The New Mexican staff and other newspapermen through New Mexico can heave a sigh—sigh, nothing; it's more of a groan—of relief.

President Truman's revelation today that it was an atomic bomb THEY were working on on The Hill ended what was probably the strictest censorship ever imposed upon the press of this state. There was practically no limit to the lengths that the guards went to and the situation at times became fantastically involved including the famed "Battle of the MPs."

Notwithstanding the censorship, the news of Los Alamos had scarcely raced about the Plaza this morning when the membership of the "I-Knew-It-All-Along" club began growing by leaps and bounds. As a matter of record, the most recent rumor, No. 6,892—straight from the horse's mouth last week—was that Alamos was working lickety-split, night and day, in the production of windshield wipers for submarines.

The taboo on the mention of Los Alamos was final, complete and until today, irrevocable and not susceptible to any exceptions whatsoever.

A whole social world existed in nowhere in which people were married and babies were born nowhere. People died in a vacuum, autos and trucks crashed in a vacuum and the MPs baseball team materialized out of a vacuum, trained in a vacuum and after their games at Fort Marcy Park, returned to the vacuum. Even the graduates of Los Alamos Ranch School, the institution which preceded Uncle Sam's Atomic Bomb Project Laboratory, ceased to be graduates of Los Alamos; they bounded direct from Public School No. 7 clear into the classrooms of Harvard and Yale.

And on days when the Alamos experimenters threw their atomic bombs about a little too vigorously and the windows of Santa Fe rattled ominously, this paper's phones would ring but the whole staff could just "no speak English".

The chain of secrecy about the project was maintained from the big cities in East where workers were recruited clear through to the delivery of these same workers on The Hill. The Alamos Bus stop was at Sena Plaza and people laden with luggage and youngsters clinging to their arms, frequently barged into offices of that Plaza and inquired, "Where do we go to work?" One of the earliest bits of Alamos lore was that of the dude Wac who had never been farther west than Albany, N. Y.; she chose the moment when The Hill bus was turning the highest point on the Jemez mountains to peek out—and fainted dead away.

Under these conditions of secrecy rumors multiplied like maggots in one of Mel Hagman's garbage cans. Gas warfare, rockets, jet propulsion, death rays and — atomic bombs — were among the guesses most frequently voiced. During the last Presidential campaign, Alamos—no foolin'—was sometimes a Republican internment camp.

In the early days of the project, even the "outside employes" who knew no more of what was going on than the Japs in the foxholes of Guadalcanal, were sworn never to reveal what they didn't know anyway, for the rest of their lifetime. Our own B. B. Dunne got tangled in the wringer for so much as mentioning that "there were a lot of scientists in town".

Then there was the time when the New York Daily was whipping up a Sunday feature on Nobel prize-winners in the U. S. It queried The New Mexican for a brief summary of what Prof X was doing now. The staff recognized the Alamos postoffice box number—that famous postal box where babies were born and to which whole crateloads of furniture assigned—but it was decided to give the professor a whirl anyway on the old "You can't shoot me for trying" principle. A letter went out to Professor X in which an interview was asked.

The next morning at 8:09—their watches must have been slow,—two guards jumped the cityroom. After a heap of protestations and avowals of innocence, it was agreed that the following telegram could be sent the News:

"Your man working for Mr Whiskers on extremely hush-hush project. No soap."

The telegram was delivered in New York by a Western Union boy flanked by a covey of guards. These men then began spilling all over the News cityroom like oranges out of a busted crate.

How, they wanted to know, did the News staff explain such Dick Tracy huggermugger stuff?

The News' difficulty was that the girl who had sent the telegram had gone on vacation and couldn't be reached. The News explained it after two clouded weeks in which, by report, you couldn't toss a cigaret in a wastepaper basket without setting fire to a guard.

The tantalizing little that Santa Fans knew about The Hill, only heightened their interest. There were the lights to be seen from miles away; there were the days when fires raged and smoked billowed in the mountains and always the mysterious explosions — Lady Holmes moved to Tesuque and had moments when she thought she was back in bomb-shattered London!

The payoff, however, came in the "Battle of the MPs". More than a year ago a boxing card was arranged in which the Santa Fe High athletes took on the Alamos MPs. The sluggers from The Hill must have been missing out on their vitamins or the Demons were packing an atomic punch because the MPs were knocked cold, two or three of them in one round and one punch practically.

Unfortunately for Mel Rhine and his Santa Fe MPs—as distinct from the Alamos MPs—soldiers read the sports pages and the next Saturday night, there was an epidemic of free-swinging in the bars and restaurants.

Frantically Rhine demanded that The New Mexican print an explanation that the one-round pushovers were decidedly NOT his MPs but he ran smack into the Alamos secrecy ban.

For hours Rhine sweated over a document which, by the time it complied with censorship requirements, rambled for no less than 700 words or so—and meant exactly nothing to anybody. It was a masterpiece of obfuscation. Of course, the boys were still swinging at the so-called "one-round MPs" for weeks before they discovered their mistake.

## The Weather

New Mexico: Partly cloudy with widely scattered thunderstorms mostly over mountains during afternoon and evening; otherwise fair tonight and tomorrow; no important change in temperature.

**City**

High 90, low 56.

**Airport**

High 82, low 62.

# PROLOGUE

The presses of the *Santa Fe New Mexican* broke down in the excitement of that day in August 1945. The news of the dropping of the Atom Bomb on Hiroshima was the big story everywhere, but for the *New Mexican* it was doubly so and they were trying to produce extra editions. They were able to tell their readers, not only of the dramatic possibilities of an immediate peace, but also the amazing fact that the new weapon had been designed, built, even tested, no more than twenty-five miles from Santa Fe itself. In almost total secrecy a city of six thousand inhabitants had been built up from scratch at a place called Los Alamos in the New Mexico mountains where the bomb had been made. There had been some rumours certainly. Only three weeks earlier, people had heard and seen what looked like a big explosion some distance away in the desert, but this had been reported in the papers the next day as an explosion at an ammunition dump.

As to the six thousand people there had been only the slightest sign. There had always been a mixed bunch of military men and civilians passing through the foyer of 'La Fonda', the hotel in the centre of Santa Fe; there were often small groups and families waiting outside a small office in East Palace Street but who they were, or where they were going, no one really knew.

The names in the *New Mexican* of the men responsible for the new weapon were as unfamiliar in Santa Fe as they were elsewhere. For the first time they heard of General Leslie R. Groves, the military director of the project, and of Dr J. R. Oppenheimer, the theoretical physicist from the University of California who was credited with the 'implementation of atomic energy for military purposes'; he had directed the secret laboratory at Los Alamos. Both men were virtually unknown to the general public. Groves had been the construction engineer responsible for building the Pentagon. Oppenheimer had a good academic reputation but was known only to a select group of scientists. Overnight they became international figures.

Both acquired journalistic tags: Groves became known as the 'Atom General' and Oppenheimer as the 'Father of the A-Bomb'. For a time, in the autumn of 1945, they were constantly in the news but then Groves slowly disappeared from public view and left the army to become a businessman. Oppenheimer, however, continued on the public stage. During 1946 he was deeply involved in high-level attempts to introduce a system of international control for nuclear weapons. In 1947 he was appointed director of the prestigious Institute for Advanced Study at Princeton, where men as eminent

OPPOSITE *The front page of the* Santa Fe New Mexican *announces the dropping of the atomic bomb on Hiroshima*

7

as Einstein and Piaget worked, and also became Chairman of the General Advisory Committee to the newly formed Atomic Energy Commission. In this position his effect on the whole US Arms strategy was enormous and for more than five years he probably wielded more power than any other scientist has ever done.

Yet only nine years after his name had first appeared in the newspapers as the progenitor of the Atom Bomb, he was to become the subject of a security inquiry, called by President Eisenhower himself. It was an inquiry which became, in effect, a trial for treason. Robert Oppenheimer who had successfully directed the efforts of the scientists at Los Alamos was accused of being a Soviet Agent, even of being an accomplice of the atom spy Klaus Fuchs. It was an amazing fall from grace, the origins of which go back to Oppenheimer's early life and his years as an academic in the 1930s. This book will try to throw some light on the enigma of J. Robert Oppenheimer.

# THE EARLY YEARS

## CHAPTER 1

The brilliant and complex character of Robert Oppenheimer inspired two distinct and contradictory responses among those who knew him. There is a substantial majority which remembers him as a great man, someone who was gifted with a superb intellect, considerable personal charm, and great personal integrity – someone whom many of them professed to have loved deeply. There is a minority, however, which, while admitting to his intellectual powers – no one disagrees over this – remembers him as arrogant, calculating and selfish. These people remember him as an actor who, however skilfully, was always playing out a role. To them he was incapable of proper emotion and had betrayed not only friends but causes – maybe even his own country – for his own ends.

At first sight, two such extreme views seem irreconcilable. There are certainly no obvious divisions between the people who hold such differing views. Both polarities can be found among those who knew Oppenheimer during each of the different phases of his life and among those who occupied all of the very varied milieus in which he moved. Yet another difficulty is that many of those who, at one time, thought one way about him came, in the end, to hold a totally opposite view of him.

But those who were surprised by Oppenheimer's behaviour rarely knew him well enough to see his actions against the perspective of an unusual and sheltered family background and would not have realised how much he had to struggle both to suppress and disguise an emotional immaturity.

It would be hard for anyone visiting the apartment where Oppenheimer grew up in the first decade of this century to realise that his grandfather was still a peasant farmer and grain merchant in the German town of Hanau. The apartment was on the eleventh floor of a block on Riverside Drive, a predominantly middle-class residential area of New York overlooking the Hudson River. The atmosphere was subdued, tasteful, correct. The rooms were well-furnished with fine examples of European furniture and the walls were hung with paintings by Vuillard, van Gogh and Derain, a choice which, in the early 1900s, indicated good taste rather than a particularly fat wallet.

Two relations of Oppenheimer's grandfather had taken the bold decision to come to the New World to seek fame and fortune and settled in New York sometime around 1870, starting up their own business importing cloth for the

*Riverside Drive, New York, where Oppenheimer grew up in the early 1900s*

*Robert Oppenheimer as a baby*

clothing industry. By the late eighties they were well established and were able to offer a place in the business to Oppenheimer's father, Julius.

Julius came to New York in 1888, a young man of seventeen, tall, gangly, uncoordinated, hardly speaking a word of English. His first job was in the storeroom, unpacking and classifying bolts of cloth, but he was not to remain in this situation for long. For one thing, the firm itself, which specialised in the importing of men's suit linings, was riding on the crest of the newly developing demand for ready-to-wear clothes. For another, Julius Oppenheimer was imbued with a great zeal for self-improvement. By the time he was thirty he was a relatively prosperous man, always immaculately dressed, and known to his employees as a 'proper gentleman'. He now had a good command of English, had read widely and developed an interest in the arts.

Indeed, it is possible that his first meeting with Ella Friedman took place at an art exhibition. Like Julius, she was also of European Jewish descent, but her family had been in the United States for several generations. Photographs show her to be a considerable beauty, though she always wore long chamois gloves to conceal an incompletely developed right hand. In spite of this disability, she was a painter of some distinction who had studied in Paris and who, at the time she married Oppenheimer in 1903, was teaching at her own studio in New York.

It was on the night of 22 April 1904, after a long and difficult labour, that Ella gave birth to their first child, a son. Julius first intended calling him simply Robert but, feeling that this was lacking in distinction, added his own initial at the front – J. Robert Oppenheimer.

Not long after Robert was born the couple moved to the Riverside Drive apartment where he was to grow up. Even making allowances for the period clothes and the photographic style, the pictures of the family do communicate a feeling of correctness, preciousness and claustrophobia. As Oppenheimer himself described it, he became 'an abnormally repulsively good little boy' whose home life offered 'no normal healthy way to be a bastard'.

One friend, Paul Horgan, recalled how his parents and the house appeared to him.

She was a very delicate person . . . highly attenuated emotionally, and she always presided with a great delicacy and grace at the table and other events, but a mournful person. Mr Oppenheimer was . . . desperately amiable, anxious to be agreeable, and I think essentially a very kind man . . . The household was run with luxury but simplicity at the same time, every comfort and great style and charm . . . and a sadness: there was a melancholy tone.

At the age of five he went on a trip to visit the family home in Germany, and his grandfather, Ben, gave him a small collection of minerals. It triggered a hobby which was to last for years – mineralogy – a solitary pursuit for a solitary child. Oppenheimer was to spend hours on his own collecting samples, cataloguing and polishing them. By the age of eleven, he had been elected a member of the New York Mineralogical Club, and one year later delivered his first paper there.

There was no doubt that Oppenheimer was clever and at school he was a star

*Robert Oppenheimer at an early age*

*Robert Oppenheimer with his father Julius, described by one family friend as 'desperately amiable, anxious to be agreeable'*

pupil. Although both his parents were Jewish, they had rejected orthodox Jewish society and culture, and had sent Robert, and later his brother Frank, who was eight years his junior, to the school run by the New York Society for Ethical Culture. The school's founder was another German immigrant, Felix Adler, whose educational philosophy was based very much on the cult of the individual. He believed that human values did not require a dogma to render them important, nor did values of good and evil need to depend on theology. Instead, he taught that man should form his own attitudes towards the unknown and life's mysteries. It was heroic, it was high-minded, this ethical-humanist philosophy of Adler's, and in later years Oppenheimer was to tease his father about it. For one of his birthdays, Robert composed a song for him, to the tune of 'The Battle Hymn of the Republic', in which one line went, 'And he swallowed Dr Adler like morality compressed. . . .'

Nevertheless, over a period of ten years there can be little doubt that the values imparted at that school had a considerable effect on the serious, solitary, scholastic Oppenheimer. With his voracious appetite for knowledge, he immersed himself in the whole range of subjects on the curriculum. With his Greek teacher he spent time after school reading Homer and Plato. By the age of eleven he was able to challenge an older cousin to 'ask me a question and I will answer you in Greek'. A chemistry tutor, Augustus Klock, developed his interest in science and one summer Oppenheimer spent the entire holiday with him helping to set up a small laboratory.

He had no taste for sports. He was driven everywhere, attended by servants, and even the school staff became critical at his avoidance of physical activity. On one occasion, Adler lost his patience with him because he would not use the stairs, always preferring to wait for the lift. Home came the abrupt note, 'Please teach your son to walk upstairs; he is holding up class'. As a reaction to this, his parents did try to encourage him to play outdoor sports, but he lacked co-

J. ROBERT OPPENHEIMER

ordination. He tried tennis, but played badly, and he seemed to have a distaste for doing anything badly.

However, there was one sport that he took to and became expert at – sailing. The family had taken a holiday home at Bay Shore, Long Island, a beautiful spot described in those days as 'entirely free of malaria', and Oppenheimer slowly became one of the very best yachtsmen in the area.

By the time he was eighteen, his father had given him a twenty-eight-foot sloop which he christened *Trimethy* – predictably derived from the name of a chemical compound, trimethylene dioxide – and Oppenheimer and his small brother, Frank, would sail all over the area.

The teenage Oppenheimer had developed a taste for danger. He was no nonchalant daredevil – somehow he needed to challenge some suspected weakness within himself. A summer storm would send him out across the bay, riding the tide race through the inlet at Fire Island and taking his boat right out into the roaring Atlantic. On one occasion that his brother Frank remembers, the two of them took the boat on the tide race out through the inlet to Fire Island. Once out to sea they spent five hours trying to force *Trimethy*, heeling to the point of capsizing, back into the bay. It was an act of recklessness which alarmed both parents greatly. Perhaps this was the reason he did it, but if so then he would have been disappointed with their reactions. Even after his father had coerced the crew of the local revenue cutter to go out looking for him Frank remembers no cross words.

*Oppenheimer as a child – he described himself as 'an abnormally repulsively good little boy'*

Indeed he was something of a trial for his parents during these years. Polite, bookish, diligent, he was also arrogant and snobbish. A boyhood friend who knew him during the long summers at Bay Shore remembered that 'we were thrown together a lot and yet we were never close. He was usually pre-occupied with whatever he was doing or thinking.' He also had a dark side to his character. He hardly ever laughed. His taste in literature was typically soulful – T. S. Eliot, Chekhov, Katherine Mansfield. At such an early stage in life, his taste for propriety and academic activity, his seriousness of mind and purpose, were firmly fixed. Indeed these traits so firmly set him apart from his contemporaries that at summer camp when he was fourteen he was taunted mercilessly. The harassment culminated in his being locked naked in an icehouse overnight.

His last year at school was spent in an orgy of learning and he graduated with ten straight 'A's. That summer, his parents travelled with him to Germany again where he took the opportunity to escape, alone, into the Harz mountains, on a mineralogical field trip. He returned after a period of time, extremely ill with trench dysentery. This gave rise to colitis and from that time on he was always to have problems with his digestion.

Back in New York, it was decided that he was too ill to go to Harvard that year, so, much against his will, he had to stay in the apartment alone with his books and his thoughts. He became rebellious, rejecting his mother's attentions, locking himself in his room and being boorish with everyone. The following spring his father, now desperate for some solution to his son's dark

moods, asked the English teacher at the Ethical Culture School, a husky young man called Herbert Smith, to take Oppenheimer west to the mountains, to recuperate.

For weeks the two roamed the mountains of Colorado and New Mexico on horseback, camping out at nights or staying at guest ranches. At one, the élite Los Pinos ranch, north of Santa Fe, Oppenheimer became infatuated with the woman who ran it, Katherine Page. It was an unrequited teenage passion, but it took the young boy out of himself. The whole experience of those western mountains: the horse riding, the camping, the grandeur of the mountains themselves, and of course Katherine Page, made an indelible impression on Oppenheimer. He was to return to those mountains time and time again.

In the autumn of 1922, when he was eighteen, Oppenheimer finally enrolled at Harvard. His summer in the New Mexico mountains had hardened him considerably. Indeed, Herbert Smith had been enormously impressed by the boy's grit and stamina, and with his natural ability with horses. He seemed to have a fatalistic attitude towards physical danger which made him practically fearless. Physically he was still very tall and thin, but he had fine blue eyes, and a thick mop of black curly hair. In later years, women were to find the strange mix of Byronic good looks and intellectual arrogance very attractive, but, for the time being, Oppenheimer's own immaturity prevented any major emotional affairs.

He arrived at Harvard intending to major in chemistry. He had only decided on this last course of action after testing out such varied possibilities as becoming an architect, a classics scholar, and even a poet and painter. In the end, however, he settled for science and for chemistry and settled down to the task of completing the four-year course in three years. He worked himself mercilessly. He appeared at the laboratory at eight a.m., way before anyone else. He would stop only to lunch off a 'black and tan' – an open toast sandwich covered with peanut butter and topped with chocolate sauce – which he considered the most wonderfully concentrated food. Friends who knew him at that time do not recall him once taking a girl out in his three years at Harvard. One of his friends from this period, Jeffries Wyman, has recalled:

He found social adjustment very difficult, and I think he was often very unhappy. I suppose he was lonely and felt he didn't fit in well with the human environment. We were good friends, and he had some other friends, but there was something that he lacked, perhaps some more personal and deep emotional contact with people than we were having, because our contacts were largely, I should say wholly, on an intellectual basis . . .

He was still uncertain about chemistry and even about a career in science. Friends still thought he might throw it up and turn to writing but then towards the end of his undergraduate course he began attending a course on advanced thermodynamics given by Percy Bridgman, the distinguished experimental physicist. It was his first brush with Bridgman, who impressed him greatly, and with physics. The subject appealed to the philosopher in him. It seemed

OPPOSITE *Oppenheimer at Harvard in 1925 – the year that he graduated in chemistry, completing the four-year course in only three years*

*Ernest Rutherford, the New Zealand physicist who was the director of the Cavendish Laboratory in Cambridge where Oppenheimer went after leaving Harvard*

altogether less pragmatic, much more fundamental than chemistry. 'It was the study of order, of regularity, of what makes matter harmonious and what makes it work,' he said.

In his final year he started working on a research project with Bridgman and even decided that he would apply to the Cavendish laboratory in Cambridge, England to continue his postgraduate work there in physics. Indeed Bridgman was so impressed with Oppenheimer's capacity for sheer hard work that he wrote a letter of recommendation to Ernest Rutherford, the director of the Cavendish. However he also noted that this capacity for hard work was accompanied by the kind of precocity born of immaturity. Oppenheimer was prone to show off his knowledge by asking too many questions. He would then agonise about his own gaucheness.

Bridgman recounted one story as an example. Once Oppenheimer visited Bridgman's house and admired a picture of a Greek temple. Bridgman mentioned its date and style at which Oppenheimer responded impulsively, 'Oh, that's interesting, because from the style of the capitals I would have put it fifty, a hundred years earlier than that.'

Oppenheimer was quite capable of tortuous reflection on such an exchange and he must, from time to time, have been miserable within himself over such things. However he could, nevertheless, be extremely cutting and deliberately so. He could not tolerate either crudeness or banalities of any kind and if he believed someone was guilty of either of these sins he was ready to cut them in mid-conversation. The hurt of such a snub was doubly felt as a contrast to his normal courteousness.

Apart from an unsuccessful brush with a university literary magazine, most of Oppenheimer's time at Harvard was given over to work. It was no great surprise to anyone, therefore, when he graduated *summa cum laude* in chemistry after three years. In his Year Book, a particularly American phenomenon where undergraduates try to outdo one another in their extravagant claims on posterity, Oppenheimer simply wrote, 'In college three years as an undergraduate.'

Those years of hard work had taken their toll. There had always been a danger that Oppenheimer would enter into a destructive cycle of self-absorption – so far something had always occurred which had broken it – but that year, when he was twenty-one, it came close to consuming him. In that summer of 1925, he sailed for England for the Cavendish laboratory, Cambridge. He was trained basically as a chemist; he did not have a proper grounding in physics or in the maths which accompanied it yet he was going to one of the great international centres of physics which was a mecca for the most brilliant students and researchers in the field.

It had been arranged that he would study theory and mathematics in the hope of compensating for the shortcomings in his Harvard education, and it was also arranged for him to work on an experimental project for the Nobel Laureate J. J. Thomson. For this he had to prepare very thin metallic films to investigate the penetrating power of electrons, but to his chagrin, he discovered

J. ROBERT OPPENHEIMER

he was not good at the work. As well as this, his theoretical endeavours brought him face to face, for the first time, with the true nature of creative physics. He has described how he would stand, alone, in front of a blackboard, chalk in hand, waiting for inspiration for hours on end. He would wake from his reverie to realise that the day had passed in silence. At other times, as the minutes passed, he would hear his own voice telling the blackboard, 'the point is, the point is, . . . the point is, . . . .'

His loneliness, his homesickness for America, his realisation of his own limitations, brought him to a state of despair. By Christmas, it did not seem out of the question to his friends that he would commit suicide. He himself has described how he went to Brittany that holiday and how he clearly remembered walking along the bleak winter shoreline 'on the point of bumping myself off'.

The immediate crisis in Brittany passed but on that same holiday trip to France an extraordinary incident took place. He had met up with one of his oldest friends Francis Fergusson in Paris. In the course of an ordinary conversation Oppenheimer had suddenly leapt on Fergusson with the clear intention of strangling him. Fergusson had managed to fend off the attack but this bizarre incident coupled with his obvious despair over how his work was progressing demonstrated clearly to Fergusson how mentally troubled he was.

Back in England he sought psychiatric help first in Cambridge then in London. Here the psychiatrist diagnosed *dementia praecox*, a now discarded diagnosis where the symptoms were somewhat akin to those of schizophrenia. The condition was thought to be triggered by too much studying or ill-health, and to be hereditary. It was considered, almost always, to be incurable. The psychiatrist, believing further treatment likely to do more harm than good, ordered that treatment should be stopped.

If Oppenheimer had not then decided to take a holiday in Corsica, it is difficult to know what might have happened. He and two friends – John Edsall and Jeffries Wyman – travelled by train via Paris to Nice and from there took a boat across to Corsica. They hiked down the full length of the island, sleeping in small inns and peasant huts or out in the open. The holiday provided just the break that Oppenheimer needed and his two companions began to note a certain improvement in his state of mind.

Then an incident occurred which, for them, clinched the matter. John Edsall was picked up by the police while taking pictures of the fortifications at Bonifacio. The other two went to the police station with him and as they were sitting out in a corridor they could hear Edsall pleading with the guards that he was not a spy, but an ordinary American tourist. The situation was so absurd that Oppenheimer's companion could not control his mirth; and when he looked up, through his tears of laughter, he was astonished to see Oppenheimer moving about, slapping his thighs. He was chuckling, something that his companions had never seen him do before. He was definitely on the mend. However, shortly after this another strange and ambiguous incident occurred. It had been intended that the three friends should go on to Sardinia but on their last night in Corsica Oppenheimer became quite agitated, saying he must return to Cambridge at once. The reason which he gave later in the evening, when he had relaxed somewhat, was that he had left a poisoned apple on Patrick Blackett's desk and must return to make sure that Blackett was all right. Was this some elaborate metaphor that Oppenheimer had constructed or was it hallucination? Neither Wyman nor Edsall could ever be sure but nevertheless he returned to Cambridge leaving them to go on to Sardinia.

One other thing reputedly happened on that holiday. Oppenheimer met a girl. Years later, with a fullness of phrase which itself is indicative, Oppenheimer was to write:

The psychiatrist was a prelude to what began for me in Corsica. You ask whether I will tell you the full story or whether you must dig it out. But it is known to few and they won't tell. You can't dig it out. What you need to know is that it was not a mere love affair, not a love affair at all, but love.

Certainly this girl was his first serious love, indeed his first affair of any kind apart from his infatuation for Katherine Page and a vain attempt of his mother's to arrange a relationship for him. At twenty-two he was immature even by the standards of half a century ago. Friends attribute this difficulty to his relationship with his mother. She had been a strong influence on him, this lovely, cold, intelligent woman, as was demonstrated when she was dying of leukaemia in 1931. 'I am the loneliest man in the world,' he told his old teacher Herbert Smith shortly before she died. In spite of this influence on him theirs was not a close relationship and friends believe she had imprinted the notion of the 'virgin queen' in her son's mind. This may be a somewhat glib explanation, but in its defence it must be said that throughout his life he was to find considerable difficulty in achieving a satisfactory relationship with any of the women with whom he became close.


On his return from Corsica, Oppenheimer was sufficiently recovered from his depression to re-assess his future and make the decision not to continue beyond the summer at Cambridge. Instead, he chose to accept an offer from Max Born to continue his work at the University of Göttingen. Like Cambridge, Göttingen was one of the great European centres of physics, but, while Cambridge had a tradition of experimental work, Göttingen was above all a theoretical centre.

By the time I decided to go to Göttingen [Oppenheimer recalled] I had very great misgivings about myself on all fronts, but I clearly was going to do theoretical physics if I could. . . . I felt completely relieved of the responsibility to go back into a laboratory. I hadn't been good; I hadn't done anybody any good, and I hadn't had any fun whatever; and here was something I felt just driven to try.

He couldn't have picked a more stimulating time to make this transition. When he arrived at Göttingen, theoretical physics was in a ferment. For more than ten years now, all research into the structure of matter had been governed by

J. ROBERT OPPENHEIMER

A group of physicists in Copenhagen in the late 20s, which shows the internationalism of physics. Heisenberg (front row, third from left) and von Weizsäcker (directly behind him) were to be in control of the German A-bomb project. Oliphant (second row, second from left) and Frisch (second row, second from right) were to play important roles in the Allied project. Oppenheimer knew this group well

the theory of atomic structure proposed by the Danish physicist, Niels Bohr. Indeed, only the year before, one of the professors at Göttingen, James Franck, had shared the Nobel Prize for work which had provided an experimental basis for Bohr's theory.

Then early that year of 1926, the German physicist Erwin Schrödinger had proposed a revolutionary theory of the atom which seemed to explain so many of the things that Bohr's theory did not. Instead of Bohr's 'planetary' model of the atom with the nucleus surrounded by electrons all moving in defined orbits, Schrödinger had proposed that the electrons could more precisely be thought of as a wave curved all round the nucleus. Its exact position was always uncertain – it was in all parts of its orbit at once, so to speak. Schrödinger had gone as far as developing a mathematical description of this ever-fluctuating atom, called *quantum* mechanics, and it was Schrödinger's theory and his mathematical interpretation which was the main preoccupation at Göttingen that year.

Oppenheimer had already done some work in this area at Cambridge. It had been a great boost to his confidence when, just after his return from Corsica, the Journal of the Cambridge Philosophical Society had published two of his papers, which dealt with various aspects of Quantum Theory. His reputation preceded him and, on his arrival at Göttingen, he found he was immediately accepted in the weekly seminars between staff and students as someone of standing.

Furthermore, with a subject as new as this one, he found that professors and students were learning from one another. It was the perfect situation for the quick-minded American. He entered the discussions with an abandon which

*Paul Dirac, an important contributor to the development of quantum theory. Oppenheimer met him at Cambridge and they became good friends*

*Ed Condon, a fellow student of Oppenheimer's at Göttingen in 1927. Their paths were to cross dramatically during the war*

initially caught everyone's attention, but then, as he appeared to be unstoppable, became a source of irritation. As others had done before, they thought he was showing off, putting on a performance. Eventually his colleagues were driven to submitting a written petition to the professors, requesting that the 'child prodigy's' flow should somehow be checked. Child prodigy. There were few people at Göttingen over the age of twenty-five. There was even a ditty composed for one of the student revues by the English mathematician, Paul Dirac, who was a couple of years older than Oppenheimer:

> Age is of course a fever chill
> That every physicist must fear
> He's better dead than living still,
> When once he's past his thirtieth year.

Still Oppenheimer was younger than most of them, he was only twenty-two and looked younger, and he was American. He was also wealthy and made no effort to disguise the fact. He wore clothes which, although ill-fitted to his spare frame, were expensive. While other students had difficulty in paying for the books they needed, Oppenheimer had all he wanted, and specially bound for him as well.

His eccentricities made him a natural subject for gossip. At the villa where he and some of the other students, including Paul Dirac, had lodgings, his highly-developed table manners, his very particular behaviour, made some of his fellow students feel like barbarians. Yet again they also noticed how he would suddenly cut someone dead when they said something he thought of as banal. He was seemingly totally intolerant of stupidity and pretension of any kind. He was also arrogant. A fellow American student, Ed Condon, noted that 'the trouble is that Oppie is so quick on the trigger intellectually that he puts the other guy at a disadvantage. And, dammit, he is always right, or at least right enough.'

Condon also remembered another incident which highlighted how sheltered and élitist Oppenheimer's early life had been. He invited Condon and his wife out for a walk one day, but Emilie Condon had to refuse because she had to look after their new baby. 'All right,' said Oppenheimer, 'we'll leave you to your peasant tasks.'

He also had the reputation of being an intellectual snob, carefully choosing his closer friends from those whom he considered to be his intellectual equal – or almost. One of those whom Oppenheimer cultivated was Paul Dirac, who only ten years later was to win a Nobel Prize. They spent a great deal of time together, the conversations dwelling almost exclusively on physics. Indeed, Dirac found Oppenheimer's catholic interests very difficult to understand. It was then that Oppenheimer and two other students were spending a great deal of time reading Dante in the original. Oppenheimer had even gone to the lengths of learning Italian for the purpose. He had also made attempts to write poetry of his own, and to Dirac this represented a lack of clear purpose in his thinking. 'How can you do both – poetry and physics?' Dirac is reported as saying on one occasion. 'In physics we try to tell people things in such a way that they understand something that nobody knew before. In the case of poetry it's the exact opposite.'

Not everyone would agree with Dirac's definitions, but they do serve to highlight something special about Oppenheimer's approach to his subject. He did have a broad-based education; he had specialised comparatively late in his life. He had kept up many of his non-scientific interests and now they were leading him to look for a much broader-based synthesis within the technical insights provided by physics. In the years to come, his philosophical view of his science was to have an enormous appeal to his own students.

During his time in Göttingen, Oppenheimer met another girl who was to play an important part in his life for the next few years. Her name was Charlotte Riefenstahl, a fellow physics student. As Charlotte was to recall they first met on a train journey when a group of students were travelling back to Göttingen from a seminar in Hamburg. The group's luggage was collected together on the platform when amongst the bags and battered suitcases Charlotte spotted an immaculate pigskin grip. Charlotte asked whose it was and she was told that it belonged to Oppenheimer.

Later in the journey she found herself sitting next to him and they struck up a conversation, during which she mentioned his handsome piece of luggage. He looked puzzled but nothing more was said. A little later, Charlotte mentioned the luggage to another student who wagered that now Oppenheimer would try to give her the bag. It was another of Oppenheimer's well known peculiarities that, if anyone admired something of his, he would find some pretext of making a present of it. Sure enough, this was precisely what happened. As she was about to leave Göttingen, he came to her flat and gave her the grip.

Throughout that year, Oppenheimer paid court to Charlotte in a formal, old-fashioned way. Fellow students recall him fussing around her, tending to her slightest whim. But in spite of mainly happy experiences at Göttingen, towards the end of his time there he began to experience certain mixed feelings about Germany.

Although this society was extremely rich and warm and helpful to me, it was parked there in a very miserable German mood . . . bitter, sullen, and, I would say, discontent and angry and with all those ingredients which were later to produce a major disaster. And this I felt very much.

It was perhaps partly as a reaction to this feeling that he became extremely homesick and just a little chauvinistic, infuriating some of the other students with his superlatives about the United States.

'According to him, even the flowers seem to smell better back there,' one student remarked. Then in the spring of 1927, after a flare of indignation over the fact that Oppenheimer had not remembered to register as a student and was therefore not officially eligible to take his doctorate, the university authorities gave him his doctorate 'with distinction' and Oppenheimer sailed for home.

He was followed after a few months by Charlotte, who had obtained a teaching post at Vassar, one of America's leading women's colleges. Oppenheimer was there at the dockside to meet her and one or two other student friends. One of these was the Dutchman, Samuel Goudsmit.

We all got the real Oppenheimer treatment, but it was for Charlotte's benefit really [he recalled]. He met us in this great chauffeur-driven limousine, and took us downtown to a hotel he had selected in Greenwich Village. Then he took us to dinner at the Prince George Hotel and introduced us to what he thought were special American treats, corn-on-the-cob and that sort of thing. And there we sat, in the kind of restaurant I've hardly ever been to before or since, looking at the lights of Manhattan. Very memorable.

Goudsmit and the others were to move on, but Charlotte stayed, to be fêted in the most extravagant way by Oppenheimer. She was taken on a round of expensive hotels and restaurants and then taken home to the Riverside Drive apartment to meet his parents.

The young couple must obviously have thought about marriage, but during these weeks in New York, Charlotte became convinced that Oppenheimer was still too immature to share himself with anyone. She saw how, at home, his parents cosseted him and went to great lengths to protect his privacy. She found it almost impossible to extract information from him about his past, and an inquiry, for instance, about his mother's covered right arm was put right out of court. So the affair that had begun a year earlier petered out. Oppenheimer went to Harvard as a research fellow and Charlotte to her teaching post at Vassar.

At the beginning of 1928 Oppenheimer's National Research Council Fellowship took him, after Harvard, out to the West Coast to the California Institute of Technology, where he both taught and did research. It was while he was here that he started receiving offers of university posts, ten from American universities, two from abroad. From the range of options open to him he chose to take up an assistant-professorship on another West Coast campus, the University of California at Berkeley. It appealed particularly because, as he put it, it was 'a desert. There was no theoretical physics and I thought it would be nice to try and start something.' Also Berkeley had agreed to release him to go down to Pasadena each spring to teach at the California Institute of Technology.

However, his experiences at Cal. Tech. pointed up some weaknesses particularly in his mathematics so he asked for his Fellowship to be renewed and to return to Europe for another year before taking up his post at Berkeley. His request was granted but that summer he was diagnosed as having TB and went, along with his brother Frank, to the mountains of New Mexico to try to hasten a cure. While he was there he again made contact with Katherine Page at Los Pinos, and one July morning she took him to visit a log cabin which was for rent. It was set at the top end of a rising meadow of rough grass and wild flowers. Behind it on two sides was a pine wood and in front was the most

magnificent view out across the rolling pine-clad slopes of the Sangre de Cristo mountains. Their name, 'blood of Christ', derives from the way the setting sun touches their snow-clad peaks in wintertime. The cabin itself – Oppenheimer used to refer to it as the ranch – was made of hewn timber, with a large porch and two rooms downstairs, and two bedrooms upstairs. The sanitary arrangements were non-existent.

It was an ideal spot and Oppenheimer took the lease immediately. He nicknamed the place Perro Caliente, Spanish for 'hot dog', and years later he bought the freehold outright. It was to be a holiday home for the family for the next forty years.

That summer, Oppenheimer and Frank, now aged seventeen, used the ranch as a base for expeditions over the whole area. In spite of their frail physiques, the two brothers had a considerable reputation as horsemen in the district. They talked while they rode of physics, of poetry, of Cummings' anti-war novel *The Enormous Room* and Frank began to form his first clear adult impression of his older brother.

He wanted everything and everyone to be special and his enthusiasms communicated themselves and made these people feel special. He was the least lazy person I have ever

*A recent photograph of the Perro Caliente ranch*

*Wolfgang Pauli, with whom Oppenheimer studied in Zurich in 1929 – a period Oppenheimer described as 'just very, very good indeed'*

met. Once he had accepted someone as worthy of attention or friendship, he would always be ringing or writing to them, doing them small favours, giving them presents. He couldn't be humdrum. He would even work up those enthusiasms for a brand of cigarettes, even elevating them to something special. His sunsets were always the best.

In that description of Frank's, there is one phrase which holds the key to so much of the Oppenheimer phenomenon. 'He wanted everything and everyone to be special.' This statement, with its implications of someone living according to some preconceived ideal, judging potential friends, students, girlfriends, colleagues, by whether they fitted that ideal, seems to explain so many things in Oppenheimer's life and provides some reason, at least, for the polarities of opinion about him that I mentioned at the outset of this chapter. Put simply, the mutually self-selecting group that formed Oppenheimer's close circle of friends and students, whom he allowed to come close to him, found him kind and warm and were beguiled by his intelligence and charm. However, those who did not find themselves part of this circle were often antagonised by Oppenheimer, his clique, and the ethos he projected.

At the end of that long summer, a medical examination showed that, for the time being at least, Oppenheimer's TB had been held in check and he left once again for Europe. He went first to Leiden to study with Einstein's friend, Paul Ehrenfest. He had then intended going on to study with Niels Bohr at Copenhagen but Ehrenfest sent him instead to Wolfgang Pauli in Zurich for 'more discipline and more schooling . . .'

Then in the summer of 1929 he returned to America. After spending three of the last four years abroad he was not to leave the United States again for nineteen years. He drove westward to take up his professorship at Berkeley – a ferryride across the bay from San Francisco.

# THE RADICAL PROFESSOR

Those who remember Oppenheimer's earliest efforts in the classrooms at Berkeley in the autumn of 1929 recall that he was far from an immediate success as a teacher. He seriously overestimated his audience. There were continuous complaints that he was inaudible, that he went too fast, and that he was impossible to follow. One of his earliest graduate students, James Brady, recalled that 'since we couldn't understand what he was saying we watched the cigarette. We were always expecting him to write on the board with it and smoke the chalk, but I don't think he ever did.'

Many of the students were driven to complain to the head of the physics department, Raymond T. Birge; but Birge knew that Oppenheimer himself had already appreciated that he was not getting through and so waited for things to improve. Sure enough, after two or three months, he began to interact with his audience, dropping his pace of delivery, taking pains to make the links between ideas clearer. Not that he was ever to become a great popular lecturer, but in a short time he was attracting a small group of some of the brightest students who found him the most stimulating lecturer they had experienced.

*The University of California at Berkeley, where Oppenheimer taught in the distinguished physics department from 1929 to 1943*

25

I didn't start to make a school [Oppenheimer has explained], I didn't start to look for students. I started really as the propagator of the theory (Quantum theory) which I loved, about which I continued to learn more, and which was not well understood but which was very rich. . . .

But the growing excitement of the Berkeley Physics department was compounded by the presence of another remarkable physicist, Ernest Lawrence.

'SPEED HYDROGEN IONS TO BREAK UP ATOMS' was how the *New York Times* had headlined its story in September 1930, reporting on the first of Lawrence's great atom-smashing machines. These cyclotrons, as they were called, worked by continuously accelerating electrically-charged atomic particles in a magnetic field and then aiming them at an atomic target. The sub-atomic pieces that were broken off on impact were to provide clues to the internal structure of the atoms.

One of the first machines Lawrence had built had an eleven-inch cyclotron chamber, for which the magnet required weighed two tons, but in rapid succession he had escalated to more and more powerful machines – thirty-inch cyclotrons, thirty-seven-inch cyclotrons, sixty-inch cyclotrons, each with even more enormous magnets. These machines were at the time some of the most expensive pieces of scientific equipment ever built and it was Lawrence's enormous enthusiasm and energy which had ensured the funds for these projects. He was in so many ways the opposite of Oppenheimer. He liked sport and going to the movies. He was very much an experimentalist, a fine scientist but a non-intellectual in his approach. Yet in spite of these differences the two men were to become firm friends. Scientifically, they catalysed one another's activities, Lawrence providing the experimental material for Oppenheimer and his theoreticians to work on, while in turn the theoreticians proposed new directions for the experimenters. It was an enormously fruitful relationship which throughout the 1930s produced scientific results of great importance and in less than a decade made Berkeley one of the great international centres of physics.

But while the excitement of the physics was an important factor in Oppenheimer's success as a teacher, his hold on his students extended well beyond the lecture room and it is not hard to see why.

During his four years in Europe, he had worked with and studied under some of the greatest names in physics. Not only did he have new and exciting concepts to communicate, but he had also become thoroughly Europeanised. He knew about wine, about French mediaeval poetry, about food. He had even taken a course in Sanskrit so that he could read Eastern philosophy. By any standards, let alone the standards of a West Coast physics department, he was cultivated, well-read and had the money to develop his tastes into a life style. He also liked to have a coterie of students about him.

'Robert found it very difficult to form proper relationships with equals', said a colleague who knew him well at that time. 'He could be respectful and

*Robert Oppenheimer (l) and Ernest Lawrence seen here at Oppenheimer's New Mexico ranch in the early 30s*

ABOVE *Oppenheimer, in characteristic pose with a cigarette, in the lecture room*

RIGHT *A group of Oppenheimer's left-wing Berkeley students. (l–r) Joseph Weinberg, Rossi Lomanitz, David Bohm, Max Friedman. They were to figure prominently in Oppenheimer's later security problems*

deferential to one or two people like Einstein, and he was very happy to have adoring disciples at his feet. Anything else, there were problems.'

So, from early on in his teaching career, he was surrounded by this close group, normally the most talented of his students. In time many of them came, almost self-consciously, to imitate Oppenheimer's mannerisms. They imitated his loose-limbed walk. They copied his particular way of whipping out a lighter as soon as anyone started to take out a cigarette. They even developed some of his habits of speech. For instance, he had a way of punctuating a conversation when someone else was talking with a rhythmic 'ja-ja. . .ja. . .ja' pronounced with a hint of a German accent, and numbers of his students took up the same habit. They became something of a phenomenon around the campus, easily identifiable by these derivative quirks of behaviour.

They were to be seen everywhere in their professor's company – in his car, being treated to meals at expensive seafood restaurants. Oppenheimer saw all this as part of their total education and gave instruction on wine and the various cuisines. In the spring they followed him down to Cal. Tech. for his spell of teaching there. In the summer, they were welcome to visit Perro Caliente, where they rode by day and, at night, squatting on a Navajo rug under the wide porch, played their own version of tiddlywinks.

To an outsider they were indeed an extraordinary bunch, and to many their conversation, a mixture of physics and a self-conscious appraisal of other cultural matters, must have seemed unbearably pretentious. Certainly their behaviour and that of their professor antagonised numbers of people. At Cal. Tech., Robert Millikan, the Nobel Laureate and head of the Physics department, took a strong exception to Oppenheimer. He complained of Oppenheimer's 'bohemianism' and resisted any attempts to give him promotion.

There were rumours spread about him and his followers at Berkeley which seem to have their origins in spite. It was said, for instance, that Oppenheimer's little clique had a homosexual basis. These rumours were dredged up twenty years later when the FBI were scrutinising every aspect of Oppenheimer's past and appeared in one of their 1947 reports. However, they do not seem to have been able to confirm it and the line of investigation was not pursued. Perhaps such stories say more about the antagonism towards Oppenheimer's clique than about the behaviour of the clique itself.

Oppenheimer still continued to be intolerant of any kind of foolishness and his sudden sharp attacks or rudeness made outsiders harbour still further resentment. Even one of his old professors, the gentle James Franck, who had taught Oppenheimer at Göttingen, was to suffer from one of those sallies. Franck came to Berkeley on one occasion to give a series of lectures entitled the 'Fundamental Meaning of Quantum Mechanics'. During his visit, Franck also attended a lecture given by one of Oppenheimer's students and, during the discussion, asked a question which demonstrated a certain lack of understanding. From across the lecture room came the voice of Robert Oppenheimer. 'I don't intend to deliver any lectures on the Fundamental Meaning of Quantum Mechanics,' he said, 'but the meaning of that question is a foolish one.'

His own students were used to what some of them called the 'blue glare treatment' – when aroused Oppenheimer's eyes seemed to turn from a grey-blue to a vivid blue. They learnt how to play along with it, but others were thrown by his sharpness and agility of mind. On one occasion the distinguished Japanese scientist, Hideki Yukawa, came to Berkeley, and Oppenheimer asked if he would address his group of postgraduates on his latest discovery, a new particle called a meson. Yukawa had progressed for no longer than a few minutes, when Oppenheimer interrupted him and went on to finish his explanation. Nobody, excepting, that is, poor Yukawa, thought this rude. The assumption seemed to be that Oppenheimer would understand and communicate better than the original researcher. Indeed, whatever the merits of his behaviour in this particular instance, it was certainly true that Oppenheimer's greatest ability was not as an original thinker, but as a critic. He was more adaptive than creative with a particular facility for essentialising and commenting on the thoughts of other people, and he obviously enjoyed the role of teacher greatly. Slowly, as the thirties progressed, his vision of establishing a truly American school of theoretical physics at Berkeley became a reality. Under his guidance, a dozen men earned their Ph.D.'s and went on to become

*A group of Berkeley colleagues on an outing to San Diego Zoo. Oppenheimer is second from right; his one-time student and close friend, Robert Serber, is on the far left. On the right is Luis Alvarez who was to work on the bomb project with Oppenheimer and was later to give evidence against him*

*The scientific staff of the Berkeley Radiation Laboratory in the magnet of Ernest Lawrence's 60″ cyclotron. (l–r and top to bottom)*
*A. S. Langsdorf,*
*S. J. Simmons,*
*J. G. Hamilton, D. H. Sloan,*
*J. R. Oppenheimer,*
*W. M. Brobeck, R. Cornog,*
*R. R. Wilson, E. Viez,*
*J. J. Livingood, J. Backus,*
*W. B. Mann, P. C. Aebersold,*
*E. M. McMillan,*
*E. M. Lyman, M. D. Kamen,*
*O. C. Kalbfell,*
*W. W. Salisbury,*
*J. H. Lawrence, R. Serber,*
*F. N. D. Kurie, R. T. Birge,*
*E. O. Lawrence, D. Cooksey,*
*A. H. Sneill, L. W. Alvarez,*
*P. H. Abelson*

some of the best theoretical physicists of their day. By the end of the 1930s, it was no longer obligatory for any promising graduate student to go to one of the European centres to complete their training. They could now come to Berkeley or Cal. Tech.

Although he completed some excellent work as a researcher, Oppenheimer was never in that top league who were in the running for the coveted Nobel Prize. Other Nobel Laureates freely admitted that he had one of the finest minds of his generation, but somehow one vital ingredient was missing. David Bohm, one of his graduate students at that time, believes the main reason for this relative failure was paradoxically the very same reason for his great success as a teacher. 'He was a dilettante. He just would not take his coat off and really get stuck in. He'd got the ability certainly, but he hadn't got the staying power.'

Perhaps even Oppenheimer's earliest sallies into politics were in some way a compensation for his failure to realise himself as an original scientist. Certainly this was true of later developments in his career, but his initial explorations into politics cannot for certain be put down to that reason. They were inextricably mixed up with his turbulent relationship with a girl called Jean Tatlock, because it was she who introduced him to the whole field of left-wing politics.

J. ROBERT OPPENHEIMER

Oppenheimer and Jean met in 1936, at a time when it seemed to a great number of people that Communism offered the only viable alternative to the Fascism which was gaining so much ground in Europe. The 'capitalist' nations, such as Britain and France, seemed to be spent forces on the international scene. They had done nothing about the German intervention in the Spanish Civil War. Instead, it was the Communist Party which had channelled and directed the men and resources into Spain to fight against Franco.

*The Radiation Laboratory at Berkeley, in which Ernest Lawrence built the early cyclotrons. It has since been demolished*

Nearer home, the Communist Party espoused a number of good causes. In California these ranged from the plight of the grossly exploited farm workers, to unemployment among young graduates leaving university. As a consequence the Party had attracted a large number of liberal-minded people to the activities and causes with which it was associated. Indeed, in 1935 the Communist International had realised the importance of these kinds of activities and had established the Popular Front as a way of fostering the links between the Party and left-wing liberal groups. It was an enormously successful policy, and even the news of the Stalinist purges, which was slowly emerging from Russia, did little to shake the belief amongst a wide range of people that here was a movement with great potential for constructive social change.

There were, of course, some people who saw the Popular Front as little more than a clever manoeuvre to extend the sphere of Communist influence, but in the mid-thirties this was a minority view. The Stalinist purges were seen by many as a necessary evil in the forging of a new political system, and there was a broad base of political and public acceptance for Communism.

The level of public acceptance was such that in the United States both the main political parties, Democrats and Republicans, at one time or another had formed political alliances with the Communist Party. In California in 1939, for example, the Democratic Congressman, Clyde Doyle, sat down with Communist officials to work out a campaign to elect a Democratic Governor for the State. Ten years later, in 1948, that same Clyde Doyle was a member of the anti-communist House Un-American Activities Committee.

When Jean Tatlock met Oppenheimer in the spring of 1936, she was in her mid-twenties, working for her doctorate in psychology on the Berkeley campus. Her father, John Tatlock, was a professor of mediaeval literature at Berkeley and well known locally for his right-wing views. His daughter, however, had become increasingly involved in left-wing activities, and by the time she met Oppenheimer she was an active member of the Communist Party. Details about her or her relationship with Oppenheimer are difficult to come by, but those who knew her described her as a 'beautiful girl' and 'real nice as well'. She was tall and slender, with green eyes, a combination of dark-haired beauty and intelligence which Oppenheimer found irresistible.

Up to that point in his life, Oppenheimer had remained remarkably ignorant of politics. He lived in an apartment where there was no telephone, no radio, and he read neither magazines nor newspapers. There is a story told by Ernest Lawrence that Oppenheimer did not hear about the Wall Street Crash of 1929

THE RADICAL PROFESSOR

*Haakon Chevalier in 1936. Professor of Romance languages at Berkeley and close friend of Oppenheimer's, he was later to become a central figure in Oppenheimer's security problems*

until six months later, when Lawrence told him. As Oppenheimer himself put it, 'I was interested in man and his experience, but I had no understanding of the relations of man to his society.'

However, two things had impinged on him directly and awakened his conscience. Firstly, his relatives in Germany were suffering directly from the Nazi oppression of the Jews and what they told him aroused in him what he later spoke of as a 'smouldering fury'. Secondly, the Great Depression drastically affected the kind of jobs available to his own students on graduation. 'Through them,' Oppenheimer said, 'I began to understand how deeply political and economic events could affect men's lives. I began to feel the need to participate more fully in the life of the community.' However, as he described it, he had 'no framework of political conviction or experience to give me perspective in this matter.'

So he found himself having to lean on others, and Jean Tatlock in particular, for guidance in channelling his new-found desire for political action. Within a year of meeting her, he had become involved in such organisations as the Friends of the Chinese People, the Western Council of the Consumers' Union, and the American Committee for Democracy and Intellectual Freedom. This last was concerned with the plight of German intellectuals but, like the others, it had links with the Communist Party. Very much in response to the hardship he saw among his own students, he played a part in setting up a local branch of the Teachers' Union, and it was through this organisation that he met yet another character who was to play an important part in his life.

Haakon Chevalier was a member of the modern languages faculty at Berkeley and, when Oppenheimer met him in 1937, he was president of the Teachers' Union. Chevalier had a French father and Norwegian mother and had spent the early years of his life in France and Norway before running away to sea at eighteen. He had eventually settled in America and became an academic specialising in French literature. He had already achieved something of a reputation as a translator of the works of André Malraux and had written a book on Anatole France. He had a reputation as a man who was 'charming, congenial, enthusiastic, and cultivated', and who 'knew French poetry, French wines and intelligent people'. He was described as intelligent but not brilliant and, bearing in mind Oppenheimer's predilection for friends of a similar intellectual calibre to himself, some people found it surprising that the two men became such firm friends. Perhaps it was their common interests, and Chevalier's respect for Oppenheimer which bordered on hero worship, that kept the two men so close for the next five years.

At this time, Oppenheimer was not satisfied with any token role in the Union and indeed became the branch's recording secretary. Chevalier remembers him working well into the night on such routine tasks as addressing and stamping envelopes.

Jean also introduced Oppenheimer to some of the leading West Coast left-wing figures – to men like Thomas Addis, Rudy Lambert and Kenneth May. These were the men who were declared Communists and whom some people suspected of manipulating the Popular Front to serve more specific Party ambitions. Ten years later their names were to be heard again in the hearings of the House Un-American Activities Committee.

Oppenheimer was to become very friendly with some of those men, in particular with Dr Thomas Addis who was a medical researcher studying kidney diseases at Stanford. From time to time the two would meet and, according to Oppenheimer, Addis would bring him up to date on matters such as the fighting in Spain – usually painting a desperate picture of the situation facing the Loyalists. Oppenheimer had already been giving money to various Spanish war relief groups, but now he was persuaded to make his donations through Addis and the Communist Party. From his ample bachelor's income of $15,000 a year (of which only $5,000 came from his teaching post, the rest from private sources) Oppenheimer donated around $1,000 dollars a year to various funds associated with the Communist Party. Addis was replaced as the intermediary in these deals by Isaac Folkoff, whom Oppenheimer was later to identify as a Communist Party functionary.

Whether these meetings were as innocent as Oppenheimer made out will probably never be known, but, whatever else he may have done, Oppenheimer always stopped short of becoming a Party member. This was not to be the case with his younger brother Frank.

Frank had always been very much overshadowed by his older, more brilliant brother. In retrospect he has come to feel that in so many ways Robert became something of a father figure, offering him personal advice, directing his career and so on. Once, some years before, when he was about to enter college to read physics, Frank had written asking advice on everything from art and greatness to the nature of humanity. In elaborate sentences, Robert had replied to the specific questions and then, anticipating Frank's personal uncertainties, had written:

I haven't answered everything you wrote, nor given you any brotherly advice. That's because I think you know pretty well what I should say: Discipline, work, honesty, and, towards other people, a solicitude for their welfare and as complete an indifference as possible to their good opinion.

It is as fulsomely paternal a piece of advice as one could find. On another occasion, Frank remembers asking his brother's advice because he felt he couldn't talk easily to girls. Robert's authoritative comment was, 'It's not your responsibility – it's theirs.'

Later, when he was finishing his postgraduate work at university, Frank became aware that his brother was fixing things for him, but without consulting him. Even now he is uncertain just how much his brother was responsible for his being appointed to some of the most important of his academic posts at Cal. Tech. and Stanford.

Perhaps it was as a reaction to his brother's overpowering presence that Frank decided to marry a girl of whom he did not approve. Jacquenette Quam was a Canadian who had majored at Berkeley in economics. When she met

*Oppenheimer's brother Frank (r) who joined the Communist Party in 1936*

*Frank Oppenheimer's wife Jackie, also a one-time Communist Party member, seen here at the Oppenheimers' New Mexico ranch*

Frank she became aware that Oppenheimer seemed afraid of losing his brother.

He tried to put us off from getting married [she said]. He was always saying things like 'Of course, you're much older than Frank' – I'm eight months older actually – and saying that Frank wasn't ready for it. Later he used to refer to me as 'the waitress my brother has married' because to pay my way I was working at a café on campus.

In spite of Oppenheimer's reluctance, the couple were married in September 1936. A few months later, they had both joined the Communist Party. Frank drove up to Berkeley to tell his brother the news. The response was predictable. Oppenheimer was upset. He thought his brother was being very foolish.

It was through Frank and Jackie that, according to Oppenheimer, he attended what was in his own words the only function 'recognisable . . . as a Communist Party Meeting'. It was at Frank's house and the main discussion concerned racial segregation at the local municipal swimming pool in Pasadena. Oppenheimer thought the meeting a rather pathetic event, and as he and a friend left the meeting, his friend echoed his own feelings. 'What a sad spectacle,' he said.

According to Oppenheimer, he never attended another Party meeting. Why did he have this apparent resistance to party membership and its regular functions? Friends have suggested that it was because he distrusted organisations of the size of the Communist Party and that he was too intelligent, too individualistic to be restricted by Party dogma. He also had no

J. ROBERT OPPENHEIMER

taste for local humdrum issues. They lacked the vision he needed to excite him.

However, years later the fact that he was never a member of the Party was to be overlooked. He was charged with having been 'a sufficiently hardened Communist' who probably 'volunteered espionage information to the Soviets or complied with a request for such information'.


Jean Tatlock has, so far, only been mentioned in her role as Oppenheimer's political mentor, but their love affair was to continue tempestuously for three years. 'We were at least twice close enough to marriage to consider ourselves engaged', recalled Oppenheimer; but each time marriage was imminent it was Jean who shied away. Much of the problem stemmed from her severe bouts of depression. According to those who knew her, she conformed to a classic manic-depressive pattern and, from time to time, became so unstable that she underwent treatment. She had also undergone psychoanalysis and Jackie Oppenheimer, who knew Jean well, remembers that, to Jean's horror, the analysis revealed latent lesbian tendencies. It seems that those tendencies were never fulfilled. At times of crisis in her relationship with Oppenheimer, Robert Serber, an ex-student and friend of Oppenheimer's, recalls that 'she disappeared for weeks, months sometimes, and then would taunt Robert mercilessly. She would taunt him about who she had been with and what they had been doing. She seemed determined to hurt him, perhaps because she knew Robert loved her so much.'

Part of the problem was the all too familiar one – Oppenheimer had put Jean on a pedestal and treated her with reverence. His gifts of flowers and perfume and jewellery in the end came to infuriate her. She wanted to be treated more robustly, more as an equal, but, as has been pointed out already, Oppenheimer seemed incapable of sustaining such a relationship. Eventually, in early 1939, their affair came to an end. It was Jean who finished it. During the past three years, there had been high spots, certainly, but, for much of the time, they had been two melancholy people who, while they could not bear to be apart, were miserable together.

However, the end of his affair with Jean did not mark the end of his left-wing political activities. Certainly he continued with his Teachers' Union work and maintained his donations to various funds through his Party contacts.

Looking back now [he wrote years later], I am not sure that the friendliness and attention to me on the part of some Communist Party members was as casual and natural as it then seemed. On the local scene, I had a certain minor prominence; I had a little money; I was engaged in work which, however abstract it appeared to me, was in time to lead me into the heart of secret military research. For all these reasons, Communists might have sought to cultivate my friendship in the hope they could in one way or another take advantage of it.

In retrospect there were those who were to wonder whether Oppenheimer could have really remained so naïve in his dealing with the Party and how he was seemingly able to come to terms with what was going on in the Soviet Union. For instance in 1938 two scientists, Victor Weisskopf and George Placzek, paid a long visit to the Perro Caliente ranch. They had just returned from an extended stay in Russia and what they told Oppenheimer of concentration camps, purge trials, and the lack of personal and professional freedom appalled him. He described their reports as 'so solid, so unfanatical, so true, that [they] made a great impression.'

The Russo-German pact of non-aggression in August 1939 shocked him as it had done many others who had looked to Russia and Communism as the main hope against Fascism. Indeed, at the time there was a reaction against the Communist Party in the United States. A number of its leaders were victimised. There was a great deal of hysterical criticism in the newspapers, but Oppenheimer did not follow this trend. Indeed, even the start of the war in Europe, with Russia and Germany ranged against the French and the British, did not seem to shake his faith. In early 1940, the College Faculties Committee of the Communist Party of California issued a series of pamphlets entitled *Reports to our Colleagues* which were circulated around the campuses. The author was alleged to be Robert Oppenheimer and if they represent anything of his personal views at the time they make fascinating reading.

The Communist Party is being attacked for its support of the Soviet policy. But the total extermination of the Party here cannot reverse that policy: it can only silence some of the voices, some of the clearest voices, that oppose a war between the United States and Russia. What the attack can do directly, what it is meant to do, is to disrupt the democratic forces, to destroy unions in general and CIO unions in particular, to make possible the cutting of relief, to force the abandonment of the great program of peace, security, and work that is the basis of the movement toward a democratic front.

Throughout, the author tries to dissociate the Party's social ambitions from the political ambitions of the Soviet Union, and it is possible to interpret this in at least two ways. It can be seen as an attempt by a hard-line Communist to preserve the Party, come what may. It can also be seen as the desperate attempt of a social idealist to preserve something of what he had been striving for. Whatever the interpretation, these articles do indicate a much deeper involvement in the political thinking of the Party than Oppenheimer was ever to admit to.

After parting with Jean, Oppenheimer had several short affairs. Then in August 1939, while teaching at Cal Tech, he met Kathryn Puening at a colleague's garden party. Kitty Puening was German. In fact, according to Kitty, she was a German princess and her uncle was General Keitel. She was born in 1910, and her parents had come to the United States when she was two and she grew up in Aspinwall, a suburb of Pittsburgh. Her father was an engineer working in the steel industry.

After graduating from high school, her life became a confused succession of

J. ROBERT OPPENHEIMER

new experiences. She started her college education in Pittsburgh, but after a year went to France, first to the Sorbonne, then to the University of Grenoble. In Paris her 'friends for the most part were musicians. . . . I spent little time on school work.' She then returned to Pittsburgh, but after a few months again decided to return to the excitement of the large European cities. It was then that she married for the first time, to a musician, but the marriage only lasted for a few months. Kitty discovered that her husband was a drug addict and their marriage was annulled. The court proceedings of the annulment were considered sufficiently obscene at the time to be struck from the public record.

In 1933, she returned more or less permanently to the United States where she enrolled at the University of Wisconsin and this time she decided to major in English. Over the Christmas of 1933, Kitty stayed with old friends in Pittsburgh and she and a friend, Zelma Baker, decided to hold a New Year's Eve party.

While we were making these plans [Kitty wrote years later] Zelma told us that she had met a Communist whom, she thought, we would find interesting. . . . The consensus

*Kitty Oppenheimer. Robert, whom she married in 1940, was her fourth husband*

was that none of us had ever met a real live Communist, and that it would be interesting to see one. At any event, Zelma brought him to the party.

The 'Communist' was Joe Dallet, son of a wealthy investment banker. He had been educated at Dartmouth, and five years before had destroyed his family ties to devote himself to union activities amongst the Pittsburgh steelworkers.

'Joe was three years older than I,' Kitty recalled. 'He was tall and big, with dark hair and eyes. He was, I thought, good-looking. I fell in love with him at this party, and I never stopped loving him.'

Two months later, Kitty threw up her course at Wisconsin and went to Pittsburgh where she and Joe were married.

I did the best I could to help him with his work [she was both an organiser for the union and for the local Communist Party]. I typed letters, mimeographed leaflets, and did general office work.

These were days of poverty such as I had never before experienced. We lived in a house, part of which we rented for $5.00 per month. Our only income was a relief payment of $12.40 every two weeks [in contrast to Oppenheimer's $1,200 a month]. The house had a kitchen, but the stove leaked and it was impossible to cook. Our food consisted of two meals a day which we got at a grimy restaurant. The price was 15 c each and the meal consisted of soup, meat, potato, cabbage, a doughnut and coffee. This house had two bedrooms. Joe and I had one of these and the other was occupied by John Gates and Orval Hallberg (two future national Communist Party leaders). Hallberg finally moved out because Gates was so filthy. . . . Because of Joe's insistence, I was finally permitted to join the Party, but not until I had done a number of tasks which were extremely painful to me, such as selling the *Daily Worker* on the street and passing out leaflets at the steel mill. . . .

As time went on, although Joe and I continued to be very much in love, the poverty became more and more depressing to me. . . . Finally in June, 1936, I told Joe that I could no longer live under such conditions and that I was separating from him.

She went to England where her parents were then living and after a short while returned very much to her old life-style. She started at a school of dress design and that winter went skiing in Switzerland. For some months she heard nothing from her husband until she discovered her mother had been intercepting his letters. Desperately unhappy, she wrote asking Joe to take her back, but then she heard that he was coming to Europe himself – to fight in Spain.

The two had a brief reunion in Paris in June 1937, then Joe went to Spain and they both hoped that she could join him there. But this was not to be. In October, she was summoned to Paris for what she thought was the first leg of her journey to Spain, but on arrival she was given a telegram telling her of Joe's death in action.

At first she did not know what to do, but a friend of Joe's, another Communist, Steve Nelson, was passing through Paris and for two weeks stayed to help her get over her grief. She then returned, via England, to the United States, and in 1938 resumed her university studies, this time in biology at the

*Steve Nelson in the early 1950s. In his youth he was an organiser with the Alameda County Communist Party in California and a good friend of Kitty Oppenheimer's*

J. ROBERT OPPENHEIMER

University of Pennsylvania.

Later that year she renewed an acquaintance with a British doctor, Richard Harrison, whom she had known since she was a teenager. In November they married – it was Kitty's third marriage. This marriage Kitty described as 'singularly unsuccessful from the start'. The couple lived apart for much of the first year, Kitty finishing her degree, Richard Harrison studying for his National MB at a hospital in Los Angeles. When Kitty met Robert Oppenheimer in August 1939, she and her husband had just moved into an apartment together.

The effect of that first meeting at the Pasadena garden party was electric on both of them. 'I fell in love with Robert that day,' Kitty wrote, 'but hoped to conceal it. I had agreed to stay with Dick Harrison because of his conviction that a divorce might ruin a rising young doctor.'

The concealment did not last for long. The following summer, Oppenheimer asked the Harrisons, both of them, to spend the summer with him at the ranch in New Mexico. However, Harrison was studying for his final medical exam and could not go. According to those who knew her, Kitty then engineered a visit to the ranch on her own for health reasons. According to Kitty, 'Dick had, however, personal reasons for wanting me to go without him.'

Whatever the circumstances, Kitty drove up with friends to the ranch and 'it was then that Robert and I realised that we were both in love.'

On their return Kitty took the initiative and went to Reno to wait the statutory period of residence prior to obtaining a divorce. At that time she probably knew she was pregnant. On 1 November 1940, she both divorced Richard Harrison and married Robert Oppenheimer. This was her fourth marriage.

The speed of their romance took everyone by surprise. Some people were shocked by it, but there were numbers of others who felt that at last Oppenheimer had been humanised. He had run off with another man's wife. His flesh was as weak as the next man's. But how had it happened, this humanisation? Even though Oppenheimer had had a number of affairs he still found it difficult to relate on anything like equal terms to women; friends who saw this relationship take shape felt he was nevertheless extremely vulnerable to a direct and forthright sexual approach. They saw this as his first truly sexual affair in which Kitty, an experienced woman, had taken the initiative.

Within a short time, friends noted a definite change in Oppenheimer's social habits. He began to see less and less of some of his old friends, in particular some of his old political colleagues. Instead, the couple began to move in a different circle: less intellectual and more social. Naturally this was seen very much as Kitty's doing and a degree of resentment built up against her. With very few exceptions, everyone I met who knew her, actively disliked her.

Kitty was a schemer [said Jackie Oppenheimer]. If Kitty wanted anything she would always get it. I remember one time when she got it into her head to do a Ph.D and the way she cosied up to this poor little Dean of the biological sciences was shameful. She never did the Ph.D. It was just another of her whims. She was a phoney. All her political convictions were phoney, all her ideas were borrowed. Honestly, she's one of the few really evil people I've known in my life.

In May 1941, after a difficult pregnancy, Kitty gave birth to their first child, a son they christened Peter, but who was nicknamed Pronto, from the speed of his arrival after their marriage. Oppenheimer was suffering from mononucleosis, and they both wanted very much to escape to New Mexico to recuperate. For a time it seemed out of the question, but then the Chevaliers, Haakon and his wife Barbara, came to the rescue, offering to look after the two-month-old Peter while the couple were away.

It was an incident-packed holiday. Kitty had a motoring accident, Oppenheimer was kicked by a horse. They met the physicist, Hans Bethe, in the area and asked him to come and visit. Later they were to be glad of so many memorable incidents and therefore so many alibis, as it was claimed that the couple were not in New Mexico at that time at all.

Back in Berkeley, the couple moved into a new home on Eagle Hill. Shortly after they had moved in, Kitty heard that Steve Nelson, the man who had comforted her in Paris after Joe Dallet's death, was in the area. He was now an organiser with the Alameda County Communist Party but, notwithstanding, Kitty invited him, his wife and baby out to the new house for a picnic. It was the first time Oppenheimer met Steve Nelson and according to Kitty 'the conversation was purely social'. Later she met Nelson again on several occasions – on his own in a low-price restaurant and at his apartment with his family.

This was at a time when Oppenheimer was beginning to become involved in war work, but Kitty was to state that she 'never discussed Robert's war work with Steve' and that Nelson 'evidenced no interest in Robert or in Robert's work.' Yet soon after this, Nelson was to attract the attention of the FBI and their reports were to indicate a strong interest by Nelson in the highly secret war projects being developed at Berkeley.

As we shall see in the next chapter, Oppenheimer had first become involved on the embryo atomic bomb project through Ernest Lawrence. Lawrence had been asked to commit his cyclotron to use as a means of separating out uranium for the bomb and initially he asked for Oppenheimer's assistance over some theoretical problems. In October of 1941 he had then taken Oppenheimer to a meeting of all the top scientists on the project at General Electric's laboratory at Schenectady.

It was the realisation that America must surely soon join in a life or death race with the Germans to produce the most deadly weapon ever conceived, and that he could play a key role in that race, that more than anything changed Oppenheimer's attitude towards his other political activities. Up to that time he had maintained his regular meetings and payments to Communist Party officials but this new project made the cause of the scattered and defeated Spanish Republicans seem even less relevant than it had been.

On the night of 6 December 1941, Oppenheimer returned from a Spanish War Veterans Rally feeling acutely disillusioned with these activities. It was to be the last meeting of its kind that Oppenheimer would attend. Within hours, the news was announced of the Japanese attack on Pearl Harbor and the United States entered the war in earnest.

'I decided that I had had enough of the Spanish cause,' Oppenheimer said, 'and that there were other and more pressing crises in the world.'

*Veterans of the Lincoln Brigade returning to New York from fighting against Fascism and Franco in Spain. Such a diverse group as this indicates the wide appeal of the allied causes of Communism and anti-Fascism*

# CHAPTER 3 THE BEGINNINGS OF THE BOMB

Early in 1939, Oppenheimer had attended a Physics Conference in Washington where he heard a review paper on the latest European work on fission. Even then there had been a great deal of discussion about the possibility of an atomic weapon being developed, but at that time the French work, confirming a fission chain reaction, had not been published.

When Joliot Curie's letter did appear, in the 22 April edition of the British scientific journal, *Nature*, it confirmed without doubt that such a weapon was possible. With atomic fission, vast amounts of energy were liberated, and between, on average, 3 and 4 more neutrons per fission. Joliot Curie had shown that enough of these neutrons encountered other atoms, causing them to fission, producing more energy and more neutrons to produce a chain reaction. In the tiniest fraction of a second, the chain reaction would generate enormous amounts of energy – it would be an explosive reaction of unprecedented power.

The *Nature* letter was read within days in centres of physics throughout the world.

## THE EARLY HISTORY OF THE BOMB

1931 Cockroft and Walton split the atom.

1932 James Chadwick discovers the neutron.

1934 The Joliot-Curies discover artificial radioactivity – by bombarding a target with alpha particles, as a result new elements were produced.

1934 Enrico Fermi extends the Joliot-Curies' work and bombards elements not with alpha particles but with the newly discovered neutrons. When he did this with uranium as the target he reported finding several different artificially radioactive elements as products.

1938 Hahn and Strassmann prove that what Fermi had observed 4 years earlier was the 'bursting' of the nucleus. The first paper from them describing what was to become known as 'Atomic Fission' was published internationally on 22 December 1938.

1939 Frisch and Meitner describe the mechanism for this 'fission' and indicate that large amounts of energy are given off by the process. The big question was whether neutrons were liberated which could then cause a further fission, a further release of energy and so on to produce a chain reaction.

1939 Leo Szilard confirms that the neutrons are produced and an explosive chain reaction is likely.

1939 22 April: a letter in *Nature* from the Joliot-Curies confirming that 3.5 neutrons are produced by every fission. The chain reaction is confirmed.

In Germany, it precipitated a high-level meeting within a week of publication. The meeting took place secretly on 29 April in the Ministry of Education's headquarters in Berlin, and resulted in a decision to commandeer all existing stocks of uranium, and to obtain fresh supplies from the newly captured mines in Czechoslovakia.

It was indicative of the times that one of the scientists at the meeting tried to censure his fellow Germans, Hahn and Strassmann, for freely publishing their research on fission and thereby making it available to the whole world. He gained practically no support for his motion. In spite of the international situation, and the obvious strategic importance of the work, scientists were still very unwilling to relinquish their tradition of open exchange of information.

At Otto Hahn's institute in Dahlem, Dr Siegfried Flugge heard about the secret meeting, and the decision made there, with considerable dismay. He had little faith in his own government and their ability to act responsibly, so he decided to do what he could to ensure that the whole world would know of what work was going on in Germany. In June of that year, with a freedom which seems amazing nowadays, the German periodical *Naturwissenschaften* published an article by Flugge reviewing the potential for nuclear energy. It had an effect that Flugge could not have guessed at.


In the United States, Leo Szilard, the Hungarian immigrant scientist, had been furious about the letter published by the French scientists in the April edition of *Nature*.

In February 1939, working in a borrowed laboratory, with a borrowed sample of radium, he had proved most of what the French had now published. However, instead of publishing, Szilard had been so frightened by his own discovery that he had campaigned furiously for a moratorium on the publication of any more work associated with nuclear fission. He had been reasonably successful in the US, perhaps because not much of this work was going on there, and he had then written to various European centres, including Paris, proposing the same policy. For their own internal political reasons, the French had chosen to ignore his proposal and had gone ahead and published. In all probability the Germans would very soon have covered the same ground as the French workers and confirmed the chain reaction themselves, but Joliot Curie's paper was seen, with good reason by Szilard, as the starting flag in the race to produce the first nuclear weapon.

Indeed, all the indications from Germany that summer pointed to the fact that they were taking the bomb very seriously. Firstly it was heard that they had banned all exports of uranium from the Joachimsthal mines in Czechoslovakia. Then because of a minor indiscretion at Hahn's laboratory in the presence of a visiting British scientist, it became known that the Germans had held a high-level secret meeting on nuclear energy. Finally, in June, Flugge's article in *Naturwissenschaften* appeared. Far from being interpreted as an attempt to keep the nuclear fission debate out in the open, it was taken to

*Albert Einstein (l) with Leo Szilard in the late 1940s re-enacting the writing of the letter to President Roosevelt in 1939. This letter led to the setting up of the American atomic weapons programme*

be an indication of just how advanced the Germans were. If they can publish this much with impunity, the thinking went, just how much more do they know?

Szilard now felt most strongly that some positive action was necessary. For one thing, the United States must ensure that it had access to the mines of the Belgian Congo, the only other substantial source of uranium outside Czechoslovakia. This would mean contacting the Belgians and Szilard knew of only one person with good contacts there and that was Albert Einstein. He was a personal friend of the Belgian Royal Family and when approached by Szilard, he agreed to help in any way he could.

But then Szilard's fertile mind thought of another use for Einstein. Along with the banker, Alexander Sachs, Szilard had already drafted a letter to President Roosevelt urging that the American Government join the race to produce a nuclear weapon. Sachs had the contact with Roosevelt but felt that the letter needed Einstein's scientific weight behind it. Again Einstein agreed to help – a step which in later years he was to regret bitterly. However, in the

J. ROBERT OPPENHEIMER

short-term it had the desired effect. After an initial reluctance, Roosevelt eventually saw the significance of the request.

'Alex, what you are after is to see that the Nazis don't blow us up?' Roosevelt is reported as saying.

'Precisely,' said Sachs.

It was then that Roosevelt called in his attaché, General 'Pa' Wilson, and, pointing to the Einstein–Szilard–Sachs document, said, 'Pa, this requires action!'

Which, of course, is how all good American stories go, but somehow this one subsequently went adrift. While the Germans were making such rapid progress, Roosevelt's commanding presidential statement simply heralded the beginning of two years' messy and unproductive in-fighting.

The responsibility for implementing the presidential edict went to Lyman Briggs at the Bureau of Standards and he invited some of the country's best physicists to serve on a Uranium Committee. Briggs was a respected figure but at the time he was plagued by ill health. From the beginning he failed to fire his Committee with any sense of urgency. He was also obsessed by secrecy – so obsessed, in fact, that only a tiny fraction of the people asked to work on the Committee's projects had any idea that they were working on a bomb. 'This aspect was played down', said Dr Sam Allison of the University of Chicago, who was an actual committee member. 'We weren't told. I thought we were making a power source for submarines.'

Briggs was also unwilling to spend money and so all the projects were hampered, not only by secrecy, but by a shortage of funds. At the end of nearly two years the committee had managed to spend only $50,000.

How long this state of affairs would have continued is difficult to say, but in July 1941 a group of scientists from Britain came to try and provoke the Americans to greater activity. The British had very quickly realised the possibility of a nuclear weapon and, in early 1940, had established the Maud Committee, a rough equivalent to the Uranium Committee. For more than a year, it had reported valuable experimental work, both on the construction of a weapon and on ways of separating the rare uranium isotope which would constitute the core of the bomb. However, with the country stretched to its limits they simply did not have the resources to move on to the manufacturing stage. For some time the British had been disappointed at the progress being made in the United States, and so they had sent this mission headed by the Australian scientist, Marcus Oliphant, to try to provoke more action. Very quickly Oliphant recognised that Briggs and the Uranium Committee were unlikely to respond as necessary. He went instead to an old friend, Oppenheimer's colleague at Berkeley, Ernest Lawrence, and impressed on him the urgency of the situation and the reality of the German threat.

Oliphant had little difficulty in winning over Lawrence and, in turn, Lawrence had to decide how best to outflank the Uranium Committee and ensure that some action was taken. In the end he seized on the opportunity provided by a degree ceremony in Chicago to talk to James Conant, the senior

*Ernest Lawrence (r) and Marcus Oliphant, the Australian scientist who, in 1941, used his friendship with Lawrence to provoke the Americans into more action on the A-bomb*

*Arthur Holly Compton, Head of the Metallurgical Lab. at Chicago from 1942. It was Compton who invited Oppenheimer to join the bomb project*

scientist to whom the Uranium Committee reported. Lawrence confronted Conant in September 1941, in the living room of Chicago's Dean of Physics, Arthur Compton. According to Compton, Lawrence first reported his conversations with Oliphant on how feasible the bomb was and how, if the Germans made it, they 'would have in their hands the control of the world'.

Conant was reluctant [Compton wrote]. As a result of the reports so far received he had concluded that the time had come to drop the support of nuclear research as a subject for wartime study. . . . I rallied to Lawrence's support. I confirmed his interpretation of the new scientific results [from Britain] as indicating the practical feasibility of the atomic bomb. I described the rough estimates that had been made of the destructive power of such a weapon. I told of the evidence that the Nazis were making a major effort of the atomic programme. They would not do so in the midst of war unless they believed they might succeed. Conant began to be convinced. . . . He turned to Lawrence, 'Ernest, you say you are convinced of the importance of these fission bombs. Are you ready to devote the next several years of your life to getting them made?' Conant had put his finger on the crucial point. The question brought Lawrence up with a start. I can still recall the expression in his eyes as he sat there with his mouth half open. Here was a serious personal decision. . . . He hesitated only a moment, 'If you tell me this is my job, I'll do it'.

In fact, to some extent James Conant was only pretending to need convincing because he had already begun to implement changes to the Uranium Committee, reinforcing its membership in crucial areas. But, following that September meeting with Lawrence, he determined to send a small mission to see the work in Britain at first hand. Then he helped Vannevar Bush, the presidential adviser on science, to prepare for a meeting with Roosevelt on

*Scientific leaders of the bomb project discussing electro-magnetic separation of uranium in 1940. (l–r) Ernest Lawrence, Arthur Compton, Vannevar Bush, James Conant, Karl Compton, Alfred Loomis*

J. ROBERT OPPENHEIMER

9 October 1941. At that meeting they managed to convince Roosevelt of the urgency of the situation, and Bush came away with an order to expedite the development of a nuclear weapon in every way possible. That meeting was a crucial step on the path that led to Hiroshima and Nagasaki.

Meanwhile, as good as his word, Lawrence returned to Berkeley and started planning to convert his latest cyclotron, very much his pride and joy, from its use as a research tool into a machine for extracting the rare U-235 isotope of uranium needed for the core of the bomb. He also began trying to analyse the implications of the British work described to him by Oliphant and, to help him, he called on the services of Robert Oppenheimer. This was Oppenheimer's first involvement with the nuclear weapons project but, in the next two months, he attended a number of top-level meetings all aimed at trying to work out a proper strategy for developing the new weapon. The most important meeting was at General Electric's laboratories at Schenectady on 21 October 1941, where Oppenheimer provided the calculations for the amount of U-235 that would be needed for an effective weapon. The final report of that meeting, which contained Oppenheimer's calculations, was the blueprint for the bomb design and provides a remarkably good plain man's guide to how they hoped the bomb would work.

The basic conclusion of the report, written by Arthur Compton, was that 'a fission bomb of superlatively destructive power would result from assembling quickly a sufficient mass of Uranium-235.'

The word 'sufficient' is the interesting one because it contains the key to the whole principle of the bomb. As already described, the crucial reaction which makes an explosive chain reaction possible is the one between a neutron and a Uranium-235 atom.

$$n + U^{235} \longrightarrow 2 \; \underset{116}{Barium} + 3n + Energy$$

The neutrons produced by the first fission travel out across the uranium until they collide with another uranium atom when another fission will take place, and so on. It is hard to imagine but the hard uranium metal is very largely space – it consists of atomic nuclei linked by powerful inter-atomic forces but with relatively enormous spaces between them. This means that there is only a limited chance that each neutron will collide with a uranium atom to produce further fissions. Indeed, the lump of uranium has to be a 'sufficient' size for there to be enough of a chance of a collision to create a fast enough chain reaction. This was the size that Oppenheimer calculated.

He estimated that a piece of uranium weighing a hundred kilograms would be sufficient. This mass was called the critical mass. Below it there would not be sufficient collisions to start the chain reactions and a majority of the neutrons would fly off into the space beyond the metal. Above it there would be an explosion.

The other key word in the report's summary was 'quickly'. How do you assemble this explosive critical mass quickly?

Very simply – at least in theory:

$$50 \text{ kg} \quad + \quad 50 \text{ kg} \quad = \quad 100 \text{ kg}$$
$$\text{subcritical} \qquad \text{subcritical} \qquad \text{critical}$$

The practical problems of assembly, however, are immense. If the two pieces came together too slowly, then a stray neutron emerging from one piece could trigger a localised nuclear reaction in the other piece which would be enough to blow the bomb apart and prevent the major reaction from taking place. This 'pre-detonation', as it was called, was to be one of the big initial problems that the bomb designers had to overcome. The other major problem they foresaw was how to produce enough of the precious Uranium-235 isotope. It was, they knew, present in ordinary uranium ore in a ratio of one part in three hundred, but because Uranium-235 is chemically identical to the common Uranium-238 isotope, which makes up the rest of the uranium metal, it was going to be enormously difficult to separate the two. Ernest Lawrence intended to use his giant cyclotron to bring about the separation.

By the end of the Schenectady meeting they had also worked out the likely force of the bomb. In theory one kilogram of uranium could produce an explosive energy equivalent to several hundred tons of TNT, but, because even the best reactions blew themselves apart after a very short time, they estimated that no explosion would produce more than a tenth of that available energy. This still meant that a bomb of the size Oppenheimer had indicated – about one hundred kilograms – would produce an explosive energy equivalent to several thousand tons of TNT. It was the first time scientists had come face to face with the realities of the weapon they were about to create.

In the months following the Schenectady meeting, Oppenheimer continued to perform calculations and offer advice to Lawrence and Compton. By January 1942, Compton had been sufficiently impressed by him to ask him to come and work full-time on the Bomb Project. As part of the reshaping of the Uranium Committee, Compton was putting his own men wherever he felt there was a weak point and he put Oppenheimer to work alongside Gregory Breit, supervising the construction of the bomb mechanism. Breit, whose official title of Co-ordinator of Rapid Rupture caused Oppenheimer some amusement, was an extremely cautious, touchy man. For both of them, the next four months were to prove extremely difficult. Breit must have felt threatened by Oppenheimer and yet Compton gave him no backing. For his part, Oppenheimer had to contend with Breit's awkward personality and his obsession with secrecy.

Breit was always frightened something would be revealed in the seminars [said Allison, now a member of Breit's team]. Oppenheimer was frightened something would not. I backed Oppenheimer and challenged Breit to cut the censorship. He accused me of being reckless and hostile to him. I failed – the seminars became uninformative.

Eventually, it was Breit who gave in. On 18 May 1942, he resigned and left the bomb project entirely. Oppenheimer was left in sole charge of the programme.

*The Co-ordinator of Rapid Rupture, Gregory Breit. He and Oppenheimer did not get on and his eventual resignation in May 1942 left Oppenheimer in charge of developing the bomb mechanism*

Only six months after attending his last Spanish War Veterans Meeting on the eve of Pearl Harbor, Oppenheimer was occupying a central position in the bomb project. In early 1942 he had finally stopped the payments via the Communist Party into various charities. Years later there were to be those who construed this not as a sign of dwindling interest or even of political expediency but as a preparation for Oppenheimer's new role as Communist within the system.

However, by no means all his actions were consistent with this theory. Sometime early in 1942 he was asked to fill in a security questionnaire and in this he freely admitted that, although he had never been a Communist Party member, he had been 'a member of just about every Communist Front organisation on the West Coast'. Such a full and ready admission does not, on the face of it, seem consistent with someone preparing to infiltrate a secret project.

In October 1941, a meeting took place which was to be crucial to the future of the German effort towards producing a fission bomb.

By this stage in the war the Germans, unlike either the Americans or the British, had been running a full research programme on the bomb and were very well advanced. They had designed and built their first atomic pile, and they now had the industrial capacity to produce a ton of uranium a month with which to fuel it. The scientist in charge of the work, Professor Werner von Heisenberg, was later to say 'it was from September 1941 that we saw the open road ahead of us, leading to the atomic bomb'.

This realisation precipitated a moral debate amongst the German scientists,

*Werner Heisenberg, a leading German atomic scientist who, in 1941, sought Niels Bohr's advice on the moral question of working on atomic weapons in wartime*

*A group of eminent physicists in 1920. Lise Meitner is in the centre, Niels Bohr on her right and Otto Hahn, one of the discoverers of fission, immediately behind her*

and at the end of October Heisenberg travelled to German-occupied Denmark to speak with Professor Niels Bohr. Bohr was one of the most distinguished and respected of physicists who at one time or another had taught many of the senior scientists working on both the Allied and German projects including Heisenberg. So far he had uneasily sat out the war in German-occupied Denmark, resisting any attempts by the Germans to involve him in the war effort. Thus when Heisenberg visited him it was, as someone described it, as if Heisenberg, the 'high priest' of German science, was going to seek absolution from his Pope. According to Heisenberg, he went to seek guidance from the uncommitted Bohr on whether a physicist had a moral right to work on the problems of atomic bombs in wartime. He even obliquely proposed to Bohr that there should be an international agreement among scientists not to work on these projects but, for whatever reason, Bohr refused to be drawn by this proposal.

Apparently Bohr suspected a German attempt to neutralise the Allied superiority in nuclear physics and thus, to Heisenberg's surprise, replied that military research was inevitable everywhere and was thus proper too. Heisenberg returned to Germany without the advice he claimed to be seeking and the German bomb effort proceeded apace. For his part Bohr was left with a firm conviction that Germany was on the brink of producing a fission bomb, a conviction he was to convey as passionately as he was able when two years later he escaped from Denmark to join the Allies.

When Oppenheimer took over from Breit he was well aware of the need for a complete re-evaluation of the work on the bomb mechanism. For instance, ever

*Le Conte Hall, Berkeley. It was in the attic rooms of this building that Oppenheimer's study group met in the summer of 1942 to discuss the theoretical aspects of the fission bomb and came up with the possibility of atmospheric ignition*

J. ROBERT OPPENHEIMER

since his own theoretical calculations on the critical mass of the uranium weapon, there had been no experimental work to confirm or disprove his calculations. This meant that the scientists still did not know something as basic as whether they were going to need two, twenty or two hundred kilograms of uranium.

A team in Chicago was set to work on this problem, while Oppenheimer called together a team of theoretical physicists to see how far they could go in developing an exact specification for the bomb which the engineers could then start work on.

This group met at regular intervals throughout that summer in two attic rooms at the top of Le Conte Hall, the administrative block on the Berkeley campus where Oppenheimer had his office. They met under what, for those early days, were considered strict security arrangements. The windows were all clad in wire mesh, including the exit on to the small balcony outside, and the door was fitted with a special lock with a single key which was given to Oppenheimer.

The group that Oppenheimer brought together for those discussions was a distinguished one. Among it was the aristocratic Swiss physicist, Felix Bloch; Robert Serber, a former student of Oppenheimer's who was now working with him at Berkeley; John van Vleck, one of the future Nobel Laureates in the group; the German physicist Hans Bethe; and the Hungarian, Edward Teller.

At the start of their sessions, they had before them the results of mainly small scale and disparate investigations, which included research from several of the groups that had been working for Breit; but some of the most significant results came from Britain.

At the start, they tried to evoke an idea of the scale and impact of the weapon they were devising. They began by studying the effects of past explosions, like that of the fully-loaded ammunition ship which had gone up in the harbour of Halifax, Nova Scotia, in 1917. On this occasion, 5,000 tons of TNT had completely destroyed two and a half square miles of the centre of Halifax and killed up to 4,000 people. The new weapon could be expected to produce several times the blast, so, using scale laws, they multiplied up the effect of the Halifax accident. These calculations were to enable Oppenheimer and his colleagues to visualise in much greater detail the devastating potential of the new weapon.

Next they dealt with elementary aspects of how the bomb would look, its basic structure, its size and so on. They envisaged it, at the instant before explosion, as a sphere of uranium inside a heavy metal shell which would both contain the explosion for crucial milliseconds and reflect back the escaping neutrons into the fissioning uranium metal. They even had a rough estimate, from the British, of the average theoretical distance a neutron would have to travel before colliding with an atom and producing another fission. The figure was ten centimetres (four inches), meaning that a sphere eight inches in diameter should contain enough neutrons for a chain reaction to go ahead.

They were also able to give more precise figures for the length of time in

DATE 2-13-42

*Robert Oppenheimer at the time he joined the bomb project. It was then that he admitted in a security questionnaire that he had been 'a member of just about every Communist Front organisation on the West Coast'*

*Robert Serber was a member of Oppenheimer's Le Conte study group. He was to become one of Oppenheimer's closest colleagues at Los Alamos*

*The devastated harbour of Halifax, Nova Scotia, in 1917. A munitions ship carrying 5,000 tons of TNT collided with another ship in the harbour and exploded. The Le Conte Hall study group used this explosion to project the likely effects of the A-bomb*

BELOW RIGHT *Felix Bloch (r), the Swiss physicist with George Uhlenbeck (l) and Enrico Fermi*

BELOW *Hans Bethe who also took part in the Le Conte Hall meetings. He later became head of the Theoretical Division at Los Alamos*

which the bomb would have to be assembled and detonated – less than a millionth of a second. The specifications for the weapon would have to be very tight indeed. Also in those tiny moments of time the core of the bomb would be converted from metal, to liquid, to gas, while the fission process was still proceeding. They had to try to work out just how well the fission reaction would continue under such disruptive physical forces, but Hans Bethe, who had done original research on the reactions inside the sun, already had a fairly precise model worked out of what would be happening.

As the weeks went by the group worked out and collated not only what was known, but what stages still had to be gone through if the weapon was to be made. Robert Serber was one of those who was impressed by the progress they were making, and he very quickly marked this down to Oppenheimer's abilities as Chairman. Edward Teller was another who noticed how well they were progressing and he also attributed the success to Oppenheimer.

'As Chairman, Oppenheimer showed a refined, sure, informal touch,' he said. 'I don't know how he had acquired this facility for handling people.

Those who knew him well were really surprised. I suppose it was the kind of knowledge a politician or administrator has to pick up somewhere.'

Yet again, Oppenheimer's phenomenally quick mind, his ability to grasp other people's ideas and then to clarify and direct them was proving invaluable. The politeness he had shown in his early years had matured into a grave but urbane charm which he now knew how to use to great advantage. All those abilities were about to be severely taxed when, early in July, Edward Teller mentioned a new idea that had been his increasing preoccupation.

Almost a year earlier, he and the Italian physicist – and Nobel Laureate – Enrico Fermi had been enjoying a quiet lunch together and hypothesising about what might lie beyond fission.

Both of them were familiar with the work of scientists such as the Russian, George Gamow, and Teller's friend, Hans Bethe, on the source of energy in stars. This energy, they believed, came from intense heat which caused light nuclei, such as hydrogen, to fuse and in the process to release incredible amounts of energy. Perhaps it was possible, Fermi had suggested, for the detonation of a fission bomb to create the intense heat needed for the fusion reaction here on earth. The result would be such a release of energy that it would overshadow even the enormous potential of fission. A rough calculation indicated that, weight for weight, a fusion reaction in deuterium gas (a heavy form of hydrogen) would produce five times as much energy as a fission reaction in uranium; and deuterium is much cheaper and more easily obtainable than uranium. In that lunchtime conversation, the idea of the thermonuclear weapon, the 'super' as it came to be known, was born. While Fermi had other preoccupations, Teller was to become increasingly fascinated by this idea for a new weapon.

Teller first mentioned the bomb to the Berkeley group because of its economic advantages, but as July wore on he came more and more to monopolise the group's time with endless discussions of various aspects of the 'super'. After a while, some of the other members of the group became impatient. They were not, in their view, doing what they set out to do. But then, at the end of July, Teller came up with some information that totally disrupted the meetings and threatened to finish the weapon programme altogether.

Teller had been doing some calculations on the heat build-up in a fission reaction, as part of his assessment of how effectively a fission reaction would set off the consequent fusion reaction. His calculations showed that not only would the fission reaction cause the fusion in the deuterium, but it would also create enough heat to cause a reaction between the deuterium and nitrogen. And so? you might ask. Nitrogen makes up eighty per cent of the earth's atmosphere. According to Teller's figures, the initial fission reaction would create enough heat to set light to the earth's atmosphere.

Immediately Oppenheimer called a halt to the discussions until they had time to check Teller's results and work out the consequences. Hans Bethe was set to work on the calculations, the kind of task for which his absolute reliability

*Enrico Fermi, the Italian physicist and Nobel Laureate whose discussions with Teller led to the idea of the H-bomb*

made him ideally suited, while Oppenheimer went and sought out his immediate superior, Arthur Compton.

A series of long-distance telephone calls revealed the fact that Compton was on holiday in a lake cottage near Michigan and Oppenheimer eventually caught up with him at the local general store.

As our car [Compton recalled] pulled into the local store where the keys were kept, the 'phone was ringing. It was a call to me from Berkeley. Oppenheimer and his group had found something very disturbing. How soon could he see me? I gave him the directions and told him I would meet him at the train the following morning.

I'll never forget that morning. I drove Oppenheimer from the railroad station down to the beach looking out over the peaceful lake. There I listened to his story . . .

Compton was appalled by the vision of atmospheric and perhaps even oceanic ignition conjured up by the calculations made at Le Conte Hall.

This would be the ultimate catastrophe. Better to accept the slavery of the Nazis than to run a chance of drawing the final curtain on mankind!

We agreed there could be only one answer. Oppenheimer's team must go ahead with their calculations. Unless they came up with a firm and reliable conclusion that our atomic bombs could not explode the air or the sea, these bombs must never be made.

It looked as if the American bomb project could be stifled at birth.


In May 1942, three months before the Le Conte Hall meetings, von Heisenberg and Professor R. Dopel performed an experiment which indicates just how far ahead of the Allies they were. They had already built three prototype atomic piles but the fourth – pile LIV – was bigger than the others. These piles, although they looked nothing like the pile which had yet to be built in Chicago, nevertheless worked on basically the same principle.

During that particular experiment the pile, encased in two hemispheres of aluminium securely bolted together, was lowered slowly into a large tank of water. The neutron source which it was hoped would initiate fission within the uranium metal in the pile was introduced into the pile's centre through a sealed shaft, and measurements began.

Their measurements showed that the pile was producing more neutrons than were being injected by the neutron source at its centre. The experimenters had achieved the beginnings of a chain reaction and they calculated that if they increased the size of the pile by a factor of approximately fifteen they would be able to build the first chain-reacting pile in the world. Already Heisenberg and Dopel were the first experimenters to obtain a positive neutron production from a pile and they saw no reason why the scaling up of the present pile should not be possible.

# ENTER GROVES

On the morning of 16 September 1942, Colonel Leslie R. Groves of the Army Corps of Engineers emerged from a Congressional hearing on military housing. He had recently heard that he was to be offered a combat assignment and needed to obtain the approval of his senior officer, General Brehon Somervell. By chance, outside the hearing room, Groves met Somervell and took the opportunity of raising the matter with him. To his great surprise, Somervell told him that he could not leave Washington. As Groves recalled, he went on to say

> 'The Secretary of War has selected you for a very important assignment and the President has approved the selection.'
> 'Where?'
> 'Washington.'
> 'I don't want to stay in Washington.'
> 'If you do the job right it will win the war.'
> My spirits fell as I realised what he had in mind.
> 'Oh, that thing,' I said. Somervell went on,
> 'You can do it if it can be done. See Styer and he will give you the details.'

The Army had only become involved in building the atom bomb when senior government scientists, like James Conant and Vannevar Bush, began to realise the sheer scale of the project they had spawned.

The amount of construction involved was simply beyond their experience, and now that America had entered the war in earnest the situation was complicated by that terrible wartime bureaucratic menace – priorities. Everything from destroyers to anti-aircraft guns had top priority – indeed there seemed to be nothing that had anything less – and American industry was trying to cope with orders equivalent to $100 billion a year. For scientists inexperienced in the workings of the Washington procurement labyrinths, attempting to mount a project to build a new weapon, particularly one where they still had no clear manufacturing procedures developed, was doomed to failure and Conant and Bush recognised this.

So, in June 1942 the Manhattan District was set up, so named because the offices of its first military boss, General George Marshall, were in New York. But it became clear, very quickly, that Marshall, while a good engineer, was little better at fighting the priorities war in Washington than the scientists themselves, and so the job came to fall on Leslie Groves.

*Colonel Leslie R. Groves, a picture taken while he was still supervising the building of the Pentagon. A year later in September 1942, he was promoted to General and appointed head of the bomb project*

Groves was forty-six years old, the son of a Presbyterian army chaplain. He had studied engineering first at the University of Washington, Seattle, then at the Massachusetts Institute of Technology and had then gone to West Point Military Academy. Ever since he had graduated fourth in his class from that Academy, he had steadily accumulated a reputation as a good engineer and a man who would get something done if it was humanly possible. How he achieved his objectives, however, was a different matter. He could be blunt and ruthless, with no patience with sloppiness of any sort. Of those who worked with him, most feared him and few liked him, but this suited Groves who seemed only to demand respect from his colleagues. Kenneth Nichols, a professional soldier and a trained engineer, who worked with Groves from the beginning of his involvement with the Manhattan Engineering District, describes him very forcefully:

*Colonel Kenneth D. Nichols (r) seen here with Groves*

He's the biggest sonovabitch I've ever met in my life, but also one of the most capable individuals. He had an ego second to none, he had tireless energy – he was a big man, a

J. ROBERT OPPENHEIMER

heavy man but he never seemed to tire. He had absolute confidence in his decisions and he was absolutely ruthless in how he approached a problem to get it done. But that was the beauty of working for him – that you never had to worry about the decisions being made or what it meant. In fact I've often thought that if I were to have to do my part over again, I would select Groves as boss. I hated his guts and so did everybody else but we had our form of understanding.

Because of this capacity to get things done on time and according to specification, he had been put in charge of the construction of the Pentagon and, by 1942, was responsible for all aspects of military construction throughout the US. This included the building of camps, airfields, chemical manufacturing plants, ports and so on. In total, Groves was responsible for the expenditure of an amazing $600 million a month.

Only one small item blotted an otherwise splendid reputation. Groves had recently been subject to a Congressional inquiry because of alleged overspending. He had come out of it unscathed, but a perfectionist like Groves was determined it was never going to happen to him again.

Yet in spite of the enormous power he wielded he had been in his own words 'like every other regular officer, extremely eager for service abroad as a commander of combat troops'. Certainly, taking charge of a speculative new weapons project which was expected to involve expenditure of little more than $100 million altogether, could have had little appeal.

However, the Army had the trump card. Despite his strong reputation, promotion had come slowly for Groves. At one time, he had spent more than ten years as a lieutenant, and he was one of the older of the Army's colonels. So Groves was offered promotion to Brigadier-General. It did the trick. Before setting off on a tour of the project, Groves waited only for his promotion to come through, but in the meantime he went to visit Vannevar Bush.

Bush was Chairman of the National Defense Research Committee, responsible not only for the A-bomb, but for much of the other American wartime scientific effort. Groves assumed Bush would know of his new appointment but:

through some oversight, he had not been informed and consequently was quite mystified about just where I fitted into the picture and what right I had to be asking the questions I was asking. I was equally puzzled by his reluctance to answer them. In short the meeting was far from satisfactory to both of us.

Indeed after the meeting Bush rang Somervell asking who Groves was. He was told that Groves' appointment was official to which his comment was 'then God help us'. But Groves was moving fast. He very quickly settled the question of the site for a plant in Tennessee which would produce purified uranium. Then he pushed through an order for the highest priority to be given to all Manhattan Engineering District requests. When his promotion came through on 23 September, he set off on his tour of the laboratories. It was to be a most discouraging trip.

Most of the laboratories Groves was to visit on his trip were involved in experimental work on processes for separating out the fissionable U-235 isotope from the main mass of U-238 isotope. As already noted the two isotopes are chemically indistinguishable, and so the separation processes being developed had to rely on the tiniest physical differences between the two, namely the small differences in their atomic weight and their size.

The first process was being developed by Westinghouse Research Laboratory at Pittsburgh, and depended on the fact that, under high centrifugal forces, the heavier U-238 atoms should be separated from the lighter U-235 atoms. Here, it became apparent very quickly that the results were so far inconclusive and, furthermore, that the Pittsburgh researchers were not working with the zeal that Groves expected. On his return to Washington, he recommended that research on this method should be abandoned. The programme was dropped soon afterwards.

The next laboratory on his list was at Columbia University in New York, where work was going on into the gaseous diffusion process. In principle, this method was well tried. It relied on the slight difference in the size of the atoms of the two isotopes. When forced through a fine porous barrier, the slightly smaller U-235 atoms should pass through faster. The first portions of the mixture reaching the other side of the barrier will thus contain more of the U-235 isotope. This enrichment process had to be repeated many times before almost pure U-235 could be obtained (*see diagram* p. 61).

Well tried though the method might be, the particular problems that arose with uranium were almost overwhelming. Firstly, uranium is not a gas but a hard metal and so had to be converted into one of its compounds which was a gas. The only one of those that was at all suitable was uranium fluoride, but this was so corrosive that no pipe, or pump, or even diffusion barrier, had yet been designed that would contain it. Everything would have to be redesigned from scratch and even then the size of the plant required to produce just the few pounds of uranium would have to be gigantic. A chemical plant employing literally tens of thousands of skilled men was going to be needed. Yet the confidence of John Dunning who was designing the process was infectious, and Groves responded to it. But it was apparent that if this gas diffusion process

*Two views of the experimental gaseous diffusion equipment used by John Dunning to extract the precious Uranium-235 isotope. This equipment is now in the Smithsonian Institution Washington DC*

J. ROBERT OPPENHEIMER

*Dr John Dunning (l) of Columbia University, advocate of the gaseous diffusion method of isotope separation*

was to be possible at all it was not something which would happen overnight. While not advising abandoning the work, Groves held out little hope of it ever being practicable.

A somewhat chastened Groves set out westwards by train to Chicago – to the newly-formed Metallurgy Laboratory to examine the work going on to develop an atomic pile. The pile would serve a dual purpose. Firstly, it would allow the scientists to examine experimentally the physics of a controlled fission chain reaction, something which had only been possible, so far, using theory. Secondly, it would be a source of the new fissionable element, plutonium.

Working on this project were some of the finest scientific minds in the world: Leo Szilard, who had awakened Government concern about the bomb back in 1939; the Italian Nobel Laureate, Enrico Fermi; and another Hungarian, Eugene Wigner. The presence of these three physicists had enabled Arthur Compton, who ran the project at Chicago and was himself a Nobel Laureate, to recruit some of the brightest of the country's young physicists and he had now accumulated a total staff of more than twelve hundred.

On his arrival, Groves was first shown round the laboratory and then met some of the leading scientists. Although he was impressed by what he saw, he was also conscious of indecision, an indecision that seemed rooted in the open-mindedness of the true researcher but which to a practical engineer like Groves seemed unnecessarily delaying.

He also came across the same huge uncertainties about the size of the weapon and its critical mass that had existed a year before at the meeting at

*A painting by Gary Sheahan reconstructing the scene when the prototype reactor built by Enrico Fermi's team in Chicago went critical for the first time on 2 December 1942. This experiment confirmed that an atomic explosion was possible. The reactor was also the prototype for those used to produce the new element plutonium, used as an alternative to uranium for the core of the bomb*

Schenectady. They were still only able to give an answer that was accurate to a factor of ten and, as Groves was graphically to point out to the illustrious company assembled in the conference room that afternoon, it was as idiotic as sending for a caterer for a wedding reception, then telling him 'We don't know how many guests are coming – maybe somewhere between ten and a thousand – but see to it that you have the right amount of food for them'.

By the time they sat down to discuss what he had seen, Groves was thoroughly antagonised. Furthermore, the feeling was reciprocated by the scientists. At one point during the meeting, one of the nuclear physicists was going through a calculation on the board for Groves' benefit. It says much for Groves' maths and his basic grasp of physics that he was at least keeping up. But suddenly he spotted a figure in an exponent that seemed to be copied incorrectly on the following line. Straight away Groves thought it was a trap, that he was being tested, but, taking his courage in both hands, he questioned the error.

The scientist quickly glanced at the board and came back immediately 'Oh, you're right – that's an error'. Groves felt somewhat vindicated but still mistrustful. Thus before the meeting ended he felt compelled to make a strong bid to put the relationship between himself and the scientists on the right basis. 'There is one last thing I want to emphasise,' he said. 'You may know that I don't have a Ph.D. Colonel Nichols has one, but I don't. But let me tell you that I had ten years of formal education after I entered college. *Ten* years in which I just studied. I didn't have to make a living or give time for teaching. I just studied. That would be about equivalent to two Ph.Ds wouldn't it?'

This statement was met with silence from the assembled scientists but, after

J. ROBERT OPPENHEIMER

Groves had left the meeting, Leo Szilard exploded with indignation, 'How can you work with people like that?'

From Chicago, Groves headed west, towards Ernest Lawrence's Radiation Laboratory at Berkeley. Lawrence met Groves on his arrival at San Francisco railroad station and took him straight to the Radiation Laboratory. From the start Lawrence's approach and personality delighted Groves. He was open, candid, full of boyish enthusiasm and not at all the traditional idea of the Nobel Laureate; furthermore, after the frustrations and disappointments of Pittsburgh, Columbia and Chicago, he actually offered to show Groves separation in action.

Lawrence drove Groves across the Bay to Berkeley in his own car. It was a drive that Groves was to remember for a long time. Lawrence, foot hard on the

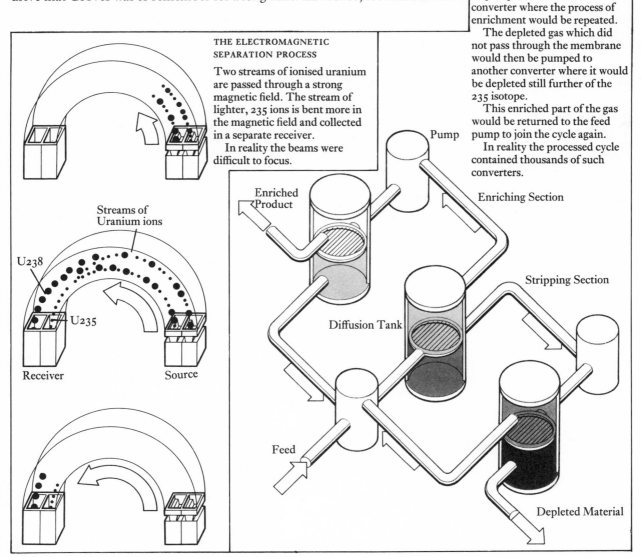

**THE GASEOUS DIFFUSION PROCESS**
The Uranium Hexafluoride gas would be pumped under pressure through the membrane in the converter. The gas on the far side would contain slightly more of the lighter 235 isotope and would be pumped on to another converter where the process of enrichment would be repeated.

The depleted gas which did not pass through the membrane would then be pumped to another converter where it would be depleted still further of the 235 isotope.

This enriched part of the gas would be returned to the feed pump to join the cycle again.

In reality the processed cycle contained thousands of such converters.

**THE ELECTROMAGNETIC SEPARATION PROCESS**
Two streams of ionised uranium are passed through a strong magnetic field. The stream of lighter, 235 ions is bent more in the magnetic field and collected in a separate receiver.

In reality the beams were difficult to focus.

Streams of Uranium ions

U238

U235

Receiver

Source

Pump

Enriched Product

Enriching Section

Stripping Section

Diffusion Tank

Feed

Depleted Material

*The Calutron. Ernest Lawrence used the giant magnet of his proposed 184″ cyclotron for a device to separate uranium isotopes electromagnetically. The device, the Calutron, was named after California University*

pedal, drove at breakneck speed through the traffic all the time talking with enormous enthusiasm straight at Groves about all his plans.

On arrival at the laboratory Groves, severely shaken from his drive, was taken to see the newest of Lawrence's great machines – the 184-inch calutron. It was a truly impressive sight. In an enormous experimental hall fringed with gantries the giant magnet, which provided the separating electromagnetic field, towered twenty feet above the floor. Above it hung a huge red gantry crane and the hall was alive with technicians putting the final touches to the great machine.

Lawrence set about explaining how the machine worked – how the atoms of uranium gas accelerated through the vacuum in the central circular chamber to a speed of many thousands of miles per second, and how at this speed they entered the immensely strong magnetic field generated from the vast magnet. The trajectories of the two isotopes were then affected differently in the field and on the far side of the field there were two containers, one to collect the stream of heavier atoms, the other to collect the lighter ones.

Lawrence even set the machine running for Groves and showed him the blue arc inside the machine which contained the rapidly accelerating atoms. It

J. ROBERT OPPENHEIMER

was an impressive performance from Lawrence, and from the machine, but at the end Groves asked,

'How long does this thing have to run to get real separation?'
'Well, it takes a long time to make a vacuum in the machine itself,' Lawrence replied.
'It'll take from fourteen to twenty-four hours to get a vacuum that's sufficient'.
'But how long do you run it?'
'It's never been run for more than ten or fifteen minutes.'
'What about separation?' asked Groves 'How much do you get in these baskets?'
'Well, actually, we don't get any sizeable separation at all. I mean not yet. This is still all experimental you see. . . .'

It was now a seriously depressed Leslie Groves who went on to his next appointment at Berkeley. So far his trip had been little short of disastrous. He had decided to abandon the centrifuge approach. At Columbia and now at Berkeley he had seen experimental methods which contained so many uncertainties and yet were so expensive to implement that it seemed to be courting disaster to go any further with them. Yet, in the first flush of his enthusiasm after his appointment, Groves had already done so. The site in Tennessee which Groves' predecessor, Marshall, had dithered about throughout the previous summer and which Groves had decided on immediately, was to house the machines developed from Lawrence's experimental and so far unproductive calutron. And building work had already started. For the cost-conscious Groves, the Manhattan Project, as the weapons programme was to be called, was fast becoming a nightmare.

His next appointment held out the prospect of still more insuperable problems. It was with the scientist in charge of designing the bomb – the Co-ordinator of Rapid Rupture, Robert Oppenheimer.

Two months before Oppenheimer had returned from his meeting with Compton in Michigan to face the difficult problem of making realistic calculations on just how likely was the chance of a nuclear weapon setting light to the atmosphere.

He had discussed it with Hans Bethe, who had discovered what he believed was a flaw in Teller's calculations. In calculating the heat build-up in the reaction, Teller had ignored certain heat losses through radiation. Further calculations by the group made even the basic deuterium fusion that Teller needed for his new bomb somewhat uncertain and almost completely ruled out the possibility of the reaction with the air. But just how completely did they rule it out? Compton has told how the physicists in the group hummed and hawed over the problem, then on his direction they computed a three-in-a-million chance. A three-in-a-million chance of destroying the world, yet Compton felt this was a low enough chance to take and ordered work on the weapon to proceed. But Teller tells a different version and in part is backed up by Hans Bethe. Teller says that his calculations never created any great problems and that the group very quickly corrected them and were then able to dismiss the prospect of atmospheric ignition entirely.

Yet over the next three years, various scientists were to make the same calculations as Teller and, because the initial scare at Le Conte had been kept secret, time and time again they were to come to Oppenheimer in a high state of alarm. The issue even found itself back on to Teller's desk when, in early 1945, Oppenheimer asked him to compute exactly how atmospheric ignition would come about. Certainly his calculations showed that the heat build-up needed was of an order greater than that achievable in a fission reaction, but neither the secrecy surrounding the initial scare nor the fact that Teller was asked to make those final calculations in 1945 supports his thesis that the matter was firmly laid to rest in 1942.

Nevertheless, by the time Groves arrived at Berkeley, the problem had been pushed into the background, and Oppenheimer was ready with some fairly clear evaluations of both the fission and the fusion weapons.

It is difficult to imagine two more contrasting and conflicting types than Oppenheimer and Groves. Oppenheimer was tall and ascetic in appearance, a radical intellectual. Groves was also tall but extremely bulky, a conservative military engineer from a Presbyterian background with absolutely no taste for intellectual or artistic pursuits. Yet, in spite of their great differences, the chemistry between these two men somehow worked – and that was almost certainly because Oppenheimer wanted it to.

During the year that he had been associated with the bomb project, Oppenheimer had been excited not only by the technical and administrative challenges of the work but by a new-found sense of direction. Furthermore, the job of co-ordinating and directing the efforts of others suited him. His ability to charm and to persuade meant, as he had shown during the summer, that he could mould a committee of very disparate individuals into an effective working group. His quick mind allowed him to shape all discussions and keep them to the point. Also, the range of problems that such applied weapons research threw up suited his dilettante approach to science more than pure research. So for a whole complex of reasons Oppenheimer wanted to remain in a central position on the project and, although there is no record of the meeting, it is a reasonable supposition that he had carefully worked out how he would handle Groves.

At this stage in his tour Groves was confused as well as depressed and he was looking for guidance. He found, in Oppenheimer, someone with a marvellously clear view of the technical options, who was not trying to sell a particular pet method and who was prepared to take the time to explain the scientific intricacies to him. They met for the first time in Berkeley on 8 October and Groves was so impressed that a week or so later, after paying a return visit to Chicago, he arranged to have Oppenheimer flown from Berkeley to join him on the Twentieth Century Limited, the famous passenger express, as he travelled on from Chicago towards New York.

In the cramped conditions of the tiny compartment on the train, Groves and his two military aides, Nichols and Marshall, sat talking for hours with Oppenheimer about how best to organise the project. One problem which Oppenheimer had already experienced was the way in which the high level of security thought necessary for the project had a stultifying effect on research. He had seen how morale was affected in a laboratory where researchers were working on something whose final significance was known to hardly anyone and he was determined to avoid such a situation arising again. So he proposed that all the researchers be brought together in a single laboratory where discussion between the scientists could then be as free as desired. The laboratory should then be made as secure as possible from the outside world.

It was just the sort of scheme the General had been considering himself, and it pleased him enormously to find a scientist who not only recognised the security problem but actually thought about it practically. But for Groves this restriction in the flow of information to one laboratory had another purpose. He had come to the conclusion that the interchange of ideas that the scientific community prized so highly was a waste of time. He did not want to see the scientists under his charge take part in 'a great university where they discuss their new ideas and try and learn more from each other'. Ideally he would have liked to restrict dialogue altogether, but he had come to realise that this would not be possible. Oppenheimer's idea of the single laboratory where at least everyone would be limited to working on the project in hand provided him with a reasonable compromise.

Groves decided to act on Oppenheimer's proposal and find a site for the new bomb laboratory. It was actually beyond the brief of his assignment but that did not worry Groves. This was to be the first of many occasions where he was to behave according to the dictum 'When in doubt, act'. At the same time he began looking for a director for his new laboratory.

The man Groves would have liked to head the new unified laboratory was Ernest Lawrence, but with a terrifyingly large commitment to the electromagnetic process he felt he could not risk releasing Lawrence from his present position. After that there was really not much choice, even though in later years Groves was politely to rationalise his decisions not to consider other possible candidates. Groves was drawn to Oppenheimer even though he had no administrative experience, was not a Nobel Laureate and therefore did not in Groves' words have 'the prestige among his fellow scientists, that I would have liked the project leader to possess'. Groves decided to back him. But then there came a blow which Groves could not have expected.

On hearing that Oppenheimer was being considered for such a senior post, the FBI contacted Groves through the Manhattan Project's own security force and warned him that they thought it extremely ill-advised to use Oppenheimer on the project at all. 'As always in security matters of such importance, I read all the available original evidence,' Groves reported, 'I did not depend on the conclusion of the security officer.'

The files he read contained evidence that was partly provided by

Oppenheimer himself when he filled in his security clearance questionnaire and partly by FBI investigators. It mainly dealt with his past associations with various leftist organisations and his friendship with numbers of known Communists. The file was still growing and as the FBI expanded its espionage activities, Groves could have read new information that illustrated, more forcibly than anything from the pre-war years, Oppenheimer's potential danger.

Even though Russia was now one of the Allies in the fight against Germany and at that very moment the battle of Stalingrad was at its height, there was considerable concern in America about Communists obtaining information about secret projects to pass on to them.

Because of the recent Freedom of Information Act a large number of FBI files containing the raw data on their investigations during the war have now been cleared and they contain the material on which Groves would have based his decision.

For instance, a technical surveillance log dated 10 October 1942 reported a conversation held in the Communist Party headquarters in Alameda County, Oakland, and which, according to the report, 'was monitored through a microphone-telephone technical installation.' The participants were Steve Nelson, the same Steve Nelson who had comforted Kitty in France, Lloyd Lehmann, and a third party who was not named. The summary continues:

During the discussion, Lloyd told Steve about an important weapon that was being developed and indicated that he was on the research of it. Steve asked if 'he' suspects you to be a YCLer [Young Communist Leaguer]. Steve then talked about a man, saying he was too jittery: he used to be active, but was inactive; was considered a 'Red' and mentioned that the reason the Government lets him remain was because he was good in the scientific field. Steve indicated this man had worked in the Teachers' Committee and the Spanish Committee; and could not cover up his past. [The monitors of the technical surveillance believed that Steve was referring to J. Robert Oppenheimer].

This part of the report does indicate that the Communists did know about the weapons project, in principle if not in detail, and shows also that some of Oppenheimer's past Communist contacts were still interested in him.

Later in the same report Nelson and his colleagues began to discuss someone else working at the Radiation Laboratory.

Lloyd said he [the other person] was in favour of coming out in the open more; said he had a three month deferment on the basis of war work; was 21; and had graduated. The unknown man [the third party] then said Rossi was trained to do theoretical physics and should stay with that. Nelson said the project was extremely important and the third party said he [probably referring to Rossi] would have to be an undercover Party member as if he quit his work they did not know what political work he could do as he might be drafted.

There was some confusion between the telephone monitors on who Rossi was, or even if Rossi's name was used, but certainly the information about the man they wanted to stay 'undercover' on the project fitted Rossi Lomanitz. Until recently, Lomanitz had been a student of Oppenheimer's and Oppenheimer had recommended him for his present assignment.

In spite of evidence such as this, Groves felt that Oppenheimer's potential far outweighed a security risk and almost immediately arranged to take him on a search for a new laboratory site. However, the Manhattan Project security team were less certain about this balance of odds and, for the time being at least, refused to give Oppenheimer security clearance while they continued their investigations.

Nevertheless, the search for a suitable site had begun. There had been a number of suggestions, but all but two possibilities had been rejected. Groves had rejected the suggestion of a site just north of Los Angeles, at San Bernardino, because the temptation to break security and go into town would be too great. Another site near Reno, Nevada, had been rejected because the weather in winter was considered too bad.

Eventually, the search had narrowed to a number of possibilities in New Mexico. Here the main city, Albuquerque, was wonderfully accessible by both air and by rail, but the surrounding countryside was relatively uninhabited and inaccessible. Initially, there were five sites on the list but, by the time Groves and Oppenheimer set out to look over them, they had narrowed the list down to two possibilities: Jemez Springs, and a place Oppenheimer himself suggested, called Los Alamos.

Jemez Springs, the first of the two they visited, turned out to be a long, thin valley, hemmed in on three sides by tall cliffs and hardly ever seeing the sun. Groves was concerned about the lack of existing buildings. Oppenheimer thought it would be depressing, so they moved on.

Their unmarked car wound its way slowly up a badly surfaced mountain road away from Jemez Springs and up into the Jemez mountains towards Los Alamos. On the way, the little party passed through the countryside that Oppenheimer had grown so attached to during the past fifteen years. The Pecos ranch was only twenty or so miles away on the other side of the Sangre de Cristo mountains and over the years Oppenheimer had criss-crossed this area many times on horseback. He was taking Groves to see the Los Alamos Boys School set seven thousand feet up in the mountains. Accommodation was already available on site and there were supplies of both water and electricity.

The car finally arrived at a level plateau among the mountains and there they found a sprawling complex of log houses and school buildings. The school had a reputation for giving its students a stoic outdoor upbringing and in the fields around the schoolboys, dressed in traditional Boy Scout uniforms, turned to look at the little group that clambered out of the car and proceeded to pore over maps and look out over the surrounding countryside. It was the most beautiful situation with magnificent vistas over the mountains, but Groves was concerned only with practical matters. The school buildings were a wonderful bonus, but there were drawbacks. The water supply was only just

*Los Alamos Ranch School for boys: a graduation ceremony featuring Indian dances. This building, Fuller Lodge, was to become the social centre for the scientists*

adequate for the present population. Power lines would have to be brought in. The road up to the school from Santa Fe was little more than a donkey trail and would have to be relandscaped completely.

Oppenheimer had drawn up a rough plan for the laboratory and he believed that he would need only thirty or so scientists, plus back-up personnel, to accomplish the task ahead. So, on that basis, Groves decided there and then that Los Alamos should be the site of the new laboratory. Only a few months later, for various reasons, Oppenheimer was to change dramatically his estimates of the staff required for the project, but by that time the compulsory purchase of the school had been completed and construction work had begun.

A short time after Oppenheimer's return to Berkeley an event took place which, although trivial at the time, was to turn into one of the most important incidents in his life.

Early in 1943, his friend Haakon Chevalier and his wife came round to the Oppenheimers for dinner. At some point in the evening, Oppenheimer went out into the kitchen to prepare martinis, something he made quite a speciality of, and Chevalier followed him.

Exactly what was said between the two men is not known, because their accounts of it differ somewhat. However, they do agree that Chevalier told Oppenheimer that he had recently been talking to a British engineer, named George Eltenton, who was working for the Shell Development Corporation in Berkeley. Eltenton was a friend of Chevalier's and was also an acquaintance of Oppenheimer, and he had, for a time, lived and worked in Russia and was now

OPPOSITE *Aerial view of present-day Los Alamos, still isolated amongst the canyons and mesas of the New Mexico mountains. Originally Los Alamos occupied only part of the central finger-shaped mesa*

ENTER GROVES                    69

involved in the Teachers' Union on the West Coast. Chevalier told Oppenheimer that Eltenton had said that he had means of getting technical information to the Russians.

However, according to Chevalier he did not approach Oppenheimer in the hope that he would agree to pass on information about his war work but merely as something 'he should know of'. Oppenheimer certainly made it quite clear that he would have no part in any such dealings.

The conversation – which came to be known as 'the Chevalier incident' – was brief and seems to have soon been forgotten in the pleasantries of the evening. However, just how innocent was Chevalier's approach? Chevalier recalls that his response to Eltenton's proposal was an unqualified 'No . . . that I was not one to involve myself in such a thing, and that I was sure Oppenheimer would be horrified at any suggestion of this kind.'

This is how George Eltenton described the incident from his point of view when interviewed by the FBI four years later. He described how a Russian, Peter Ivanov, had approached him, saying that the Soviet Government (which was an ally and in dire straits at the time) 'did not feel it was getting the scientific and technical co-operation which it felt it deserved.' Having, as he put it, 'convinced myself that the situation was of such a critical nature that I would be in my own mind free in conscience to approach Haakon Chevalier', he did so, putting Ivanov's arguments and asking whether he thought Oppenheimer could be approached. 'With considerable reluctance, we agreed that we must try and contact Oppenheimer,' Eltenton told the FBI.

Why were they reluctant? The implication is that they were only going to approach Oppenheimer as some last measure, but should they have approached him at all?

The question of the transmission of any possibly obtainable data [Eltenton continued] was discussed and I informed Mr Chevalier that Mr Ivanov had given assurances that such data when available would be 'safely' transmitted through his channels. This involved photo reproduction and subsequent transmission by means unknown to me.

It is my belief that Haakon Chevalier approached Dr Oppenheimer because a few days later the former dropped by my house and told me that there was no chance whatsoever of obtaining any data and Dr Oppenheimer did not approve.

From this account, it can be seen that Eltenton thought Chevalier was making a definite approach to Oppenheimer and that 'such data when available would be "safely" transmitted.' His account does differ from Chevalier, but however Chevalier's role is interpreted it is difficult to see the initiation of this incident as anything but attempted espionage.

# THE BIGGEST COLLECTION OF EGGHEADS EVER

## CHAPTER 5

If Oppenheimer had been left to his own devices, it is quite probable that he would have made an interesting stab at producing a bomb with his team of thirty or so carefully chosen colleagues. Immediately following the decision to build the laboratory at Los Alamos, he seemed to have almost no idea of what the sheer administration of the laboratory would entail. Sam Allison from Chicago was involved in the project by Oppenheimer right from the start.

Just before Christmas of 1942, Oppenheimer asked me to come and help plan the preliminary layout . . . On the Mesa he and I sat down and planned the laboratory. He showed me what he called an organisation chart for a hundred personnel. I looked at it and felt sure that something was wrong, but I didn't know what. The best I could do was to poke at random. 'Where are the shipping clerks?' I asked.

He gave me a thoughtful sympathetic look, 'We're not going to ship anything', he answered. I completely underestimated the size of the installation but not so much as he did . . . I thought the idea of a desert centre was a mistake. It would have looked more sensible to me to put it in a big industrial district. Certainly it would have been more sensible economically, but there was Oppenheimer's love for that country.

Oppenheimer's inability to assess the practical requirements is understandable but his false idea of the size of scientific team needed is less so. He approached the whole matter with a loose, almost poetic impracticality. Priscilla Duffield, Oppenheimer's secretary, remembers long rambling conversations between Oppenheimer and Robert Serber on whom it would be lovely to have in the team and how one man's brilliance might mobilise another's rather more pedestrian abilities. It was as if he were casting a Broadway play rather than organising a massive scientific and technical undertaking. He had rather charming ideas of special quiet housing facilities for the 'unmarried couples' – by which it was assumed he meant childless couples.

The shortcomings of his approach began to show seriously in the early weeks of 1943 when Robert Wilson, who had been a student at Berkeley with Oppenheimer, was, at the very young age of twenty-eight, put in charge of moving the Harvard cyclotron out to Los Alamos. On 4 March, at Oppenheimer's request, he visited the site at Los Alamos to see if it was ready to receive the cyclotron, as well as to inspect the progress of construction of the other scientific facilities. He was simply appalled by the chaos he found at Los Alamos.

*Priscilla Duffield who was Oppenheimer's secretary at Berkeley and moved with him to Los Alamos*

*Robert Wilson had been taught by Oppenheimer at Berkeley. At the early age of twenty-eight he headed a team at Princeton which worked on an isotope separation method which it was later decided to abandon. His young team were a somewhat reluctant but crucial addition to the staff at Los Alamos*

On my way back I stopped at Chicago's Met Lab and discussed with John Manley not only the situation at Los Alamos but also the lack of planning as to who would be responsible for what and as to the schedule of when various things should happen. We decided to go directly to Oppenheimer to press him for some decisions which might help to mitigate the circumstances.

So we went to see him in Berkeley. Well, it seemed in those days that much that Oppenheimer did was done at a party; at least that's where we cornered him. He'd been doing his usual magic with the martinis – just the right amount of martini and a proper amount of gin and made very ceremoniously, and whether he'd had too many or it was Manley and I, I don't know, but we got into a terrible argument.

We just went after Oppie unrelentingly with all of these practical problems that we were trying to make him understand, and after a certain stage, Oppenheimer became extremely angry. He began to use vile language, asking us why we were telling him of these insignificant problems, that it was none of our business, and so on.

Both of us were scared to death. We were frightened because, if this was the leader and, if the leader was going to have a tantrum to resolve a problem, then how was anything going to be sorted? So we withdrew, John and I, and discussed some more, and decided that we would take more initiative and not look for so much leadership from Oppy.

But just as he had done twelve years earlier, when he made his disastrous start to his teaching career, Oppenheimer was to learn very quickly. By March of 1943 he had worked out a complete organisation chart and had increased the size of the laboratory from a prospective hundred to fifteen hundred men. He had also taken a grip of his other major problem – recruiting.

One of the reasons why Groves had really wanted a Nobel Laureate as the Director of the new laboratory was because it would help in attracting other scientists. All the best researchers were already involved in various other kinds of war work, from rocketry to radar, and these people had to be attracted to work on the new project. Yet Oppenheimer had a double disability in recruiting; not only did he lack this final accolade but in his approach to a possible recruit he was, for security reasons, restricted in a way which would do credit to the hero of a Hans Christian Andersen fairy tale.

In making an initial advance he was not allowed to tell potential recruits what the project was that they were being asked to work on. He also had to tell them that they would have to leave their homes and sever all connections with the outside world. Only married scientists would be allowed to bring their families – those not married would not be able to see their girlfriends or families until after the war.

It was a daunting task, but Oppenheimer approached it cleverly. He concentrated on enlisting a handful of the best scientists and then used their names as a draw for the rest. Very early on he approached Hans Bethe who had been with him in Berkeley the previous summer, and Enrico Fermi from Chicago. But he did not limit himself solely to the top brains. He also made a point of recruiting Dana Mitchell, widely recognised as a very fine scientific administrator, to run the stores. They were all interested in the new project, but some of them were concerned by one aspect. Oppenheimer had agreed with Groves that all the scientists should join the Army; he himself had even visited the Presidio in San Francisco to begin enrolling as a Lieutenant Colonel. It was yet another of the paradoxes surrounding Oppenheimer, a left-wing liberal who was yet content to join the Army. Bob Wilson remembers the logic behind Oppenheimer's decision.

*Robert Bacher, a physicist from Cal. Tech. who had been working on radar in the early days of the war. His experience made him one of the scientists who most strongly resisted the induction of the Los Alamos scientists into the Army. He was to become Head of the Experimental Physics Division*

He'd become very patriotic and his ideals had changed from being directed either at the union workers or the Spanish War Veterans. He was convinced that the war effort was a mass effort to overthrow the Nazis and upset Fascism and he talked of a people's army and a people's war, as though it were a big indigenous upsurge. This also made his previous life more plausible to us. The language had changed so little. It's the same kind of language, except that now it had a patriotic flavour, whereas before it had just a radical flavour.

But while a large number of the scientists agreed with this feeling of being part of the people's war, there were those whose own experience made them baulk at agreeing to take a rank in the Army. Hans Bethe, Isidor Rabi and Robert Bacher of Cal. Tech. had already experienced an army régime while working on radar projects and found it to be totally inhibiting. They believed that a military régime was bound to introduce inflexibility into a system that needed to be as flexible as possible. For instance, would not an army officer find it more difficult to be wrong or to change a decision? Were they not likely to be over-zealous on security matters?

So strong were their feelings on this question that they refused to join the project until it was settled. Indeed a meeting was held during February 1943 at the Waldorf Astoria Hotel in New York where Bacher, Rabi and a group of less senior scientists made their feelings very clear to Oppenheimer. Sitting in a back bedroom of the hotel, Oppenheimer listened to their protestations and by the end of the meeting he had agreed to make a case to James Conant for not joining the army. The result was a compromise – an agreement to defer the affiliation for nine months at least, which was enough to mollify the protestors. Recruitment went ahead with Oppenheimer criss-crossing the country, steadily building-up a very impressive team.

Six months earlier in Berlin there had been a meeting crucial to the development of the German A-bomb programme. In April 1942, Hitler had signed a decree expressly forbidding any development programmes that were likely only to be of post-war interest and in June a conference was called to assess the future of the bomb project in the light of this decree.

Heisenberg was the senior scientist present and Albert Speer and Field Marshall Milch, Goering's deputy, were the senior members of the military party. What Heisenberg had to say about the potential of the new weapon obviously intrigued the visitors but, according to his own account, he dampened their enthusiasm by saying that to produce a bomb in Germany was at that time an economic impossibility. 'I was pleased,' Heisenberg recalled, 'to be spared the responsibility of making a decision. The Fuehrer's orders in force at the time ruled out altogether the enormous effort necessary to make an atomic bomb.'

However, while Milch left the meeting unimpressed by the immediate potential of the new weapon, Speer nevertheless authorised construction of buildings to house the larger-scale reactor that Dopel and Heisenberg were hoping to construct after their success in producing a chain reaction a few weeks earlier. But for the time being at least the atom bomb was reduced in priority. The Germans were in grave danger of losing their slight advantage over the Allies.

Oppenheimer moved out to Santa Fe on 15 March 1943 with a number of his team from Berkeley.

Three thousand construction engineers, under the supervision of the

*Part of the early preparations for the new laboratory at Los Alamos. The rough winding track which had linked the old Los Alamos school with the nearest town, Santa Fe, had to be transformed into a proper highway*

*The roads and foot paths around Los Alamos were either like quagmires or dust bowls depending on the weather. During the war paved sidewalks were never built because of Groves' concern over costs*

J. ROBERT OPPENHEIMER

Army, had been working for almost three months putting up the main buildings. At great speed and using rough timber and building paper, they had almost completed a main building, five laboratories, a machine shop, a warehouse, a set of barracks and a set of barrack-like apartments. All the time, every kind of prefabricated army housing was arriving and being thrown up, producing something little better than a shanty town. There were no paved sidewalks and, thanks to Groves' fetish for economy measures, there was never to be any street lighting.

The construction workers had lived through the cold winter months in trailers, in total ignorance of what they were working on. Their morale was very low, and they seemed almost to resent the arrival of the scientists. They were uncooperative and there were flare-ups. Bob Wilson, with the considerable problems associated with installing the cyclotron, again found himself in the frontline of this confrontation.

Almost straight away we were in a we-they situation. I remember there was a lieutenant-colonel in charge of putting in the facilities for the building housing the cyclotron. On my first visit I spotted that the wires bringing in the power were too small – the cyclotron was off to the side some way from the power house and there was bound to be a voltage drop. Well, I pointed out the mistake to this colonel, and that the wiring would have to be re-done, and he just decided that things had gone too far and that he was going to make a fight. So we began escalating the problem, he to his superior and I to mine. On our side we went through calculations and we were convinced I was right but the other gentleman, to show how dumb I was, pointed out that I had neglected the frequency drop – he actually tried to prove that there would be an A.C. frequency drop in the current from say sixty cycles to fifty cycles. It's a great idea but impossible and once he had adopted that position, it was actually hard for us to lose. But Oppenheimer had to write a letter to Groves about it, and eventually this officer was shipped off to the South Pacific. But it was a continuing problem. I don't think the military personnel we had out there was particularly adequate, that was part of the problem. The military were just not going to put guys on this project who, as they described it, could be out winning the war.

In spite of the friction with the military, which was to continue throughout the war, there was in the early days a great atmosphere of excitement, a feeling described by some of the scientists as akin to the first few days at summer camp. They drove in or came in by train from all parts of the United States, scientists with their families, not knowing either their final destination or the true nature of the project they were to be working on. Their directions told them to go to 109, East Palace, in Santa Fe, to the US Army Corps of Engineers office. In *Tales of Los Alamos*, Bernice Brode describes her family's arrival.

In the street in front of 109, taking up more than its share of the lane, an ancient dilapidated school bus, marked 'U.S. Army', in bright paint, was parked. A big soldier was good naturedly loading his bus with awkward household purchases such as brooms, mops, mirrors, potted plants and kiddie-kars. . . .

'For cryin' out loud, lady,' the soldier was saying, 'we got a war on, remember? For

*Dorothy McKibbin (l) with Robert Oppenheimer. Mrs McKibbin ran the reception office in Santa Fe where new arrivals went, 'more hostess than chargé d'affaires' was how she was described*

this I join the army!' He threw his hands up in mock despair, but carefully lifted a small whining boy into the bus. Then he shouted like a circus barker: 'Bus leaving for the wilderness up yonder, everybody in! All aboard, hur-ry, hur-ry, hur-ry!...'

We went into the courtyard to the shabby screen door leading to the inner office of 109. There my husband introduced us to Dorothy McKibbin, who was in charge not only of the office but of many other things.... She had a quiet grace in the midst of all the hubbub – a hostess rather than a *chargé d'affaires*.

'Welcome, Brode family, and do find chairs while I phone to the site that you have arrived,' she said. 'We'll have a little peace now that the bus has left.'

Dorothy made out temporary passes for the boys and me as she chatted. 'Make this your headquarters when you come to Santa Fe. Everybody does. Leave your parcels here and meet each other here. That's what this office is really for.'... All newcomers passed through this and were sent up to Los Alamos with their misgivings replaced by trust in the unknown 'up yonder'. Dorothy was a happy choice for our introduction to the war years on the Mesa.

After a long drive up the rough, winding, dusty road, and a thorough scrutiny at the gate, the new arrivals drove three more miles through a confusion of lorries and bulldozers until they arrived at their apartment blocks or barracks, depending on what their status was. Even the apartments of the most senior

J. ROBERT OPPENHEIMER

*East Palace, Santa Fe, as it is today. The entrance to No. 109 where Dorothy McKibbin had her office and received new arrivals is immediately to the left of the pedestrians. Most of those arriving here did not know what their final destination would be*

scientists were strictly utilitarian. They stood, four in a block, their thin intervening walls allowing for little privacy. The central heating was in the hands of manic-depressive Indian stokers, who alternately turned the little apartments from ice boxes into turkish baths.

For cooking, the army had provided large cumbersome wood-burning stoves nicknamed 'Black Beauties', which were almost impossible to light at that altitude. On one occasion, Bob Wilson's wife, Jane, cornered General Groves about the problem and, rashly, he decided the ladies were too soft, and proceeded to show them how it should be done. An hour or so later, a flustered, sooty General Groves achieved success, but Jane Wilson's point had been made. In time, electric hot plates made their appearance on the Mesa.

But whatever the hardships, it all seems to have been treated very much as an adventure, at least by those whose impressions have been recorded. No one I spoke to could remember more than one particular case of psychiatric breakdown, in spite of the physical rigours and the lack of privacy. Perhaps this had something to do with the age of the staff. The average age was about twenty-five and there was hardly anyone on the site over forty. Also, the wives had their husbands with them instead of in the armed forces somewhere abroad and they all had the additional satisfaction of knowing they were taking part in a life or death race against the Germans. Given all these factors, perhaps it is not surprising that many of those on the Mesa considered themselves truly fortunate to be there.

But irritations there were and they were not inconsiderable. As Los Alamos was not supposed to exist, all post to the inhabitants had to be addressed to Box 1663, Santa Fe. All outgoing mail and phone calls were subject to censorship, and visits to Santa Fe were restricted to one a month.

Everyone shopped in Santa Fe [wrote Eleanor Jette in her book of reminiscences *Box*

*1 A typical room in the men's dormitories. Some bachelors spent more than two years living in these utility surroundings*

*2 The laundry at Los Alamos ran on a do-it-yourself principle. Shortage of a proper nappy service was a great bone of contention amongst the large number of young mothers on the Mesa in the early days*

*3 The PX store. Some foods, like meat, were relatively plentiful. However there were often sudden surpluses and equally sudden famines*

*4 Homes occupied mainly by the technical staff at Los Alamos. There was always ill feeling about the relative privileges afforded to the scientists. Notice the duckboard pathways*

*5 A living room in the kind of apartment occupied by scientists such as Edward Teller and Robert Wilson*

*1663*], which was full of men from G2; you could always spot them because they wore snap brimmed hats – straw in the summer – felt in the winter. G2 followed Hill people around town to see that they didn't speak to anyone on the street.

People from Los Alamos were supposed to cut their own parents if they met them on the street. G2 saw to it they didn't mail any letter surreptitiously and tailed them into La Cantina (La Fonda bar). . . .

The Censorship regulations were panned. The monitored phone calls were a nuisance. You'd tell Papa, or Uncle Joe, that you went on a picnic last Sunday. He'd ask you where you went and the monitor would cut the connection to caution your answer. Frequently you never were able to get your connection again.

The army and, in particular, General Groves were the butt of all complaints about security, but the feeling of antagonism was mutual. At a meeting Groves was reputed to have told his military staff that 'at great expense we have assembled the greatest collection of eggheads ever'. It was an uneasy relationship and sometimes flared up into open confrontation. One such incident involved Edward Teller's wife, Mici, and concerned some pines near her apartment. This is how she described it to Bernice Brode.

I told the soldier in his big plow to leave me please the trees here [like her husband Mici was Hungarian] so Paul [her baby son] could have shade, but he said, 'I got orders to level off everything so we can plant it,' which made no sense as it was planted by wild nature and suits me better than dust. The soldier left, but was back next day and insisted he had more orders 'to finish this neck of the woods.' So I called all the ladies to the danger and we put chairs under the trees and sat on them. So what could he do? He shook his head and went away and has not come again.

On another occasion, physicist Ken Bainbridge came home after a day's work to find that the carefully tended lawn in front of his apartment had simply disappeared. It had been lifted by the army to grace the new CO's house. Bainbridge had to fight extremely hard to have it returned.

In a short while the scientists developed a social life of their own. There were the cinema, square dances and endless parties of all shades of intellectual seriousness and innocence. In time, the Mesa was to sport a nineteen-piece band, a choir and orchestra, and a radio station; but perhaps as a result of their youth or because of insufficient things to occupy them, the population's birth rate climbed dramatically in the first year.

General Groves complained about the rapid increase in population [wrote Bernice Brode], which immediately increased the housing problem and eventually would increase the school troubles. Rumour had it that the General ordered the Commanding Officer to do something about the babies, but it was not clear what was done, if anything.

In those first few months, before the establishment of such sophistications as a Town Council, all these problems, great and small, came to Oppenheimer. It says much for his burgeoning abilities as administrator, as well as the respect in

ABOVE *An Indian dancing display attended by laboratory staff. The men, from surrounding settlements, acted as cleaners and somewhat erratic stokers*

RIGHT *James Tuck, a member of the British Mission, dances with an Indian woman, one of the much sought-after maids at Los Alamos. They were allocated not on seniority but according to need. If a wife worked in the laboratory this was a major qualification*

which he was held, that throughout that period no serious conflicts arose.

From the start Oppenheimer decided to ensure that communications between the scientists of the, now permanently isolated, Los Alamos community were as good as possible, and on 15 April – the day the laboratory formally began operations – he inaugurated a series of introductory lectures for all the new staff.

They assembled in part of the central administration complex called Main Tech where they were greeted first by General Groves. In this gathering marked particularly by the enthusiasm of the participants, his limp handshake and his short opening address struck a very sour note, as Bob Wilson recalls:

From what he said he appeared not to believe in the eventual success of the project. He emphasised that if – or when – we failed, it could be he who would have to stand before a congressional committee to explain how money had been squandered – that we should make his job in this respect as easy as possible. He could not have done worse at starting the conference on an upbeat note of enthusiasm.

The physicists on 'the hill', as the laboratory was to become known, were soon to become all too familiar with Groves' negative provocations and his concern over the project's budget.

Groves was followed by Robert Serber, whom Oppenheimer had delegated to give the introductory lectures. A thin wisp of a man with a hazy, uncertain voice, Serber seems an almost obtuse choice to fill the assembled scientists with enthusiasm. 'He wasn't much of a speaker,' says one of those present, 'but, for ammunition, he had everything Oppenheimer's theoretical group had uncovered during the last year. He knew it all cold, and that was all he cared about.'

The briefing by Serber, and by other experts in explosives and chemistry, went on for two days and it was on the second day that something came up

# INFORMATION AVAILABLE TO THE SCIENTISTS AT LOS ALAMOS IN APRIL 1943, BASED ON THE INTRODUCTORY LECTURES GIVEN BY ROBERT SERBER.

## The Bomb Materials

### URANIUM-235

A great deal was already known about this fission material.

*The Critical Mass:* It had recently been estimated that 15 kilograms would be the critical mass, though some new figures just in from Madison and Minneapolis indicated that an even larger amount might be needed.

*Preparation:* The main hope lay in electromagnetic and gas diffusion methods. Both were expensive to industrialise and they were still far from certain to succeed.

*The Explosion Mechanism:* Two important facts were still unknown about uranium-235. Were sufficient neutrons released from each fission to allow the chain reaction to multiply quickly enough? This still needed checking.
Was the time between the absorption of the neutron and the release of the energy and the new neutrons fast enough? If it was not, then the fissioning mass could blow apart before the reaction was fully underway throughout the metal. Both these questions had to be answered.

### PLUTONIUM

In April 1943 it was still not proved for certain that this element existed. Yet the construction of a whole industrial plant sited at Hanford, Washington employing thousands of people was planned to start within two months.

*The Critical Mass:* This had been calculated at 5 kilograms of plutonium, a good deal less than uranium. It was hoped that once Hanford began production, it would be more readily available than uranium-235.

*Preparation:* To be made in atomic piles, the prototype of which, designed by Fermi's team, went critical only four months earlier in Chicago.

*Explosion Mechanism:* No details known.

## The Bomb Mechanism

The mechanism most favoured for the mechanism was the so-called 'gun method' (see diagram overleaf).

The main problem foreseen at this stage was predetonation. If the two sub-critical pieces were not brought together quickly enough, the bomb would blow apart before the fission chain reaction had properly started. This would happen because of stray neutrons which initiate just enough fission to produce the energy to simply blow the bomb itself apart but no more.

These stray neutrons are produced by the interaction of particles in the metal with certain impurities also present.
Thus there were two courses of action:
1: Purification of the Metal
2: Develop techniques for almost instant assembly.

In April 1943, it was hoped the so-called gun method would be fast enough.

This principle of assembling the critical mass was used in the bomb 'Little Boy' (below).

Inside the bomb's casing was a modified artillery gun (A) which fired a subcritical uranium shy into a subcritical spherical uranium target.

When the two subcritical pieces came together (B) they exceeded the critical mass and the nuclear explosion took place.

Although the two pieces came together almost instantaneously, there was always a problem of surface nuclear reactions caused by stray neutrons (C). These could blow the bomb apart before it went fully critical.

which was to prove of considerable significance in the next eighteen months. The meeting was discussing the gun method, and whether it would provide the necessary velocity for assembling the sub-critical portions of the bomb into the critical explosive mass. Then a young physicist, Seth Neddermeyer, from the National Bureau of Standards, stood up to make a contribution. He clearly had difficulty in expressing himself and a number of those present missed the point he was trying to make, but it slowly emerged that he was trying to formulate an entirely new approach to the assembly problem.

In effect Neddermeyer was suggesting a completely different configuration for the bomb. Instead of the gun configuration, he was suggesting one where the key word was implosion. The fissionable material was to be shaped into a hollow sphere which would then be surrounded by explosive. When the explosive was detonated, it forced the subcritical hollow sphere to implode, producing a solid sphere which now exceeded the critical mass and the nuclear explosion took place. It was an assembly which should take place almost instantaneously and certainly much quicker than anything possible using the gun method.

However, no sooner had Neddermeyer's suggestion been clarified, than there were voices raising objections and problems. If the explosive did not produce an entirely even shock wave around the central hollow sphere then surely wouldn't that sphere be blown apart before it went critical? This was not a problem of pre-detonation this time but, simply, that the central sphere would be subject to such amazing forces during the implosion that only a tiny imbalance would be needed in the shock waves to tear the sphere apart. Furthermore, a number of scientists pointed out that the production of an even and symmetrical shock wave bearing down on the sphere was going to be extremely difficult, if not impossible to achieve. For Neddermeyer this negative response was very discouraging but, at the end, Oppenheimer spoke

# THE GUN METHOD

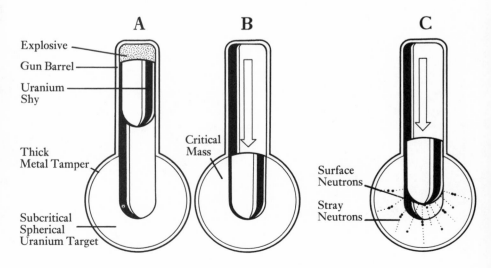

J. ROBERT OPPENHEIMER

out in his defence suggesting that he might like to work on the idea and develop it. Neddermeyer accepted gladly.

Shortly afterwards the meeting broke up and Oppenheimer was faced with an issue that would recur with monotonous regularity during the next two years.

Edward Teller had been invited by Oppenheimer to come to Los Alamos, but when he arrived, Teller found that the conditions of his employment were not what he expected. Firstly, he had thought that he was going to be allowed to continue to develop the idea of the Super, the weapon in which the fission bomb acts to initiate an even more violent 'fusion' reaction between molecules in a deuterium coating. Secondly, he believed that he was to work on his own.

On his arrival, however, he found he was expected to work on the fission weapon under his old colleague and friend, Hans Bethe, who had been appointed the Head of the Theoretical Division at Los Alamos. Teller had a confrontation with Oppenheimer and, although Oppenheimer used all the tact and charm he could muster, Teller emerged from the meeting feeling he had been cheated. He was to create problems for Oppenheimer from that moment onwards.

In those early weeks, all kinds of battle lines were being drawn, and Oppenheimer moved from one critical situation to another. One of his greatest concerns was the maintenance of the free exchange of ideas within the project. This was more or less assured at Los Alamos itself though, even here, he found resistance from the Army and the security officers it had appointed. However, in any technical discussions involving a group outside Los Alamos, the Army were to prove totally inflexible.

*A scientific meeting at Los Alamos. Oppenheimer is in the second row. In front (l–r) are Norris Bradbury, future director of the laboratory, John Manley and Enrico Fermi*

THE BIGGEST COLLECTION OF EGGHEADS EVER

Groves was, no doubt, genuinely concerned about the danger of espionage but, as the project slowly gained momentum and he saw control move inevitably into the hands of the top scientists, he must have seen security procedures as one way in which he and the Army could exercise a direct influence on the running of the project. He had already appointed an Associate Director for Los Alamos, the physicist Ed Condon whom Oppenheimer had known back in his Göttingen days. Condon had been working for Westinghouse when Groves asked him to take on the task of liaising between the scientists and the military authorities. However, he was, as Groves was to put it, 'not a happy choice'.

Condon was too experienced a scientist to sympathise much with Groves' attempt to limit contact between laboratories to a bare minimum. During the first few weeks of Los Alamos' existence there were a number of infringements of security which increasingly angered Groves to the point where he decided on a showdown.

The incident he chose was a meeting which Oppenheimer attended in Chicago. Originally, it had been intended that Ernest Lawrence and Harold Urey from Columbia should also attend but their presence was successfully blocked. Only Oppenheimer went up to Chicago, and there he discussed the likely availability of plutonium with Arthur Compton. It was an important matter, the personnel involved were of the highest level, yet it infringed the security codes. Groves came to Los Alamos and there he personally dressed down both Oppenheimer and Condon. But particularly he blamed Condon for letting Oppenheimer go. Condon objected strongly. He appealed to Oppenheimer to back him against Groves but Oppenheimer refused – for what he described as 'factional reasons' – by which it seems he meant he could not afford to fall out with Groves on such an issue. Condon resigned and the security restrictions – and Groves' grip on the project – tightened. Condon summed up the situation as he saw it in his letter of resignation to Oppenheimer:

I feel so strongly that this [security] policy puts you in the position of trying to do an extremely difficult job with three hands tied behind your back that I cannot accept the view that such internal compartmentalisation of the larger project is proper.

Groves did not stop there, however, in order to ensure that he knew exactly how Los Alamos was being run. He appointed a Review Committee. Working according to the maxim of a previous Chief of Engineers, 'I have no objections to committees as long as I appoint them,' Groves set up a five-man committee under W. T. Lewis which visited Los Alamos in May 1943. Their report both informed and reassured Groves; he now felt he knew what was going on in considerable detail and was no doubt pleased that the committee considered that the way Oppenheimer had organised Los Alamos was sound. He had split it into four divisions: Hans Bethe headed the Theoretical Division; Robert Bacher fresh from his work on radar was the Chief of the Experimental Physics Division; Chemistry and Metallurgy was in the hands of twenty-six-year-old Joseph W. Kennedy; the Ordnance Division, which would carry the engineering burden, was to be run by Captain William (Deke) Parsons, a one-time naval gunnery officer.

*Captain William Parsons, head of the laboratory Ordnance Division. He armed the bomb that was dropped on Hiroshima*

They made only one suggestion and that was to move the development of the special methods for the purification of plutonium to Los Alamos. This, coupled with the increased amount of ordnance development, effectively doubled the size of Los Alamos yet again. Where, only six months previously, Oppenheimer had envisaged a laboratory employing only one hundred people there were now gathering a total population of over three thousand.

The Manhattan Project was fast turning into the largest scientific project in history.

# CHAPTER 6  A PROBLEM OF SECURITY

In April 1943, Oppenheimer was in the very peculiar position of being at the head of one of the most secret of wartime projects and yet still without his own security clearance. Furthermore, the security officers responsible for the Manhattan Project were becoming more concerned about him rather than less.

Before wading into the depths of circumstantial evidence that security were working on, it is worth trying to get a glimpse of the perspectives of the time.

In early 1943, Russia was an ally, and one for whom there was a great deal of unalloyed admiration. General Douglas MacArthur had described the efforts of the Red Army as 'the greatest military achievement in all history'. Throughout the autumn of 1942, Americans had read daily accounts of the amazing battle for Stalingrad, and *Life* magazine, echoing General MacArthur's sentiments, had placed the Russian Army 'in the top class of fighters'. The prominent New York lawyer, Herbert Brownell, agreed to serve on a 'Thanks to Russia' committee; only ten years or so later, he became the ferociously anti-Communist Attorney General of the United States. It is therefore not surprising that a Russian War Relief Party was given in Berkeley by a radical French professor – Haakon Chevalier.

Nevertheless, some security officers on the project were almost more concerned about the long-term threat of Communism and of the Soviet Union than they were about the Nazis. One of these officers who had been reluctant to give Oppenheimer his security clearance was Colonel John Lansdale, a thirty-one-year-old Cleveland lawyer with a reserve commission who had been called into the Army to act as General Leslie Groves' aide on security matters. He had

*Stalingrad, early 1943. The Russian army's heroic resistance in this city led to a wave of pro-Russian feeling. General MacArthur described the Red Army's efforts as 'the greatest military achievement in all history'. In spite of this and even though she was an ally, the US government was reluctant to share secrets with Russia*

made his own study of Communism in action and had developed a deep suspicion of all Russophiles, who he believed could justify acts of treachery in the name of friendship for the Soviet Union and because they would be helping an ally.

Lansdale was not alone in holding this view; Colonel Boris Pash, Chief of Counter-Intelligence for the Ninth Army Corps on the West Coast, with jurisdiction over all West Coast atomic energy facilities, had the same fears.

The tight security surveillance started by the FBI on Oppenheimer was continued by the Army after he moved out to Los Alamos. Years later, a report of an interview with one of the agents, Andrew Walker, who was assigned to the Los Alamos Security Office during the war, described how Oppenheimer was covered.

There were at this time a number of CIC agents in Los Alamos, the majority of whom were apparently on undercover assignments. He said that the various CIC agents became acquainted as time went on, and that it became apparent to many that certain CIC agents were 'working' Oppenheimer's mail, and that the subject's telephone was monitored, and that he understood Oppenheimer's office was wired.

*Colonel John Lansdale, the thirty-one-year-old Cleveland lawyer with a reserve commission who had been called into the army to act as General Groves' aide on security matters*

As well as this, Walker acted as Oppenheimer's driver-cum-bodyguard, yet, through all that time, he was unable to recall one single indiscretion on Oppenheimer's part. As he described it, 'normal conversation (with Oppenheimer), if any, would relate either to the weather or the countryside'. When he was talking to another passenger in the car, 'Oppenheimer would frequently open a window in the car, which would result in a rush of air, preventing Walker from overhearing the conversation'. Walker himself assumed this to be nothing more than good security practice. Indeed, the whole impression of Oppenheimer that emerges from Walker's report is of someone who was almost beyond reproach in his behaviour.

Yet this was not the way that the Chief of Security at Los Alamos saw Oppenheimer. Captain Peer de Silva was an ambitious ex-West Point officer. He had 'film-star' good looks, fancied himself as something of a lady's man, and from the start does not seem to have liked Oppenheimer. On reading a report of an FBI interview with him, it is interesting to note that his suspicions of Oppenheimer are never based on hard surveillance data, of which he had plenty, but on circumstantial evidence and opinion.

*Colonel Boris Pash, Chief of Counter-Intelligence for the Ninth Army Corps on the West Coast, with jurisdiction over the West Coast atomic energy facilities. After some time investigating Oppenheimer he recommended that the scientist should be 'removed completely from the project . . .'*

According to de Silva [the FBI summary reads], subject evinced little pattern of political convictions, however de Silva feels subject naturally inclined along liberal lines one might expect a Marxist-Socialist to follow. De Silva noted subject as Director of Los Alamos project, exercised considerable influence in selection of scientific personnel and stated recollection, subject personally contacted MED head in interest of clearance for Martin Kamen. De Silva is of opinion subject was also instrumental in employment of Philip Morrison, Robert Serber, and David Hawkins, all considered of questionable security background by de Silva.

Certainly all the scientists mentioned here by de Silva had left-wing connections, but was this enough to call into question either their desirability or the man who employed them? Was de Silva reacting, as others had done before, to Oppenheimer's instinctive 'cliqueness' in surrounding himself with old friends with common sympathies?

There certainly seems to be an element of this in his behaviour but also de Silva was attempting one of the most difficult kinds of assessment for any security man. He was looking for the kind of traitor who was motivated by 'conscience' rather than by money, and bearing in mind the kind of men who did finally betray secrets of the project, this broad-based approach to his subject was a valid one. However, it would seem that his individual judgements were too crude, that his criteria were oversimplistic, because while he continued to worry about Oppenheimer and his friends he missed entirely the two spies who did work at Los Alamos.

John Lansdale, however, while suffering from the same preoccupation with Oppenheimer, tried to use more subtle assessments of his subject's attitudes. He made it his business to get to know Oppenheimer during the early months of his association with Groves and the Manhattan Project. Lansdale went to Los Alamos and had a number of long and rambling conversations with him. He also made it his business to visit Kitty Oppenheimer and to talk to her at length as well. Her association with Joe Dallet had not escaped the FBI's notice and Kitty impressed Lansdale as 'a strong woman with strong convictions . . . as a type of person who could have been a . . . Communist'. Years later he recalled some interviews in the sitting room, some out in the garden where she had entertained Steve Nelson. He remembers that eventually she gave him a martini. 'Not the kind to serve tea', he deduced from the way she handled her glass. He was right. Both Oppenheimers were heavy drinkers but for Kitty the pressures of the next few years were to make it a serious problem. But Kitty never made any pretence of entertaining Lansdale socially and he decided that she 'hated me and everything I stood for'. Nevertheless, she played a part and she played it well, as Lansdale recalled.

As we say in the lingo, she was trying to rope me, just as I was trying to rope her. The thing that impressed me was how hard she was trying. Intensely, emotionally, with everything she had. She struck me as a curious personality, at once frail and very strong. I felt she'd go to any lengths for what she believed in. The tactic I fell back on was to try to show her I was a person of balance, honestly wanting to evaluate Oppenheimer's position. That's why our talks ran on so long.

I was sure she'd been a Communist and not sure her abstract opinions had ever changed much. But feelings were her source of belief. I got the impression of a woman who'd craved some sort of quality or distinction of character she could attach herself to, who'd had to find it in order to live. She didn't care how much I knew of what she'd done before she met Oppenheimer or how it looked to me. Gradually I began to see that nothing in her past and nothing in her other husbands meant anything to her compared with him.

Indeed, Lansdale began to see these feelings of Kitty's as something he could

OPPOSITE *Kitty Oppenheimer, photographed during the war in the Oppenheimers' Los Alamos sitting room. A biologist, Kitty worked in the laboratories. However, she never seemed to settle at Los Alamos and was reluctant to assume the role of director's wife*

J. ROBERT OPPENHEIMER

use. In his report on these meetings which went to Groves, he wrote, 'Dr Oppenheimer was the most important thing in her life' and that 'her strength of will was a powerful influence in keeping Dr Oppenheimer away from what we would regard as dangerous associations'.

In practice, however, Kitty's influence did not prevent Oppenheimer from keeping up some of his old associations. On 12 June 1943, Oppenheimer visited Berkeley on business but after his work was finished he was followed by security agents to where Jean Tatlock, his one-time fiancée, was now living. Various people who spoke to me and who had received accounts of that meeting from security had different memories of just how complete their surveillance had been. Certainly the agents kept a watch on the house throughout the night, and the following morning they saw Oppenheimer and Tatlock leave the house and drive to the airport where Oppenheimer boarded the plane for New Mexico. However, there seems a strong possibility that they managed to bug the meeting electronically, and two people described to me how the couple talked for a long while in the living room before eventually retiring to the bedroom.

Ever since they had broken up four years earlier, Jean had been suffering increasingly serious bouts of depression and undergoing psychiatric treatment. By his own admission, Oppenheimer had continued to see her on average two or three times a year but over the last few months, even though Jean had been asking to see him with increasing urgency, Oppenheimer had not found the time from his commitments at Los Alamos to visit her. When they did meet, Jean's state of mind was such that it is hard to believe that they discussed anything other than their personal problems. The records of the meeting if they exist have not been released, and so we only have Oppenheimer's account. Ten years later he recalled simply that 'we did not talk of Communism'.

When the two parted at the airport it was the last time they were to see each other.

However personal this meeting with Jean had been, it served only to increase the doubts that security officer Colonel Boris Pash had about Oppenheimer. His responsibilities included Lawrence's Berkeley Radiation Laboratory and he was then investigating an alleged Soviet attempt to penetrate the project there. Already two of his leads had involved Oppenheimer and now he had this new information about his meeting with Tatlock. At the end of June 1943, Pash wrote a memorandum to Lansdale in Washington.

In view of the fact that this office believes that subject still is or may be connected with the Communist Party in the Project, together with the interest of the USSR in it, the following possibilities are submitted for your consideration.

The first of these possibilities was that the Communist Party was trying 'officially' to divorce Oppenheimer's affiliation with the Party. However, he might still be secretly affiliated and if so, Pash went on, 'there is a possibility of his developing a scientific work to a certain extent, then turning it over to the

Party without submitting any phase of it to the US Government'.

His second thought was that Oppenheimer might pass on the project's secrets through an intermediary. One of his final recommendations was that Oppenheimer be 'removed completely from the project and dismissed from employment by the US Government'.

Both these possibilities seem so far-fetched when related to Oppenheimer in isolation that one immediately questions Pash's state of mind. But, so far, we have not considered those other leads that had already come Pash's way from the Radiation Laboratory. The first indicated that a Soviet unit or 'cell' was being organised by Steve Nelson. The other maintained that the 'cell' supposedly involved several of Oppenheimer's ex-students. The central figure in this 'cell' was the scientist known as 'Joe'. The prime suspect was Giovanni Rossi Lomanitz, the brilliant physicist who was still only twenty-one-years-old and who was about to be made a group head by Ernest Lawrence.

Lomanitz was politically active, of that there is no doubt. Oppenheimer later recalled his 'wild' talk about how the war was so terrible he didn't care which side won. He had also been involved in setting up the Federation of Architects, Engineers, Chemists and Technicians in Lawrence's laboratory. Yet in spite of these activities he was obviously well thought of by Lawrence and on 27 July 1943, Lawrence gave him his promotion. Three days later on 30 July he received a special delivery notice from the draft board to appear for a physical examination the next day. Someone seemed very determined to get Lomanitz into the army and away from the Manhattan Project.

In desperation Lomanitz went to Lawrence, who was as puzzled as he was, and then Lomanitz telephoned Oppenheimer. Oppenheimer immediately telegraphed the headquarters of the Project stating that Lomanitz was 'the only man at Berkeley who can take this responsibility'. It was no use. Lomanitz recalls that the draft board was, itself, sympathetic to his position but that it seemed to be subject to heavy pressure from above. Shortly after this Oppenheimer received another visit from Colonel Lansdale. They talked mainly about Lomanitz but also about the more general aspects of security; during this discussion Oppenheimer made a remarkable statement. He told Lansdale emphatically that he did not want any current member of the Communist Party working at Los Alamos because there was always a 'question of divided loyalty'. To a zealous security officer like Pash or Lansdale this could be seen as an attempt by Oppenheimer to clear himself of suspicion. But suspicion of what? Did he feel, with their drafting of Lomanitz, that security was getting close and that he needed to prove himself somehow? Whatever his reasoning he was about to take a step which was to prove one of the most momentous of his life.

Towards the end of August 1943 he had to visit Berkeley, and on this occasion he visited the office of Lieutenant Johnson, the campus security officer, to ask if it would be all right for him to talk to Lomanitz who was still on the campus. Johnson told Oppenheimer that he thought Lomanitz was dangerous but gave him permission nevertheless. Then just as he was leaving,

Oppenheimer volunteered the information that there was a man in the San Francisco area whom he felt the security officers should keep an eye on. He was a man called George C. Eltenton, a British engineer working for the Shell Development Corporation and, like Lomanitz, an active member of the FAECT union.

According to Oppenheimer, the word had got around to physicists that he was in a position to supply classified information to the Russians, via the local Consulate.

It was the first time Oppenheimer had mentioned the 'Chevalier incident' to a security officer. He mentioned neither Chevalier's name nor his own.

The conversation was brief – partly because Eltenton was outside Johnson's jurisdiction and not his concern and partly because security knew about him already. Nevertheless, as soon as Oppenheimer left, Johnson contacted Pash and the two agreed to arrange to meet Oppenheimer again the following day.

Meanwhile Oppenheimer went to the Radiation Laboratory, borrowed Lawrence's office and sent for Lomanitz. Part of the background to this meeting was that Oppenheimer had arranged for Lomanitz to work at the Radiation Laboratory and had extracted a promise from Lomanitz at the time that he would avoid any political activity and concentrate on the physics. According to Oppenheimer's later account of the meeting Lomanitz repudiated the promise, admitted that he was still active as a Communist and stated that he was being framed for his union activities. Oppenheimer was angered by this response and did nothing more to help his ex-student. In a short time Lomanitz was to become Private Lomanitz, a company clerk in the army's 44th Division.

The next day, 26 August, Oppenheimer again found himself in the security office in Durant Hall, this time in the company of both Pash and Johnson – and a hidden tape recorder connected to a microphone in the telephone receiver on the desk. Oppenheimer sat down and an important conversation began. What follows is based on the transcript of that conversation.

'This is a pleasure . . . I don't mean to take too much of your time,' Pash began deferentially.
'That's perfectly all right,' replied Oppenheimer, 'whatever time you choose.'

Oppenheimer had assumed he had been asked along to talk about Lomanitz but, very quickly, Pash directed the conversation towards the 'Chevalier incident'.

Oppenheimer again volunteered that, although he had no first-hand information about it, he understood that an unnamed man attached to the Soviet Consulate had indicated that he was in a position to transmit information about the Berkeley atomic project without danger of discovery.

'To put it quite frankly,' he told Pash, 'I would feel friendly to the idea of the Commander-in-Chief [the President] informing the Russians that we were working on this problem. At least I can see there might be some arguments for doing that, but I do not feel friendly to the idea of having it moved out the back door.'

Pash then pressed Oppenheimer to be more specific about the contact with the Soviet Consulate, but Oppenheimer was cautious, 'to give more . . . than one name would be to implicate people whose attitude was one of bewilderment rather than one of co-operation.'

However, there was one name he was prepared to mention – that of the British engineer working with Shell, George Eltenton, whom he described as 'one of the channels [to the Soviet Embassy] by which this thing went'. He stopped short again at giving Chevalier's name, stating that 'to go beyond that would be to put a lot of names down, of people who are not only innocent but whose attitude is a hundred per cent co-operative'.

But Pash was not prepared to end his questioning where Oppenheimer wanted. Mindful of the fact that this man was, after all, the Director of Los Alamos, he took a persuasive line with him, assuring him repeatedly of the absolute anonymity of anything he might report. After something like minutes Oppenheimer did begin volunteering more information – tantalising and incomplete.

There had been contact, he said, with two of his close associates at Los Alamos but these approaches had not been made by Eltenton but by someone else. Eltenton was then to arrange a contact with a reliable man from the Soviet Consulate who had 'a lot of experience in microfilm work, or whatever the hell'. He was at considerable pains to impress on Pash that the flavour of these approaches to his colleagues while technically treasonable had not been presented in that light. They were simply to make up for 'defects of our official communication' on the part of US officials who 'don't feel very friendly to Russia'. Pash obviously wanted to know more about this other 'contact'.

Oppenheimer retreated, 'I think it would be a mistake. That is, I think I have told you where the initiative came from. To go any further would involve people who ought not to be involved in this'. Oppenheimer did however go so far as to say that the contact with his Los Alamos colleagues was 'a member of the faculty', but there he stopped.

Pash became insistent, wheedling and cajoling, 'I want to again sort of explore the possibility of getting the name of the person on the faculty . . . not for the purpose of taking him to task but to try to see Eltenton's method of approach.'

Oppenheimer still did not reveal the crucial name but, in order to avoid seeming positively obstructive, he did volunteer specific pieces of information, information which was to cause him considerable difficulty in the years to come. Eltenton's contact, he told Pash, had approached three people in all, two at Los Alamos, contacted within a week of each other, and a third at Berkeley who was about to join the staff of one of the project's other laboratories. To Pash it was clear that Oppenheimer knew a great deal, perhaps that he was holding back on more than just the name of the contact, and so he tried to impress on Oppenheimer just how much extra work his reticence was likely to cause. 'We could work a hundred years,' Pash said, 'and never get this information.' In the end, after some hours sparring, the meeting broke up politely as it had begun. Pash: 'Well we appreciate it and the best of luck.' Oppenheimer: 'Thank you very much.'

But while both men had been at pains to maintain the façade of affability, this had been a momentous meeting for each of them. A week later, Pash sent a special message to Groves in which he offered his thoughts on why Oppenheimer had suddenly volunteered the information about Eltenton. Pash suggested that the drafting of Rossi Lomanitz had triggered a renewed fear in Oppenheimer for the security of his own position. He had thus volunteered the information about Eltenton to 'retain the confidence of the Army personnel responsible for this project'.

On the same day Pash arranged that another memorandum was dispatched to Washington containing even more serious charges against Oppenheimer. It came from Pash's security man at Los Alamos, Captain Peer de Silva, and in his note he declared that Oppenheimer's reluctance to name names indicated that he was 'playing a key part in the attempts of the Soviet Union to secure, by espionage, highly secret information which is vital to the security of the United States'. As evidence to support this claim, de Silva pointed to the large number of 'known Communists or Communist sympathisers' that Oppenheimer had recruited to the project. He concluded that Oppenheimer must either be 'incredibly naïve and almost childlike in his sense of reality', something de Silva not unreasonably found impossible to believe, 'or, extremely clever and disloyal'.

Yet again, it is tempting to dismiss the suspicions of the professional security men as paranoia, but that would be unfair. Only ten days after the interview with Pash, on 6 September 1943, they intercepted a note from Joseph Weinberg, another former student of Oppenheimer's, working alongside Lomanitz in the Radiation Laboratory. It said:

Dear A, Please don't make any contact with me, and pass this message to S and B, only don't mention any names. I will take a walk with you when this matter is all cleared up.

Not only was this note concrete evidence in support of their general concern about security on the project but, following so closely on the Pash–Oppenheimer interview, it could not be beyond the realms of possibility that Oppenheimer himself had tipped Weinberg off.

When the two memos arrived in Groves' office in the Pentagon, it was decided that his security adviser, John Lansdale, should make his own investigation. He and Oppenheimer had already met on several occasions, but this meeting in Groves' Washington office was to have a much sharper edge to it than the discursive conversations the two men had had in Los Alamos.

It began amiably enough with Lansdale referring to Oppenheimer as 'probably the most intelligent man I ever met' but very quickly Oppenheimer was parrying questions about the 'Chevalier incident'. It was a meeting which was recorded, and many who years later read the transcript were to ask who was being questioned by whom.

Lansdale began with a bluff. He told Oppenheimer that he thought they now knew who the Eltenton contact was, but asked Oppenheimer to tell them. He didn't.

'I don't see how you can have any hesitancy,' Lansdale said, 'in disclosing the name of the man who has actually been engaged in an attempt at espionage for a foreign power in time of war.'

'I know,' was the reply. 'It's a tough problem and I worried about it a lot.'

'Well,' said Lansdale, 'if you won't do it, you won't do it, but don't think I won't ask you again.'

Lansdale then started probing Oppenheimer about who on the bomb project were Communist sympathisers. Oppenheimer first volunteered two fairly obvious names, Lomanitz and Weinberg.

'I suspected that before,' he said, 'but was not sure. I never had any way of knowing.' Then he gave Lansdale the name of a secretary who he thought was a member, then Robert Serber's wife Charlotte's name and, finally, Kitty's. It was obvious he knew Lansdale had already talked to her. When asked by Lansdale about himself his answer was an emphatic 'No!'

Then Lansdale asked him to say 'yea' or 'nay' about their party affiliations, to a list of names he had compiled.

'Do you know a fellow named Rudy Lambert?' asked Lansdale.

'I'm not sure, do you know what he looks like?'

'No, I've never seen him. He's a member of the Party,' replied Lansdale.

So Oppenheimer had avoided the question and furthermore Lansdale had then given him the answer. Lansdale then asked about Steve Nelson and Isaac Folkoff and then: 'How about Haakon Chevalier?'

'Is he a member of the Party?' asked Oppenheimer.

'I don't know,' replied Lansdale.

'He's a member of the faculty, and I know him well. I wouldn't be surprised if he were a member. He is quite a Red.'

Again Oppenheimer had first tested Lansdale's state of knowledge and then volunteered a little information, an amount he obviously judged safe.

Lansdale then asked about Jean Tatlock. Oppenheimer said he thought she had dropped out. They then talked generally about matters such as political loyalties until Oppenheimer suddenly asked,

'Why do you look so worried?'

'Because I'm not getting anywhere.'

'Well,' replied Oppenheimer, 'except on that one point, I think you're getting everywhere that I can get you.'

'Well, try to put yourself in my position.'

Lansdale then explained how, in identifying possible spies at Los Alamos, he had little else to go on but past associations and activities. To illustrate his problem he picked

the case of Dr J. R. Oppenheimer, whose wife was at one time a member of the Party anyway, who himself knows many prominent Communists, associates with them, who belongs to a large number of so-called front organisations, and may perhaps have contributed to the Party himself, who becomes aware of an espionage attempt by the Party six months ago and doesn't mention it, and who still won't make a complete disclosure.

In this 'example' Lansdale had given Oppenheimer a remarkably complete synopsis of the security dossier held on him. He was at some pains to point out to Oppenheimer that this illustration 'was personal but not pointed, you get my distinction'. Also 'I've made up my mind that you, yourself, are OK,' added Lansdale, 'or otherwise I wouldn't be talking to you like this, see?'

'I'd better be – that's all I've got to say,' was Oppenheimer's reply.

There was more discussion, more attempts to get the name of the contact, but each time it was resisted. More names were added to the list of Communist sympathisers and after two hours or so of (from Lansdale's point of view, anyway) futile sparring, the conversation wound itself down in another collection of ingratiating pleasantries. Oppenheimer offered a final explanation for his obduracy, 'It is a question of some past loyalties . . . I would regard it as a low trick to involve someone where I would bet dollars to doughnuts he wasn't involved.'

'OK, sir,' and Oppenheimer's second confrontation on the 'Chevalier incident' was at an end.

In these extracts of their two hour conversation I have picked on certain exchanges between the two men which support the view that Oppenheimer was giving only the obvious or the unimportant away, and was at the same time successfully testing the level of Lansdale's knowledge and concern. It is, however, possible to interpret Oppenheimer's role in this conversation entirely differently – to see him as a man in an impossible situation. He had not bargained for the obsessive way the security officers would pursue the name of his 'contact' and he was now desperately defending someone for whom he felt responsible.

It had only been a month or so earlier, in the middle of July 1943, that Groves had pushed Oppenheimer's security clearance through against the advice of the security forces, and he must have been viewing these new developments in the security saga with considerable misgivings. In the early days of September, before he had seen the two memoranda from Pash and de Silva, Groves had shared a sixteen-hour train journey with both Oppenheimer and Lansdale in which they had talked a great deal about security. In particular they talked about Lomanitz, and Oppenheimer, still angry about Lomanitz's folly in involving himself in political matters, had told Groves he was sorry that he had had anything to do with him and wanted to wash his hands of him.

Then they talked about the interview with Pash which had taken place a week or so earlier and, on this occasion, while still refusing to name the 'contact', Oppenheimer agreed to do so if he was ordered to by Groves himself. This posed an uncomfortable dilemma for Groves. After all, Oppenheimer had volunteered the information about Eltenton and the threat to the security of the

Radiation Laboratory; by forcing him to go further than he wanted, he might be deterred from revealing any similar problems in the future. It was also reasonable to suppose that Oppenheimer had well and truly discouraged his unnamed 'contact' from making any future overtures. Thus, for the time being at least, Groves chose not to force the issue with Oppenheimer and demand the name.

Groves certainly seems to have had a very different perspective on the problem at the Radiation Laboratory from that of his security officers, and this could well have been due to an overall view of the usefulness of information about the work going on there to another power. Lawrence's electromagnetic separation process was proving to be very much the 'white elephant' of the separation procedures. The plants being built at Oak Ridge on the basis of Lawrence's experimental calutron were soaking up a quarter of the total two billion dollar expenditure on the project. Its product was so impure that it could only be used to feed one of the other separation processes. As a measure

*The Alpha-1 racetrack at Oak Ridge, part of Lawrence's electromagnetic separation plant. Each of the 100 or so protruding ribs are magnetic coils wound with wire made from the 6,000 tons of silver Nichols obtained from the Treasury. The box-like cover around the top contains the solid silver bus bar*

of the sheer size of the hardware needed, it was discovered during the construction of the huge magnets that there was just not enough copper in the US to complete the magnet's windings. So, with a fine piece of bravado, Nichols had contacted the US Treasury. Could they provide silver for use on an important war project, provided it was returned afterwards? Yes, how much was required? came the reply. To Treasury officials used to dealing in troy ounces the figure Nichols gave them must have been totally bewildering – six thousand tons! However, the silver was delivered, and used, and returned when the war was over.

This story indicates the huge dimensions of this part of the project and any foreign power would copy it, if they could, at their peril. In 1954 Groves was to say this, under oath, about the information allegedly passed on to the Russians by Joseph Weinberg.

I would like to emphasise that the information he passed on was probably with respect to the electromagnetic process ... we were never too much concerned about this: because I personally felt that while the electromagnetic process was a process, while it was of extreme importance to us during the war, and we saved at least a year's time by doing it, that it was not the process we would follow after the war. That is one of the reasons why we put silver in those magnets, because we knew we could get it out.

It appears that Groves actually viewed the electromagnetic process as an enormous red herring, so this was information that Groves was prepared to see smuggled out to the Russians. Indeed, he seemed to have known about Eltenton for some time before Oppenheimer named him, and even to have resisted attempts by the FBI and security to close him down. 'I would rather have it there where I would know it,' he said. 'Of course, after the war I brought it to the attention of various friends in the Shell Oil Company and I believe that group was cleaned out in twenty-four hours.'

So Groves was much more sanguine about the security risks that Oppenheimer had warned of, but during the next few months he was under constant pressure from his security officers to make Oppenheimer reveal his secret. In November, Pash was seconded to an important role as military commander of the so-called Alsos[1] mission into Europe to try to discover just how far the Axis powers had progressed with their bomb. Before he left he spent two frustrating months testing every single lead on the Berkeley campus which could uncover Oppenheimer's contact. If for no other reason than to stop the waste of security's time and effort, Groves decided to act, and, on a visit to Los Alamos on 12 December 1943, he confronted Oppenheimer and ordered him to divulge the name of his contact.

It must have been with enormous misgivings that Oppenheimer gave up the name of his close friend, Haakon Chevalier. He still insisted to Groves that in his opinion Chevalier had made no further approaches other than the three original ones he had mentioned to Pash but he must have known that, from

[1] Alsos is the Greek for Groves – some people felt this was not a very good joke and an increased risk to security.

now on, because of his information, Chevalier was a marked man.

Whatever those misgivings, there is a clear indication from the only contemporary records of that conversation with Groves, that Oppenheimer still tried to protect himself and his own involvement in Chevalier's activities. The day after the conversation took place, Colonel Nichols sent three telegrams to various security officers on the Manhattan Project. They all said substantially the same thing and the one to Peer de Silva at Los Alamos read:

HAAKON CHEVALIER TO BE REPORTED BY OPPENHEIMER TO BE PROFESSOR AT RAD LAB WHO MADE CONTACTS FOR ELTENTON. CLASSIFIED SECRET. OPPENHEIMER BELIEVED CHEVALIER ENGAGED IN NO FURTHER ACTIVITY OTHER THAN THREE ORIGINAL ATTEMPTS.

At no time in his conversations with Pash and Lansdale had Oppenheimer revealed that he himself was one of Chevalier's contacts and although, years later, Oppenheimer insisted that he had told Groves he was Chevalier's contact, this contemporary record indicates that he did not reveal himself. Thus it would appear that on that cold December day in Los Alamos, Oppenheimer had been guilty of implicating his friend while protecting his own good name. Certainly this was the conclusion reached years later by an embittered and exiled Haakon Chevalier.

At the time of the Groves–Oppenheimer conversation, Chevalier was in New York waiting to hear whether he had clearance for a job in the Office of War Information. A month later he was called by an OWI official and told he had not got the necessary clearance. According to Chevalier, the official then went on to say that he had just returned from Washington where he had seen Chevalier's FBI file which contained 'allegations that were so fantastic as to be utterly unbelievable'. Chevalier remembers the official as saying, 'someone obviously has it in for you.'

# CHAPTER 7    A PROBLEM OF PREDETONATION

On 4 July 1943, Independence Day, Seth Neddermeyer began his tests on the implosion method of assembling the critical mass of the bomb.

Out in one of the dozens of canyons which dropped sharply away from that plateau on which the new laboratory had been built, he was conducting small scale experiments which, as he himself was the first to admit, served more to illustrate the problems he faced rather than provide any solutions.

He decided from the start that he could not start work on a spherical configuration as the geometry of the explosion was too complicated, so he worked on cylinders. He took lengths of thick metal piping and surrounded them with his explosive which was, in turn, surrounded by a tamping material. The explosive was detonated and the battered piece of pipe was retrieved for inspection from wherever it had been flung by the blast. In all these early experiments Neddermeyer was trying to achieve an even collapse of the pipe but the results were discouraging. Not only were the pipes badly twisted and deformed, but it became clear that he was going to need to use even more explosive to simulate the required force of implosion.

But such quantities of explosive would also completely destroy the only evidence there was of how successful the test had been, the metal pipe itself. So Neddermeyer not only juggled with varying amounts and types of explosives in a vain attempt to produce a more symmetrical implosion on the piping, but he

Neddermeyer (below, in a recent photo) proposed that a subcritical hollow sphere of uranium or plutonium be surrounded by explosive (A). This would be enclosed in a thick metal tamper.

When detonated the explosive would implode the hollow sphere which would become critical (B) and the nuclear explosion would begin.

Initially, he experimented with cylinders (C), attempting to implode steel pipe. The geometry of cylinders is simpler than spheres.

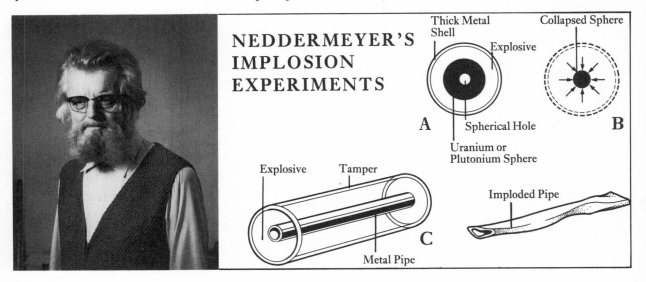

NEDDERMEYER'S IMPLOSION EXPERIMENTS

Thick Metal Shell

Explosive

Collapsed Sphere

A

Spherical Hole

Uranium or Plutonium Sphere

B

Explosive    Tamper

Imploded Pipe

C

Metal Pipe

also spent a great deal of his time thinking of automatic ways of actually recording the moment of implosion. This way he would not need to recover the pipe.

From the sidelines, Oppenheimer looked on at Neddermeyer's efforts with that high-minded indulgence which, earlier in his life, had infuriated his relatives. To him, Neddermeyer was one of those special people, someone with 'originality and a fine mind', but someone, also, whom Oppenheimer felt able to patronise. In those early months this was an indulgence that he could afford. Implosion was only a sideshow. The main effort of the laboratory was directed towards refining the 'gun' method, and almost all the early experimental results indicated that this method would work well.

In November of 1943, Bob Wilson's cyclotron group established a crucial fact about U-235. Its neutrons were nearly all emitted in less than a thousand millionths of a second, quite fast enough, using the gun method, for an intense fission reaction to take place before the bomb blew itself apart. It was a result which established almost beyond doubt that a uranium bomb was feasible.

*Glenn Seaborg, the Berkeley chemist who discovered element 94, plutonium*

As to a weapon based on plutonium, the experimental results were still in a much more embryonic stage, mainly due to the lack of any samples to work on. However, Glenn Seaborg, the physicist who had discovered the metal, brought a tiny sample to the laboratory and the first experiments with it at least indicated that plutonium did produce enough neutrons to trigger a fission chain reaction. It was thought that plutonium was likely to need a more rapid assembly than uranium and so all the work on the 'gun' at that stage was geared towards achieving the assembly velocities considered necessary for plutonium. The ordnance division were now working with newly forged barrels, and they were trying all kinds of different explosive materials to find the one which gave the quickest assembly.

In the latter part of 1943, the real problem areas on the project lay not with the bomb mechanism but with the processes for producing the fissionable material. Groves' early efforts to set up the vast industrial plant necessary to produce the material were bearing fruit. Enormous factories had sprung up employing tens of thousands of people, of whom very few, even the senior staff, knew what the end product of the labours would be.

At Oak Ridge, the site in Tennessee that Groves had so precipitately decided on, there were not one but two enormous plants being set up.

The first construction had been the plant based on Lawrence's calutron which was to produce uranium by the electromagnetic process. Stone and Webster, the engineering firm who were building the plant, had the immense problem of having to design it from scratch when the process itself was still not properly developed. Furthermore, the vacuum system was of a magnitude never before attempted, on such a scale that it had to be thirty million times better than that used in ordinary power plant equipment. The magnets, the new ones on which the silver windings were used, were two hundred and fifty feet long, they weighed between three and ten thousand tons and each one had between twelve and twenty-one tons of silver windings. On entering the halls

workers could feel the pull of the magnets on the nails in their shoes – hairpins suddenly flew into the air, leaving elaborate coiffures to collapse ignominiously.

The plant had been completed in less than a year. When it began operating in August 1943, it used as much power for its magnet as a large city, and there were thirteen thousand people employed in running it. And yet the fruits of this vast labour were a few grams of black powder – a teaspoonful – which was still only about fifteen per cent pure Uranium-235. Furthermore this black powder represented only ten per cent of the material produced – the remaining ninety per cent was spattered over the walls of the vast machine and was almost impossible to retrieve. Although the plant was running to capacity by the end of 1943, it was extremely erratic and susceptible to breakdown. Around Christmas it broke down completely and was out of action for several weeks.

Close by the electromagnetic (Y-12) plant the gas diffusion plant was being constructed. If the uncertainties surrounding the electromagnetic process seemed formidable, they were as nothing compared with those associated with this. When Groves had cajoled the engineers of the M. W. Kellogg company to take on the work, there was still no answer to the immense problems of corrosion from the uranium fluoride gas, a problem which affected the design of every pump and valve on the plant as well as the separation barrier itself. As 1943 came to an end there was still no final answer to those monumental technical problems, yet an enormous construction crew was putting up the largest building ever constructed to house it – a separation process which might never work.

Two thousand miles away at Hanford, another vast city had been carved out of a wilderness, this time to house the reactors based on Fermi's prototype which would produce the other fissionable material Plutonium-239. Construction had begun here in March 1943, only three months after the pile on Stagg field had gone critical for the first time. Here again the sheer scale of the plant provides a completely new perspective to the abilities and achievements of men like Groves and Nichols, as well as underlining the responsibilities resting on Oppenheimer and the scientists at Los Alamos.

A labour force of forty-five thousand men worked for more than a year building the plant: forty-five thousand cantankerous, cold, poorly-housed men, who had not the foggiest idea of what they were working on. There were more than eleven thousand major pieces of construction equipment gathered, enough to form a continuous column thirty-five miles long. It was estimated that they were doing work equivalent to building housing for a city with a population of four hundred thousand.

*The factory in a wilderness – the Hanford works under construction in a bleak valley of the Columbia river in Washington state*

*One of the eight mess halls at the Hanford engineering works serving the 45,000 construction workers on the site. Hanford was to produce plutonium for the bomb but even as construction was at its height, there was doubt thrown on the usefulness of plutonium*

A PROBLEM OF PREDETONATION

The Hanford plant would not be producing significant quantities of plutonium until early 1945, but a small experimental pile, which had been set up in the burgeoning industrial jungle at Oak Ridge, did begin to produce small quantities for the scientists at Los Alamos to work with in early 1944.

In one of the experiments with these tiny samples from Oak Ridge, Glenn Seaborg had detected the presence of a plutonium isotope, Pu-240, amongst the Pu-239. It was present in such tiny amounts that it was impossible to do any significant work with it. It was some months before the isotope's crucial importance was to be realised.

Edward Teller was still smarting from what he considered as a betrayal of trust by Oppenheimer in not allowing him to work on his own, on the Super.

In his own view, this was not simply a matter of egotism. He believed that the possibility of the Super as a development from the fission bomb had been a considerable factor in the rapid launching of the bomb project six months earlier. The Super, he believed, was not just some futuristic dream but had already proved itself as a powerful political lever. He resented being asked to work on the everyday problems of the fission bomb, having to work for Hans Bethe, and he focused much of this discontent on Oppenheimer.

From very early on, he told me, he was concerned about the way in which Oppenheimer seemed consciously to be building up around him a group of liberal-minded people with a common political aim. He also recalled that on one occasion, when they were discussing something that Groves had done,

*Edward Teller (c) at a Los Alamos party. His relationship with Oppenheimer began to deteriorate soon after his arrival at Los Alamos. Teller was concerned particularly by the way Oppenheimer 'manipulated people'*

J. ROBERT OPPENHEIMER

Oppenheimer had said that the 'military spirit' on the project would have to be resisted. Teller seemed to see a political significance in such sentiments, and they worried him a great deal.

Having so much admired Oppenheimer's handling of the Le Conte Hall meetings, Teller now began to question the way in which he was directing the scientific staff. His concerns do mirror those of the students Oppenheimer alienated back in Berkeley.

'Under Oppenheimer and among his students, I claim,' Teller has said, 'although they may deny it . . . you had to do anything in order to avoid looking foolish. You had to seem to talk as though you know, whether you know or don't know. This was a change of style to which I neither could nor would adapt myself.'

His feelings were shared by the Swiss physicist Felix Bloch, who had also come out to Los Alamos. An aristocrat with a traditional European academic education, Bloch may have resented the highly democratic system of open discussion that Oppenheimer operated, but his distaste for Los Alamos was so great that he was eventually driven to ask for release from the project. His wish was granted – one of the very few scientists to be released – and it was arranged that Teller would drive him to the station. It is a measure of Teller's disenchantment that when he received an invitation to dine with Oppenheimer that very same evening, he saw it as a deliberate political manoeuvre.

'I may be unjust,' he said years later, 'but the whole thing just looked like too much of a coincidence. He used friendships, he exploited friendships. Granted, he did not want me to leave Los Alamos, but obviously he manipulated people. . . .'

Eventually, Teller's resentments came to a head in a confrontation with Bethe over something he was asked to do on implosion. Paradoxically, Teller had already been pushing for greater effort on implosion because some work he had done showed considerable advantages that no one had so far thought of. Teller had calculated that the enormous pressures created during implosions would actually reduce the amount of precious fissionable metal necessary to produce the critical mass. Yet when Bethe came to him and asked him to develop this work further, he refused, point blank, to do it. Bethe, an especially patient man, was extremely angry and went to see Oppenheimer.

Oppenheimer acted swiftly and moved Teller away from Bethe and in a short while put him in charge of a small group of his own working on the development of the Super. He could have sacked him of course, but it is a measure of Oppenheimer's political sophistication that he did not. He reasoned that Teller was still extremely useful in debate and as a trouble-shooter. He also feared that if Teller left, he was a good enough salesman to set up a laboratory of his own in competition with Los Alamos. So Teller got his way and Oppenheimer had to look for a replacement. At the time good theoreticians were hard to come by and so Oppenheimer considered himself really fortunate to obtain the services of someone who already had experience of atomic weapon research. He was a German-Jewish emigré who had up until then been working

*A group of British physicists at Harwell after the war. Klaus Fuchs (far left) and Sir John Cockroft (far right). At the time this photograph was taken Fuchs was still passing information to the Russians*

in Britain on the bomb. With a wonderful irony only perceivable in hindsight, the name of that replacement was Klaus Fuchs.

Yet this was by no means the end of Oppenheimer's difficulties with Teller. Although he was kind and likeable in so many ways, many of those who knew Teller have described him as egotistical and incapable of playing second fiddle to anyone. For the next two years, Oppenheimer had to arrange special weekly meetings with Teller, the only scientist who was not a Group Head for whom he did this. Teller was to challenge him at seminars and to continue to question many of his actions and many of his motives. A relationship which had begun in friendship had collapsed into sourness and mistrust.

Teller's calculations on the effect of the pressures generated during implosion in reducing the amounts of fissionable material required did have a significant effect on the attitudes to Neddermeyer's efforts. In the autumn of 1943, Oppenheimer decided to push ahead on implosion and asked Neddermeyer to increase his efforts. Only a few weeks before, the mathematician John von Neumann had done calculations on Neddermeyer's result so far, and these showed that, if the implosion was to be successful, there could only be a five per cent variation in the symmetry of the shock wave.

This in turn indicated that an enormous volume of mathematical and experimental work was going to be needed. There seems little doubt that Neddermeyer, with Oppenheimer's backing, could have had the personnel and resources to meet this challenge but instead, he increased his team by a mere half-dozen people. The work went on much as before.

Throughout the early months of 1944, the tests continued on the small samples of plutonium that arrived at Los Alamos from Oak Ridge, and gradually a real cause for concern began to emerge.

The tests on Oak Ridge samples were compared with the results from the small sample brought down from Chicago a year earlier by Glenn Seaborg. The Italian Emilio Segrè carried out these experiments and he showed that the new samples contained a much higher proportion of the isotope Pu-240. In fact the amount of Pu-240 was shown to depend directly on how long the material was irradiated in the pile and, on that basis, it was possible to predict that the plutonium from the Hanford piles, when it arrived, would be even more heavily contaminated.

Furthermore, Segrè showed that the isotope was an alpha-emitter and therefore a source of background neutrons. Indeed it was likely to produce so many background neutrons that, with plutonium, the 'gun' method would just not be a fast enough method of assembly to overcome the ever-present problem of predetonation. The only hope of using plutonium was if the 'implosion' method could be made to work.

On 11 July 1944 Oppenheimer communicated the results of Segrè's tests to James Conant. Unless implosion could be made to work they were likely only to be able to produce one gun-type uranium bomb by the same time next year. This single weapon, even if it worked, could prove strategically useless, stiffening rather than weakening the enemy's resistance and providing the motive to use their own weapon.

*John von Neumann, the mathematician whose calculations showed that there could only be a five per cent variation in the symmetry of the implosion shock wave*

*The Italian physicist Emilio Segrè whose research showed that plutonium from the Hanford piles was likely to have such a high neutron background that only the implosion method would work*

# CHAPTER 8    ALSOS AND THE GERMANS

Boris Pash, the PE instructor turned security man, who had investigated Oppenheimer in the summer of 1943, had spent the ensuing twelve months mounting the Alsos missions into Europe. The missions' objective was to find out just how far the Axis powers had gone in developing their bomb.

So far, information about the German weapon had been very sparse. There had been early clues that the Germans were working on such a weapon, which was confirmed in 1943 when Niels Bohr escaped from Denmark to London where he reported on his abortive conversation with Heisenberg. Apart from that, there had been hardly anything more than the occasional piece of circumstantial evidence. As an indicator of how little real knowledge they had in early 1944, Pash and his colleagues on Alsos were speculating that the great bunkers the Germans had built on the French coast might have been constructed for weapons with nuclear warheads. However, with the Allied invasion of Europe, it became imperative to see how far the Germans had got.

The search in Italy had proved to be disappointing, revealing little that was not already known, so it was with eager anticipation that Pash awaited the

*The entry into Paris: Boris Pash took this photograph when he and other Alsos mission members rode behind the first five tanks*

invasion of Northern Europe. At the end of August 1944, the Allies entered Paris, and there was Boris Pash with four of his men riding in jeeps behind the first five tanks to enter the city. He was followed two days later by the scientific director of the mission, Dr Samuel Goudsmit, the Dutch scientist who had been met and fêted on his arrival in New York sixteen years before by Robert Oppenheimer.

Over the next two months the Alsos teams followed up leads which, though inconclusive, alarmed rather than reassured them. They found proof that the Germans had cornered the major supplies of uranium and also of thorium, a possible alternative to uranium. The Allied High Command became concerned that, even if the Germans did not have a completed bomb, they might decide to use the radioactive material as a chemical poison. Indeed, when drawings of the German experimental piles were first obtained, they were so unlike the American piles – so spherical and compact – that it was seriously thought that the Germans might be considering using a whole pile as a bomb and dropping it on a centre of population.

The rumours and counter-rumours continued to circulate until November, when the advancing Allied forces took Strasbourg. It was here that they believed that a number of eminent physicists, including von Weizsäcker and Fleischmann, had been working on the bomb. By good fortune, the last stage of their advance had been accomplished with great speed, and only a few of the city's inhabitants had been able to leave. Within hours, the intrepid Pash and his 'Strasbourg Task Force' had located the university's physics laboratory.

It was in the wing of a local hospital and a number of physicists were found there posing as doctors. It seemed that von Weizsäcker had made good his

*Dr Samuel Goudsmit, the physicist who had known Oppenheimer since his student days in Europe and became the scientific head of the Alsos mission*

*Boris Pash (second from right) with his 'Strasbourg Task Force'. They found a number of German physicists in the city hospital posing as doctors*

*Carl von Weizsäcker, one of the leading scientists working on the German bomb. When the Allies entered Strasbourg, von Weizsäcker made good his escape, but his papers provided evidence that German weapons research was still at an early stage*

escape but his colleague, Fleischmann, was among those captured.

Goudsmit joined Pash in the beleaguered city in the first days of December and began cross-questioning the men he courteously referred to as 'enemy colleagues'.

'The grim part of the venture,' he wrote to his wife, 'was that I had to face for the first time a small number of people like myself, but on the other side. Thank God I didn't know them personally and I kept my own identity hidden until the very end, when I had them put on a truck and taken to a camp.'

To Goudsmit's surprise and concern these 'enemy colleagues' were totally uncooperative and he was forced to sift through all their documents which he found in various offices around the university. While the Germans shelled the beautiful city from afar, Goudsmit and his colleagues sat reading through von Weizsäcker's and Fleischmann's papers by the light of candles and oil lamps. Very soon a picture of the Germans' progress began to emerge.

They revealed that Hitler had been told of the possibilities of a nuclear weapon in 1942 and that there had been a whole series of uranium pile experiments. But the crucial facts were that even as late as August 1944 the experiments were still at an early stage. The Germans had neither the certain information that an explosive chain reaction was possible, nor did they have the material or the mechanism to make their bomb. It was apparent that the project had moved forward hardly at all since 1942. There were one or two people in Washington who, when they read Goudsmit's final report, suspected that the information had come too easily, but most people believed it.

Shortly after making these discoveries Goudsmit found himself discussing the future with one of his military colleagues on the mission.

*The Alsos mission arrives at the centre of German atomic research, close to the village of Hechtingen in southern Germany. Here they are seen digging for the Germans' hidden uranium*

'If the Germans don't have the bomb then we won't need to use ours,' Goudsmit said.

'You don't know Groves,' was the reply, 'if we have such a weapon, then we'll use it.'

Unknown to most of the scientists on the project, Japan had been considered by the high-level Military Policy Committee as a target as far back as May 1943. They had concluded that the Japanese fleet concentration at Truk would be the ideal target for the new weapon. Now that the German threat had disappeared, attention was turned to Japan in earnest.

# CHAPTER 9 THE DARK HOURS

*One of the early high-speed cameras used to record implosion experiments*

*George Kistiakowsky, the Russian-born chemistry and explosives expert. Initially a consultant at Los Alamos he was drawn increasingly into the development of the implosion lens*

Ever since Oppenheimer had decided to push the implosion bomb late in 1943, Seth Neddermeyer and his small team had continued doggedly to pursue the chimera of the totally symmetrical implosion. They now had an explosives chamber in which they had been developing various high-speed photographic techniques for observing the results of their experiments. By spring 1944 they had so far done very few experiments. They were still working with the relatively simple geometry of tubes rather than the more complex problems resulting from spheres and the objective of a practicable weapon seemed as far off as ever.

Oppenheimer was in something of a dilemma. He had backed Neddermeyer in the first place and was reluctant, as he always was, to admit that he might have made a mistake in his choice of man. Not only that, but Oppenheimer had some sympathy with Neddermeyer's slow ivory tower attitude. After all, this was the self-same approach that Oppenheimer had employed when setting up Los Alamos itself, until he was bullied to think differently. However, as more and more was known about the plutonium problems the need to make progress with implosion became ever more urgent.

Oppenheimer's first move to improve the situation had been to bring in as a consultant the Harvard chemist and explosives expert, Dr George B. Kistiakowsky. Kistiakowsky was a Russian who, as a teenager, had fought in the White Army in the years immediately following the First World War. When his army had been defeated he had escaped through Turkey to Germany where he spent several years as a penniless student, studying chemistry in Berlin. On qualifying he had been encouraged to emigrate to the US where he had lived ever since.

At the time Oppenheimer approached him, Kistiakowsky was director of the National Defense Research Council's explosives group. He was frantically commuting between Pittsburgh, Florida and Washington, putting the finishing touches to some of the special equipment to be used in the D-Day landings, and was far from enthusiastic about adding Los Alamos to this commuting merry-go-round. In the end, however, the Oppenheimer charm worked yet again and Kistiakowsky came to Los Alamos for the first time in January 1944, to co-ordinate all the work on implosion.

After a few weeks of this [he recalled] I found that my position was untenable because I was essentially in the middle trying to make sense of the efforts of two men who were at each other's throats. One was Captain Parsons who tried to run his division the way it is done in military establishments – very conservative. The other was, of course, Seth Neddermeyer, who was the exact opposite of Parsons, working away in a little corner. The two never agreed about anything and they certainly didn't want me interfering and because it was so impossible I asked to be relieved of my duties.

It was at this time that the British Mission arrived in Los Alamos, a dozen or so scientists led by James Chadwick. The British had continued with the development of their own weapon until it had become apparent that the severely strained resources of the country could not bear a project with such high risks and costs. A great deal of expertise had been developed and, rather than break up the research team and set them to work on other projects, it was decided, on the basis of an agreement to share the knowledge obtained, to ship them over to America.

Scientifically, the British had fanned out among the various groups within the project and some came to work on the implosion bomb. Almost immediately, one member of this group helped further a completely new way of approaching the problem of symmetrical implosion. He was a young Yorkshireman called James Tuck, who before he left Britain had been working on armour-piercing explosives and it was his experience there with shaped charges that led to his particular proposal.

Up to this time Neddermeyer had simply been modifying the shape of the explosive, the kind of explosive, and the position and number of the detonators used, but his efforts had failed to overcome one essential problem. The shock waves which move out from a point detonator on the surface of an explosive sphere spread out into the surrounding explosive just like the waves set off by a pebble hitting water. Thus it is always a curved wave front that hits the surface of the core, not the flat even one which would produce the necessary symmetry. Furthermore, when several detonators are fired, their diverging shock waves meet and interfere with one another, causing all manner of eruptions in the explosive and destroying any possibility of symmetry.

In his jugglings with the configurations of his detonators and explosives Neddermeyer had hardly scratched the surface of this problem, yet it had already been faced by both the US and British designers of armour-piercing shells. What these men needed was some way of ensuring that the whole force of their explosive warheads was directed towards the armour and not dissipated in all directions and they had come up with something they called the explosive lens (*see diagram overleaf*). Thus, by surrounding the spherical core completely with a number of such lenses which are all detonated simultaneously it should be possible, so James tuck proposed, to produce the symmetrical and powerful shock wave that Neddermeyer had been searching for – so far in vain.

Over the next few months the initial tests on the development of the lens were most encouraging, but they did underline the fact that to convert the basic concept into a fully practical weapon was going to require an immense amount of trial and error experimentation and endless calculations to analyse the results. Indeed, if it had not been for the availability of the prototype

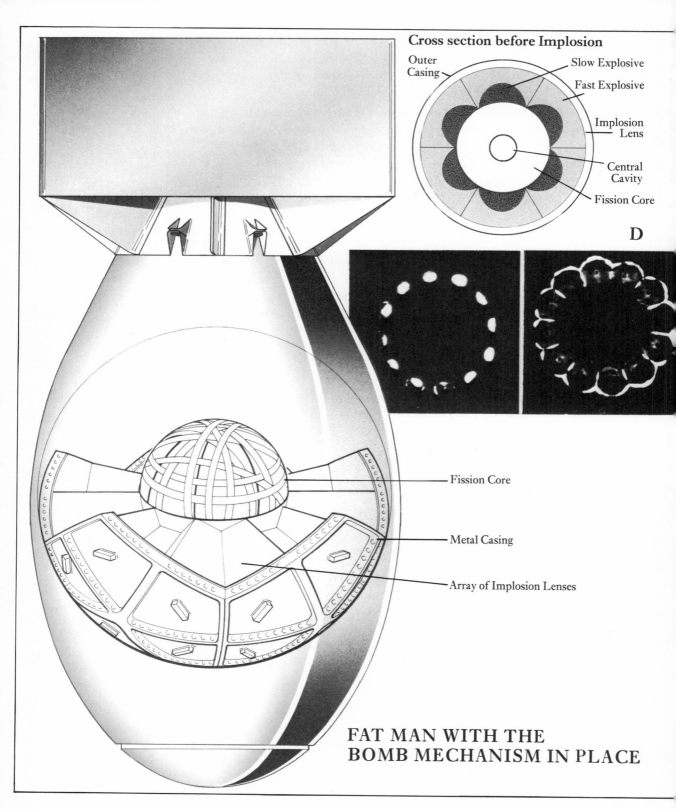

### Cross section before Implosion

Outer Casing

Slow Explosive

Fast Explosive

Implosion Lens

Central Cavity

Fission Core

D

Fission Core

Metal Casing

Array of Implosion Lenses

## FAT MAN WITH THE BOMB MECHANISM IN PLACE

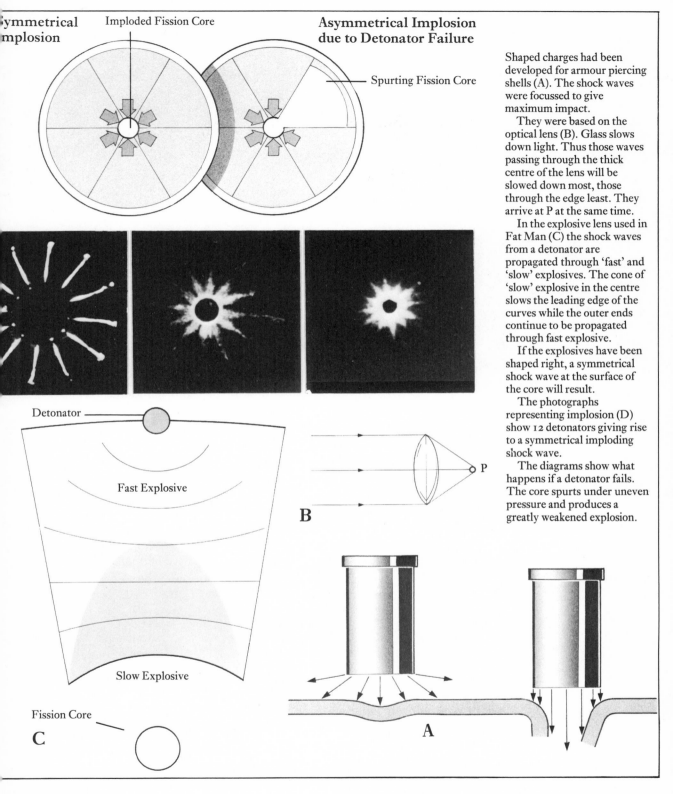

Symmetrical Implosion

Imploded Fission Core

### Asymmetrical Implosion due to Detonator Failure

Spurting Fission Core

Detonator

Fast Explosive

Slow Explosive

B

P

Fission Core

C

A

Shaped charges had been developed for armour piercing shells (A). The shock waves were focussed to give maximum impact.

They were based on the optical lens (B). Glass slows down light. Thus those waves passing through the thick centre of the lens will be slowed down most, those through the edge least. They arrive at P at the same time.

In the explosive lens used in Fat Man (C) the shock waves from a detonator are propagated through 'fast' and 'slow' explosives. The cone of 'slow' explosive in the centre slows the leading edge of the curves while the outer ends continue to be propagated through fast explosive.

If the explosives have been shaped right, a symmetrical shock wave at the surface of the core will result.

The photographs representing implosion (D) show 12 detonators giving rise to a symmetrical imploding shock wave.

The diagrams show what happens if a detonator fails. The core spurts under uneven pressure and produces a greatly weakened explosion.

*James Tuck (lower right) with colleagues on the firing ranges at Los Alamos in 1945*

computers from IBM, the further development of implosion could not even have been contemplated.

So, in the middle of the summer of 1944, Oppenheimer was facing a major crisis. By that time, he realised that he could only expect enough uranium from Oak Ridge to make one bomb within the next year. He also knew from Segrè's test that an implosion weapon was the only kind of plutonium bomb that could be made to work. Yet on the one hand he had a group under Neddermeyer who seemed to be going nowhere, and on the other he had a group which was proposing such a fundamental and difficult solution that he could only hope to achieve it by completely reorganising the laboratory.

Oppenheimer came near to despairing, and his mood affected the whole Mesa. For a while he lost his political detachment and the scenes he had with Neddermeyer, trying to stir him into action, have left a very bitter impression.

Oppenheimer lit into me [Neddermeyer has recalled]. A lot of people looked up to him as a source of wisdom and inspiration. I respected him as a scientist, but I just didn't look up to him that way. I didn't look up to him. From my point of view, he was an intellectual snob. He could cut you cold and humiliate you right down to the ground. On the other hand I could irritate him.

For most of the time at Los Alamos, Oppenheimer had managed to keep his sharp tongue in check, but now in these moments of extreme stress, when the future of the whole project was in the balance, he used his tongue to wound and made permanent enemies in the process.

J. ROBERT OPPENHEIMER

In early August, Neddermeyer reported on his latest experiments and it was quite clear that he was no nearer to achieving a symmetrical shock wave. He left Oppenheimer with only one option. He must reorganise the laboratory and organise a crash programme on implosion.

But even before the final results of Segrè's experiments were available Oppenheimer took decisive action which involved him in numerous confrontations.

First he assessed just what was going to be required to ensure at least some chance of success for this programme. There were new teams needed to work on such difficulties as ensuring precise detonation timings and for producing an initiator, a neutron source to start the chain reaction. Then completely new workshops, employing hundreds of technicians, were going to be required to carry out the precision moulding and machining of the explosives material. A final totting up of these new personnel showed that, somehow, Oppenheimer had to find six hundred more skilled men. Just finding such a number, let alone housing them and their families, was a daunting enough task.

Once he had a clear idea of the requirements of the push for implosion, Oppenheimer had to face up to the problem of who was going to run it. However much it pained him to admit it, he now realised that Neddermeyer would never be able to direct research on the scale required. But who could? Who had the necessary expertise? Captain Parsons was already fully extended putting the finishing touches to the gun mechanism and working on the modifications to the bomber carrying the weapon. Anyway, he had little sympathy with this particular project – to him it was still far too fundamental scientifically to be considered seriously as a way of producing a weapon within the time available. His only option was Kistiakowsky who was reluctant to take on an assignment where there was such a small chance of success. Again Oppenheimer used his powers of persuasion and was able to back up his plans with the offer of a much expanded division. So a somewhat reluctant George Kistiakowsky took over a division of a dozen or so men, many of them close colleagues of Neddermeyer's, and faced up to the massive problem of the implosion lens. In four months this division grew to be six hundred strong, but it was only one of three working on implosion.

I felt there was a certain kind of work involving sophisticated nuclear physics [Kistiakowsky recalled], which I wasn't competent to manage and this work was given to a new division, G Division, under Robert Bacher from Cal. Tech. Parsons' division still retained control of everything related to converting the bomb itself into an aerial weapon.

Kistiakowsky soon found himself in conflict with the conservative Parsons.

Parsons argued that what I was wanting to do was an undoable job. He believed there was something else that should be done, a kind of smoothing out of the difficulties with plutonium, minimising them rather than really overcoming them. Perhaps I am biased but I felt the way Oppenheimer handled this difference, his grasp of the technical problems, was really most impressive.

*Jumbo, the giant steel vessel designed in answer to Groves' fear that a failure in testing the new implosion weapon would waste the precious stores of plutonium. Jumbo was reckoned strong enough to contain all but the most successful explosions and the plutonium could then be retrieved. It was 25 feet long, weighed 214 tons and cost half a million dollars. Much to Groves' chagrin it was never used*

He called a big meeting of all the group heads, and there he sprang on Parsons the fact that I had plans for completely re-designing the explosives establishment. Parsons was furious – he felt that I had by-passed him and that was outrageous. I can understand perfectly how he felt but I was a civilian, so was Oppie, and I didn't have to go through him. Oppenheimer and I were simply talking, I didn't deliberately by-pass Parsons but from then on Parsons and I were not on good terms. He was extremely suspicious of me.

It was not an auspicious start to the reorganisation and one does wonder whether, with a little more careful handling, the dispute with Parsons could have been avoided. Next Oppenheimer had to face Groves who was not so concerned about the reorganisation, the starting from scratch, as he was about Oppenheimer's announcement that it would be necessary to conduct a full test of the new implosion weapon. Groves was strapped by some estimates he had given to Stimson, the Secretary for War, on when the bomb would be made available. He saw the test as a possible waste of precious plutonium which should be being used in the first practical weapon. Oppenheimer had to explain how disastrous it would be to discover at the last minute that the plutonium weapon did not work, but it was only after Kistiakowsky proposed a safety device for the test that Groves agreed to it.

J. ROBERT OPPENHEIMER

I proposed a solution of building a huge steel container, which we called Jumbo, [Kistiakowsky said] the function of which being that, if we put our bomb in the centre, and detonated it and there was no nuclear reaction, the Jumbo would not rupture and the plutonium would be inside and could be recovered. So Jumbo was built – it cost half a million dollars – and it was towed out to the site in Southern New Mexico, but it wasn't used. Why wasn't it used? Because if the bomb had worked, it would have been impossible to follow it with very sophisticated instrumentation to find out just how well it worked.

This was obvious to everyone at the time. We agreed to it. But then everyone thought the chances were a hundred to one against the bomb working.

The path was now clear for Oppenheimer to start recruiting for the new division. He was relying on two sources of men – the army, and personnel from other wartime scientific projects that were coming to an end.

At first sight, the army does not seem the most promising place to look for qualified physicists and engineers, but they had recently initiated a programme of screening the draft intake for scientifically qualified men and assigning those found suitable to the Special Engineering Detachment. Oppenheimer made full use of this programme and throughout the latter half of 1944 new detachments of SEDs were constantly arriving at Los Alamos. By the time implosion research was in full swing Kistiakowsky's six hundred-strong division consisted of no less than four hundred SEDs.

They were sent to us at Los Alamos without consulting them whether they wanted to or not – lots of them would rather have been fighting [said Kistiakowsky]. They were kids mostly, with partial college education, but there were even a few PhDs. Now Groves, who, in my view, deferred to the living comforts of civilians because he knew he couldn't get them there otherwise, took it out on these enlisted personnel, who lived in barracks built to a minimum permissible standard by the army, forty square feet per person. Not only that, but in addition to doing many long hours of work in the laboratories they were then mustered and marched and exercised.

Al Fishbein, who is still on the Los Alamos staff, was one of these SEDs.

We had reveille at six, we had drill and exercises at six-thirty and then fatigues until eight a.m. – and sometimes, working on something in the workshops, we had not gotten to bed until two or three in the morning. Our living conditions were terrible and during that very bad winter of 1944 when the water pipes to the camp froze up and there was a really big water shortage then, boy, did things get unpleasant. Imagine, thirty men living real close to one another with only a bucket of water a day each, to do everything with. We could only flush the johns once a day. It was bad enough for the civilians and their families but for us it was just terrible. Some of us used to cheat. In the passages where I was working there were decontamination showers – for accidents – and we used to take a shower in them pretty often – until we were caught in the act, as you might say, by a group of women officers.

In every respect the SEDs seemed to be getting a raw deal. While they were subjected to army rigours, the usual route for promotion away from these

ABOVE *The water supply to Los Alamos came overland through these pipes. In the hard winters they were continually freezing up*

RIGHT *The barracks of the type used by SEDs, the conscripted scientists and technicians at Los Alamos. Groves had them built to a minimum permissible standard*

horrors, the Officer Candidate School, was closed to them, presumably for security reasons. They were also viewed with some suspicion amongst the scientists, again for security reasons, and the new recruits, who had been told literally nothing about their assignment, found that their civilian colleagues were peculiarly reluctant to help.

There were some SEDs who enjoyed the outdoor existence which was the main way of relaxing at Los Alamos. 'Where else in the army could one, on a moonlight night, go skiing a few hundred yards from your barracks?' wrote one. 'But there were those who were accustomed to city living and city delights and for them life was disappointing. There were dances but there was a shortage of the vital ingredient – women.' Bob Wilson, who was at one stage the elected chairman of the Town Council, remembers a similar difficulty that came up before them.

Of the many problems that were presented to us during my term of office, the most memorable was when the MPs who guarded the site chose to place one of our women's dorms off-limits. They recommended that we close the dorm and dismiss the occupants. A tearful group of young ladies appeared before us and argued to the contrary. Supporting them, a determined group of bachelors argued even more persuasively against closing the dorm. It seems that the girls had been doing a flourishing business of requiting the basic needs of our young men – and at a price. All understandable to the army until disease reared its ugly head, hence their interference. By the time we got that matter straightened out – and we did decide to continue it – I was a considerably more learned physicist than I had intended to be a few years earlier when going into physics was not all that different from taking the cloth.

Eventually the SED problem did come to a head and Oppenheimer and Kistiakowsky found themselves facing a mutiny. The focus of the discontent had become the commanding officer.

He was a typical enlisted man, a character from South Boston, very Irish, with an inbred hatred of Harvard and academia and everything. So the senior among the enlisted men finally came to me [remembers Kistiakowsky], and said they were going

J. ROBERT OPPENHEIMER

FAR LEFT *Winter sports around Los Alamos. 'Where else in the army could one go skiing a few hundred yards from your barracks?' wrote one soldier*

*Staff at Los Alamos riding among the mountains surrounding Los Alamos. These were the mountains Oppenheimer had known for over twenty years*

to write a petition to the army to remove this officer. I made it clear straight away that a petition in wartime may be regarded as mutiny. 'Don't do it,' I said, 'let me talk to Oppenheimer.'

Which he did, and when Groves next visited Los Alamos, Oppenheimer approached him – to be told tartly that this was none of his business, it was an army matter. So, for the preservation of the common good, Oppenheimer stepped sideways and allowed Kistiakowsky to continue this particular battle.

*The Leisure Centre at Los Alamos*

I asked permission to ride with Groves in his car from Los Alamos to Albuquerque and so, one night after midnight we went in that car and started our argument. I kept saying that the conditions were affecting the junior technical personnel, that I was the boss, and that if things didn't change I would leave. 'You know, General,' I said, 'I didn't ask to come here and what's more you can't keep me here. I'm too old to be drafted,' I said, 'and I'll leave.'

Groves' response was grunts and violent attacks on me for transgressing my authority as a civilian, meddling in army affairs. But the outcome was that the officer was removed, put in charge of the officers' mess. Q.E.D.

The removal of that particular commanding officer made a tremendous difference and life for the SEDs became almost agreeable.

'I didn't used to sleep in barracks, after a while,' said Al Fishbein, 'instead, I had a bed set up under the bench in the laboratory. I even cooked meals there. It was great.'

Reveille was dropped and the latrines were now cleaned by civilian employees [wrote Val Fitch, another SED]. We still had the chore of manning the stores in the barracks . . . in the tradition of the army, the platoon sergeant was supposed to assign a detail to keep the stores going. In one barracks we all contributed toward paying one of our willing members to take care of them.

Saturday morning inspection also remained on the schedule but became devoid of spit and polish. The new company commander would stride down the length of the barracks at something just less than the speed of light and that was it – for another week.

One of the SEDs enjoying this new relaxed lifestyle was a draughtsman working in the drawing office attached to Kistiakowsky's division. His name was David Greenglass and in the latter months of 1944 he had enjoyed a rare treat at Los Alamos. His brother-in-law, Julius Rosenberg, had paid $150 for

J. ROBERT OPPENHEIMER

Greenglass's wife Ruth to join him in Albuquerque for their second wedding anniversary. Not until their fourth day together, while they were walking along the Rio Grande, did Ruth mention that Rosenberg was a Russian spy and that he wanted Greenglass to help him by passing on all he could about the work at Los Alamos.

Greenglass had been a member of the Young Communist League and ever since his teens had been under the influence of his domineering elder sister Ethel and her husband Julius, both dedicated Communists. Even so, he initially baulked at this request, but then the all too familiar arguments, arguments we have heard already in this story, helped him to overcome his scruples. The Russians were allies – he would simply be helping them. He also, incidentally, appreciated the favour of his wife's visit, bestowed on him by his brother-in-law, and so over the next few months he passed on everything he could about implosion and explosive lenses.

Rosenberg was so pleased with the information he received that he offered to send Ruth back to Albuquerque and set her up in an apartment so her husband could visit her. At the same time he made plans for Greenglass to have his own special courier and, in spite of the armies of security men who posed as waiters and shop assistants and added substantially to the irritations of life around Los Alamos, those meetings continued throughout the rest of the war, undetected.


During the autumn months of 1944, the canyons around the Mesa echoed with the seemingly endless series of explosive tests as work on both implosion and the gun reached a climax.

The discovery that a plutonium gun was not possible meant that, at least in this area, the task of the scientists became less rather than more complicated. They no longer had to try to achieve the extremely high velocities plutonium demanded and by December they were testing the real weapon.

These tests showed without a doubt that there was little or no chance of predetonation and, provided the uranium metal was produced in sufficient quantities at Oak Ridge, then the uranium weapon would work. But Oak Ridge were behind on the deliveries and facing enormous technical problems. They were unlikely to produce enough uranium for the first bomb until August 1945.

As to implosion the full-scale effort got off to a very uncertain start and tests throughout October and November gave no indication that the explosive lens approach would easily produce the necessary symmetry. Then, on 14 December, the team ran a series of trials using a whole range of new testing methods and for the first time the symmetrical shock wave seemed a possibility. A few days after this Groves and Conant visited Los Alamos and made their own assessment of progress. Although making a public show of optimism and even betting Oppenheimer that he could not produce the implosion weapon before the gun, Conant and Groves were in private extremely melancholy about the future. At most they thought implosion would produce a weapon that would yield only about eight hundred and fifty tons

*General Groves visiting the Radiation Laboratory in early 1944. With him are Sir Marcus Oliphant, Sir James Chadwick, who headed the British mission at Los Alamos, and Ernest Lawrence*

equivalent of TNT and perhaps even less. Indeed, there was such a shortage of staff and materials that they seriously wondered whether the weapon would be produced in 1945 at all. The problem of procurement had become really serious, industry could now see the end of the war and was beginning to wind down its war effort.

As far as staff was concerned, Oppenheimer had done well by the SEDs but was still short of men. He could not offer salaries that even approached those available in industry, and the conditions at Los Alamos that winter were, to say the least, uninviting. During November and December he managed to recruit two hundred men but, by February 1945, one third of these had resigned, stating hardship as their reason for doing so.

All the irritations and inconvenience of life at Los Alamos seemed to be compounded by flagging morale in the long winter of 1944. Housing shortages continued to be a problem. In December, the McKee Construction Company finished its third phase of housing, but with the influx of new people it was as if they had never begun. Further dissension was caused because the 'scientists' were given priority in housing matters over the 'technicians'. The 'technicians' were even offered a $100 bonus if they were prepared to come to the Mesa without their family, but that did little to relieve the pressure.

Then there was a continuing water shortage which, in winter, with the main supply pipe running overland through permanently snow-covered mountains, threatened to become a total stoppage. Notices appeared in the *Daily Bulletin*, edged in black, suggesting ways of economising. 'After bathing the baby in the deep sink, save the water for the family wash' was one such exhortation, or 'it is recommended that floors be scrubbed with water previously used for washing vegetables' and so on.

Homesickness became an epidemic. People dreamed of a lost civilisation where taps ran with clear water, newspapers and milk were delivered to the doorstep every day, and of a world unsullied by the paraphernalia and sounds of military life.

Much of the blame for these inconveniences was laid at the door of 'the G.G.' as General Groves was known – and not without reason. Groves had always thought of Los Alamos as a purely temporary phenomenon and so few proper buildings of any kind had been erected. It was because of Groves' parsimonious attitude that Los Alamos, which came most directly under his control, was widely recognised as having the worst housing on the whole Manhattan Project but it must be said that Oppenheimer probably connived in creating this situation. For whatever reason he concurred with Groves in treating Los Alamos as a temporary phenomenon.

Certainly his own domestic life was being affected by these very same pressures. The Oppenheimers lived in a large and – by Los Alamos standards – luxurious bungalow on Bathtub Row where they were isolated from the worst streets, which were, by turns, muddy quagmires or dustbowls, and protected from inadequate plumbing. Kitty had arrived at Los Alamos with a two-year-

*The Oppenheimers entertaining at Los Alamos*

old son, Peter, and during the first year had given birth to a baby girl, Toni. Thus as a mother of young children, she had suffered directly from the shortage of anything from teats for feeding bottles to an adequate nappy laundering service. Also she never properly settled into the social life on the Mesa.

As a qualified biologist, she did go and work in the laboratories but she flatly refused to take up the social role of 'Director's wife'. Instead, the official social life of the laboratory came to centre on Mrs William Parsons, whose husband Deke was the third most senior man at the laboratory. Even in the accounts of the everyday life of the laboratory, Kitty's name does not appear.

These accounts were written by women, by the wives of senior scientists and perhaps they demonstrate little more than Kitty's preference for male rather than female company. But there are people who feel it represents more than this.

She was a very intense, very intelligent, very vital kind of person [recalled Priscilla Duffield, Oppenheimer's secretary at Los Alamos], and I think there's no question at all that she was very difficult to handle. You're perfectly right, she didn't get along very well with women but she's also one of the few people I've ever heard men – and very nice men – call a bitch.

At Los Alamos I think she became very frustrated. I'm sure she had romantic ideas about herself that she didn't carry through and I think this went on for years and her frustration got worse and worse.

I don't know how much Kitty influenced Robert, but I could guess that Robert did consult her occasionally on something he was really puzzling over, and that he would give her judgement as much weight as that of anyone else whose advice he chose to ask.

*Oppenheimer's son Peter, with his father's pipe*

*Kitty with daughter Katherine, always known as Toni, and son Peter*

OPPOSITE *Oppenheimer with Kitty and son Peter. Oppenheimer was very much an absentee parent and Kitty found the children difficult. Their upbringing was largely in the hands of nannies*

Kitty's growing sense of frustration and isolation took several forms. The first to suffer, if only indirectly, were the children.

It was very hard for the children [recalled Jackie Oppenheimer, about the time she was at Los Alamos in 1945], she would go off on a shopping trip for days to Albuquerque or even to the West Coast and leave the children in the hands of a maid. They had one maid, a German one, and she was a regular tyrant. Then, when she returned, she would bring some enormous present for Peter. She must have felt so guilty and unhappy, the poor woman.

Then, more and more, Kitty began to drink heavily.

When we went up to Los Alamos [said Jackie Oppenheimer], Kitty made a dead set at me. It was known that we didn't get on well together and she seemed determined that we should be seen together. On one occasion she asked me to cocktails – this was four o'clock in the afternoon. When I arrived, there was Kitty and just four or five other women – drinking companions – and we just sat there with very little conversation – drinking. It was awful and I never went again.

She had also become very possessive of Oppenheimer. How much Kitty knew of his continuing visits over the years to see Jean Tatlock, it is not possible to tell, but her reaction to even the smallest cue could sometimes be extreme.

We came to Santa Fe when the lab was being set up and everyone, Kitty, Robert, the nurse, Peter and I were staying in the hotel [recalled Priscilla Duffield]. For some stupid reason, somebody put me in the room right next to the Oppenheimers which I don't think was very bright. There was a connecting door and Robert came through it to ask me something or another and after he'd left Kitty said, very ostentatiously, 'I think we'll keep that door locked.' That was the kind of thing she did.

However, the Jean Tatlock saga was drawing to a close. The girl who nearly ten years before had introduced him to communism and to so many of the people who were to play such an important part in his life had become increasingly ill. On a cold January day in 1944, six months after she and Oppenheimer had last met, Jean Tatlock filled the bath in her apartment in San Francisco's Telegraph Hill. Then she piled cushions next to it. That done, she took a number of sleeping pills, and sat down to write several letters, the last one without any address.

RIGHT *May 1944. The search for a test site. Turned back by snow drifts on the road, close to the rim of the Vallee Grande, Oppenheimer and Major Lex Stevens pause for refreshments*

FAR RIGHT *The search for the Trinity site. Major Lex Stevens digging out a weapons carrier, close to the rim of the Vallee Grande*

. . . . To those who loved and helped me, all love and courage. I wanted to live and to give and I got paralysed somehow. I tried like hell to understand and couldn't . . . At least I could take away the burden of a paralysed soul from a fighting world . . .

Her writing trailed off into a line. The drugs were taking effect. She managed to get across the apartment to the bath where she knelt on the cushions and plunged her head deep into the water.

Her body was found some days later by her father.

When Oppenheimer heard the news of Jean's death, he was visibly moved. He left his office and walked off to be alone among the high pine trees.

# PRELUDE TO TRINITY CHAPTER 10

In the late spring of 1944 two weapon carriers bounced their way across the arid expanses of the desert area in southern New Mexico known as the Jornada del Muerto – the Journey of Death – a name given to the area four hundred years earlier by the conquistadores as they pushed northwards into North America.

It was a party of exploration – looking for the ideal site for testing Fat Man, the nickname given to the implosion bomb. They were looking for somewhere flat and unpopulated, yet near enough to Los Alamos for all the equipment to be easily trucked across to the testing site. So far the group under Kenneth Bainbridge, the director of the implosion test, had considered sites as widely separated as a strip of sand barriers in the Gulf of Texas to the enormous sand dunes of Colorado's San Luis Valley. Now they had narrowed the field to New Mexico and were looking for the right location. As the convoy moved across the wind–swept plain with sand–devils swirling past them, they could see smoke signals passing from one adjoining mesa to another. Their progress was being marked by descendants of the Indians who had attacked and killed the conquistadores all those centuries ago.

In the party with Bainbridge was a military engineer, Major Stevens, and Oppenheimer. For Oppenheimer it was a return to a desert that he had known and loved in his youth when he and his brother had trekked all over New Mexico. The isolation and the nostalgia must have been a wonderful relief from the pressures of Los Alamos.

Return trips were made to finalise the precise location but on that occasion

*Kenneth T. Bainbridge, the Harvard physics professor who carried responsibility for the Trinity test from its inception in early 1944. Approaching forty, Bainbridge was one of the 'old men' of the Mesa*

Oppenheimer was not with them. Bainbridge pinpointed the place exactly, an area eighteen miles wide and twenty-four miles long at one corner of the Air Force's Alamogordo Bombing Range. He obtained Air Force permission to use the site, then telephoned Oppenheimer with news of his success.

Within a short time, Oppenheimer with that particular flair of his had come up with a name for the site. He took it from a sonnet by John Donne, which he had recently read.

> Batter my heart, three-personed God; for, you
> As yet but knock, breathe, shine, and seek to mend;
> That I may rise, and stand, o'erthrow me, and bend
> Your force, to break, blow, burn, and make me new.

The Holy Trinity was the inspiration for the sonnet and the name that was given to that lonely place in the New Mexico Desert.

The site was near enough to Los Alamos for convenience, accessible but isolated. It was practically uninhabited except for a few ranches, two abandoned coal-mining towns and the town of Bingham, which consisted of crossroads, store and windmill. The army set about moving the few inhabitants, on the face of it an easy task, but the ranchers did not want to go. They had no idea why they were being asked to leave their homes. Some of their cattle were still running free, so they kept drifting back. After a number of warnings, the army began a war of attrition. Marvin Davis was one of the MPs who helped persuade ranchers finally to quit the area.

They had these large water tanks where the windmills pump water, and those ranchers, they would sneak in at night and they would open up those windmills and let them

pump. And so finally the Captain got disgusted and he went over and took a .45 and shot holes in the water tanks so they were empty and there wouldn't be any water for the cattle to be attracted to.

The family most determined to hang on were the MacDonalds but incidents like these and the occasional unexplained killing of some of the stray cattle persuaded them at last to leave. By early 1945 Trinity was in the hands of the Army.

At about that time Sam Allison arrived in Los Alamos from Chicago. His work at the Metallurgical Laboratory was coming to an end, and Oppenheimer had jumped at the chance of such an able physicist coming to work at Los Alamos. He was immediately put in charge of a new advisory body called the Technical Scheduling Conference which in effect was to act as a progress chasing group throughout the project.

Later it was to become the cause of considerable resentment within the project but in the first months of its existence Allison's group was able to bring cheering news to Oppenheimer. Enrico Fermi, who had also moved his base from Chicago to Los Alamos, had done neutron multiplication tests on a small 0.9 inch sphere of plutonium from the experimental Oak Ridge pile and had produced the first experimental indications of the critical mass for an implosion bomb. He estimated it at around five kilograms, very much in line with early estimates but far less than anyone had hoped for.

Then another scientist, Luis Alvarez, finished his two-year programme of developing detonators which could fire with the millionths-of-a-second accuracy that the implosion method required. In January he reported consistently good test results with his latest designs.

The test assembly for 'tickling the dragon's tail', an experimental determination of the critical mass of the uranium bomb. A small uranium hydride slug was dropped through this almost critical assembly of slugs. For a fraction of a second the assembly went critical

*The test assembly for 'tickling the dragon's tail', an experimental determination of the critical mass of the uranium bomb. A small uranium hydride slug was dropped through this almost critical assembly of slugs. For a fraction of a second the assembly went critical*

In another distant part of the laboratories, Omega site, a series of experiments, one of the most hair-raising and dangerous of the war, was drawing to a close. Working at Omega, Otto Frisch's Critical Assemblies team were trying to produce accurate figures for the critical mass of the uranium bomb, and to do this they were performing experiments which became known as 'tickling the dragon's tail'. A small slug of uranium hydride was dropped through the open centre of an almost critical collection of other uranium slugs. The slug was guided by four rails and, for a fraction of a second, the entire assembly would become critical, generating nearly twenty million watts of energy. By measuring the output of this momentary bomb it was proving possible to work towards predicting the precise amount of Uranium-235 required, but at the same time the risk the experimenters were running was a real one. In February, so much heat was generated during one such experiment that the uranium slugs began to melt and the area had to be cleared for several days.

The buildings on Omega site were shared by members of Fermi's team and they grew progressively nervous, vacating the building during critical experiments and going on long hikes through the surrounding mountains. But

J. ROBERT OPPENHEIMER

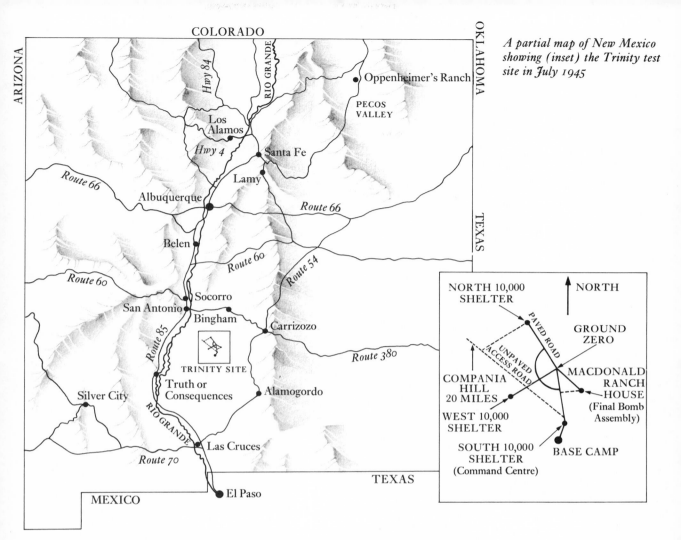

*A partial map of New Mexico showing (inset) the Trinity test site in July 1945*

these tests seemed to have a fascination for Oppenheimer and he would periodically come down to Omega and sit in the quiet of the laboratory talking physics with the experimentalists while they carried on their work.

Nevertheless almost all the different projects around the laboratory were at such a developed stage that Allison and Oppenheimer were able to draw up a day by day timetable for the next five months up to 4 July, the date projected for the test by Groves. However the implosion project still seemed to lack direction and there were worries that it was wasting scarce raw materials on following up too many approaches to the shaping of the explosive lenses. This was where friction occurred and it took place along one of the battle lines which had quite unconsciously emerged during the two years of the laboratory's existence – between a non-physicist, Kistiakowsky, and a member of the physics élite, Allison.

We were falling behind schedule with the lenses [Kistiakowsky told me]. Groves had made a prediction in August 1944 that we would have implosion by the next Spring and it was becoming clear that we wouldn't. And so I really think Oppenheimer began to lose faith in me. He told me, 'George, these people will help you,' but these people [Allison's committee] were really essentially watching what I was doing. We had one argument with these guys when they tried to accuse us of procuring materials incompetently. We left them to do it. In the end it was too difficult for them.

But I felt that was all part of being a brother physicist. On one occasion I was forced to say to Oppie in this top level council where I was the only chemist, 'You're all ganging up on me because I'm not a physicist'. To which Oppie replied smilingly, 'George, you're an outstanding third rate physicist.'

All of which in hindsight may seem trivial but it is significant that a man like Kistiakowksy, who in later years had to suffer considerable political buffeting as a Presidential scientific adviser, should remember this particular contretemps and also Oppenheimer's retort. The result, anyway, of the dispute was a decision in mid-February to freeze all new design work and concentrate on just two patterns for the lenses. However ruffled the feathers of some of the leading scientists were, this decision released enough hard-pressed staff for Bainbridge to proceed at speed with the preparations for Trinity and to get ready for a trial run with a hundred tons of TNT in early May. Although by no means as large as some accidental explosions, this trial run was the largest man-made explosion ever staged. To add to its usefulness it was decided to include amongst the explosive a quantity of radioactive material so that the scientists could perform the first studies ever of a new phenomenon – radioactive fall out.

While Fermi and Allison had been moved down to Los Alamos when there was no longer any need for their talents at the Metallurgical Laboratory, many of the scientists stayed on there. For the first time in nearly four years this group found themselves with time on their hands and they began to discuss what was going to be done with the new weapon they had developed.

This debate was catalysed, as ever, by Leo Szilard who, even in the busiest days of the project, continued to write memos and complain about its progress. 'A pain in the neck!' was how Groves described Szilard and even the statesmanlike James Conant was convinced that all Szilard was doing with his complaints was to build up a log of material with which to 'make a stink' when the war was over.

So when Szilard began to look beyond the immediate problems of the project to what would happen after the war, he had unfortunately already alienated most of those people in power who could have backed him. Nevertheless, his questioning approach rubbed off on his colleagues at Chicago and towards the end of 1944, twenty-two of the Met. Lab.'s top scientists called for a general statement to the American public revealing the existence of the Manhattan Project, the scale of the new weapon, and the way in which it was bound to affect international relations. This request and a number of other papers from the laboratory were presented to Vannevar Bush, the President's scientific adviser, and Bush did discuss the whole question of future policy with Roosevelt in September 1944. However, following that meeting nothing seemed to happen and the frustration amongst the Met. Lab. scientists began to grow.

On 9 March massed B-29 bombers conducted a raid on Tokyo. Their incendiaries started a fire storm and 83,800 people were killed. People died gasping for air in open fields far from the fire, as the great conflagration consumed all the available oxygen in the air. Sixteen square miles of the city were devastated and 1,500,000 people were left homeless. This was the scale of conventional war against which the burgeoning debate about the use of the new weapon was to take place.

*Secretary of War Henry Stimson. In 1945, when he was coping with an ailing President and making crucial decisions not only on the use of the A-bomb, but on the shape of the post-war world, he was seventy-seven*

In the spring of 1945, it still seemed to the scientists at the Met. Lab. that nothing was happening to further the debate and so yet again Szilard took the matter into his own hands and prepared a long memorandum for the President on the need for international control.

'Perhaps the greatest immediate danger which faces us,' Szilard wrote, 'is the probability that our "demonstration" of atomic bombs will precipitate a race in the production of these devices between the United States and Russia.' In Szilard's view, only a carefully designed system of international control could prevent this inevitable event from happening, and he was convinced that the sudden shock use of the weapon would seriously damage the United States' credibility in proposing such a system of control. It was a persuasive argument but in order to strengthen his hand with the President, Szilard yet again approached Einstein to ask him to write a supporting letter. Einstein agreed but, this time, nothing happened.

The President, it seems, was exhausted. In March, Henry Stimson, the Secretary of War, also had had a meeting with Roosevelt to discuss future policy. The meeting took place over lunch and Stimson thought the discussion a success but yet again no firm decision about post-war planning had been taken. It was the last time that Stimson saw the President. On 12 April 1945, Roosevelt died at Warm Springs, Georgia, and the new President, Truman, although he had been Vice-President for several months, did not even know of the existence of the new weapon.

The news of Roosevelt's death threw Szilard and his colleagues into a state bordering on despair, as they felt their chance of influencing policy slipping further from their grasp. Without any strong sense of personal conviction, Arthur Compton tried to relieve the tensions within the laboratory by taking the scientists' views to Washington, but his journey had little effect either in quelling their fears or in convincing politicians that they were failing to see the profound way in which atomic energy had changed the whole international political scene.

*12 April 1945. The flag at Trinity Base Camp flies at half mast to mark Roosevelt's death. His successor, Harry Truman, did not even know of the bomb's existence*

The day before Roosevelt died, Peer de Silva had handed over his job as security boss at Los Alamos to a new man. He was to be posted elsewhere but before he left he did two things. First he wrote a note for his successor, Thomas O. Jones, in which he declared his concern about Oppenheimer as a security risk. Then he wrote ingratiatingly to Oppenheimer himself that Oppenheimer's '. . . consideration and help . . . have, in fact, contributed much to whatever success my office has had in performing its [security] mission.'

The next day, one of the first to hear of the President's death at Los Alamos was Thomas O. Jones. He heard by phone in his office and rushed out to pass on what he had heard. On a second storey catwalk above Main Street he met Oppenheimer. 'Is it true, Thomas O.?' Oppenheimer inquired. Jones confirmed that it was and, for a few moments, Oppenheimer stood silent. Then he began talking about a meeting he had had with Roosevelt a few months previously. It was a brief conversation but Jones remembers Oppenheimer's tone of undisguised, authentic admiration, and compared it with de Silva's doubts about him. Jones came quite firmly to believe that this was not a man who could ever have betrayed his country.

A service was held by the flagpole in front of the Administration Building. Oppenheimer spoke for only a few minutes and drew from the *Bhagavad-Gita*. He spoke quietly in a voice that was difficult to hear, but the effect was powerful and memorable.

April was a good month at Los Alamos, with progress going according to schedule on all fronts and Oppenheimer was able to tell Groves that a weapon would be available by 1 August. Furnished with this information, Groves went to Washington to prepare for a meeting with the new President on 25 April. It had been arranged that Groves should accompany Stimson and two days before the meeting Groves presented the ageing Secretary of War with a status report. Throughout the war, Groves had occupied a strange position. At Los Alamos and at other laboratories on the project he was the layman continually having material explained to him but, elsewhere, he was the expert. In political circles there could have been few people who had such a grasp of the potential of the new weapon and in the crucial weeks following the change of President, Groves was to capitalise on this. Working through Stimson he was very much able to influence the debate on policy at the highest level.

For the meeting on 25 April there was concern that if Stimson and Groves went in to see the President together then reporters could put two and two together, so Groves was let into the White House by a side entrance and hustled through service corridors to a room in the West Wing to await his summons. Stimson had gone in before him and was stressing America's 'moral responsibility' in creating 'the most terrible weapon ever known in human history, one bomb of which could destroy a whole city.' However, if they could but use the weapon properly then they could be establishing a pattern which might save the peace of the world and civilisation itself.

Then Stimson asked for Groves to be brought in, and, with Truman reading one copy of his report – for the first time – and Stimson sharing the other with Groves, the General went through the whole story of the development of the weapon and how it was hoped to be used. When it came to discussing the target, Groves pointed out that Japan had been a possible target since 1943. Indeed there were reliable military estimates that, if the bomb prevented the invasion of the main Japanese islands, then more than a million lives could be saved.

It was an impressive justification for the use of the weapon but it took no account of the disagreement about how many lives would be saved. For instance, General Marshall, the Army Chief of Staff, estimated that the number of lives lost during the invasion could be as few, relatively speaking, as forty thousand. Neither did Groves mention that most scientists working on the project had been recruited through fear of the Germans, not the Japanese.

During that meeting Groves and Stimson proposed an 'Interim Committee' to consider, in detail, the country's future weapons policy and Truman agreed. From that point onwards, the main decision about America's future was moved one step away from the President.

The two scientists elected to serve along with military men and politicians on this Interim Committee were James Conant and Vannevar Bush but when approached, both these men, with great frankness, expressed the view that they did not feel themselves representative of the scientists working on the project. They proposed a Scientific Panel and, after vetting the proposed members, Stimson agreed to it. The members were Arthur Compton, Ernest Lawrence, Enrico Fermi and Robert Oppenheimer.

Shortly after dawn on 7 May 1945, the scientists carried out their dress rehearsal for Trinity, by detonating a hundred tons of TNT. That same day, the Germans surrendered unconditionally to the Allies. It brought home forcibly to many of those working on the project a crucial change in the status of their work. They were no longer involved in a life or death race with an enemy, but were working instead to produce yet another and more deadly weapon for the US arsenal. Even the hard-pressed scientists at Los Alamos began discussing it, even though, as one scientist put it, 'they were still caught up in the momentum of the project and the excitement of their technology.'

Very few had the foresight to assess the post-war political implications of using the bomb as Szilard had done. Instead their concern was based on moral grounds. It was clear to everyone that the war in Japan had to be brought to a close as quickly as possible, but was there a way this could be

ABOVE *The completed stack of a hundred tons of TNT ready for the Trinity dress rehearsal on 7 May*

RIGHT *Preparation for the Trinity dress rehearsal, 7 May 1945, using a hundred tons of TNT – one of the earliest experiments on fall-out. Here a crew is seen positioning radioactive fission products in the midst of the assembly to see how the material was spread after the explosion*

done other than by using the bomb, without warning, on a real target? Was there some kind of warning or even a demonstration that could be given?

These questions were among those that were discussed in some detail on 31 May at a joint meeting of the newly formed Interim Committee and its Scientific Panel; and Oppenheimer was to play a major part in that discussion. The Panel had been selected very much with the intention of representing the working scientists' point of view, but Oppenheimer, and, indeed, the other members of the Panel, had over the years become conditioned to a political way of thinking. Nevertheless, he knew the trust that other scientists on the project had in him as their spokesman, so how did he represent their views at that crucial meeting?

At first, the discussion centred on various technical and practical aspects of the atomic energy programme, but as the morning wore on it turned to the vexed question of whether to shock the Russians with the first use of the new weapon or whether to tell them about it. Oppenheimer observed that the Russians had always been friendly to science and he therefore thought it might be wise to hope for the best and approach them with a view to future co-operation. Here he was supported by the Chief of Staff, General George C. Marshall, who felt that there was little to be risked in telling them beforehand and even inviting them to the test, and that it might help in breaking down the barriers between the two powers. It was a suggestion which represented a significant step towards fostering co-operation and ultimately international control, but it was firmly vetoed by the President's representative at the meeting, James Byrnes. He was adamant that the Americans' best policy was to make certain that they stayed ahead in the race by every means possible. Such was his prestige that he carried everyone in the meeting with him.

Over lunch the possibility of a demonstration of the bomb rather than its

J. ROBERT OPPENHEIMER

direct use involving great loss of life came up. It had already been briefly raised by Lawrence but, painstakingly, Oppenheimer explored what real alternatives there were. He could not think of a demonstration sufficiently spectacular to convince the Japanese that this was a weapon of a completely different order. Furthermore, there were practical difficulties involved in giving a warning and then using it on a real target. The bomb might be a dud. The Japanese might manage to shoot down the delivery plane, or they might bring American prisoners into the test area. If the demonstration failed to bring surrender, the chance of administering the maximum surprise shock would be lost. Anyway would the bomb cause any greater loss of life than the raids on Tokyo?

It was on the basis of this contribution of Oppenheimer's that the Interim Committee made three crucial recommendations:

1 That the bomb be used against Japan.
2 That the target should be a military one surrounded by a civilian population.
3 That the bomb be dropped without any prior warning.

Thus at no time during this meeting had Oppenheimer represented the scientists' moral concern over using the weapon on Japan. He had dealt with it purely in terms of the political and tactical considerations involved. It could be that, at such a high-level meeting, he felt that such views would find little sympathy, or it could be that he himself was too close to the immediate problems to see the issues in any other terms. Whatever the reasons, although the scientists were to continue in their efforts to halt the use of the weapon, the decision of the Interim Committee was a crucial step on the path to Hiroshima.

Two days after the meeting of the Interim Committee in the Pentagon, on 2 June, an old second-hand Buick headed down a street in Santa Fe towards one of the bridges over the river. At one end of the bridge it stopped to pick up someone and then drove off around the town. Klaus Fuchs was meeting Harry Gold for the seventh time. The two men drove around chatting for a while and then Fuchs handed over to Gold a sheaf of documents containing a great deal of

LEFT *The bridge across the dry bed of the Santa Fe river where Klaus Fuchs met his contact Harry Gold*

BELOW *Harry Gold who was the contact for both Klaus Fuchs and David Greenglass, the two convicted spies who operated at Los Alamos on behalf of the Soviet Union*

*Trinity Base Camp, a few days before the test. Situated in one corner of the Alamogordo bombing range it had been accidentally bombed by trainee pilots. Miraculously no one had been hurt*

vital information about the implosion work at Los Alamos. At the end of their meeting Gold caught a bus to Albuquerque where he was to keep an appointment with another man on the Los Alamos payroll, but whom he had not yet met, David Greenglass.

At the Trinity site the preparations for the test were well under way. The Cowpuncher Committee, the group of senior scientists who had been appointed to 'ride herd' on the implosion bomb – hence the name – had at last fixed a date for the test, 20 July, little more than seven weeks away.

Out in the summer heat of the desert there were now more than three hundred men, GIs, physicists, weathermen, telecommunications men, working away amongst the shacks and the criss-cross of wires and crumbling adobe roads. To cope with the additional people Kenneth Bainbridge had procured seventy-five additional vehicles and the new influx of traffic had proved too much for the old tracks. This was just another thing to think of. Bainbridge had to get permission from the ever-frugal Groves to spend $125,000 laying twenty-five miles of 'blacktop' road.

Most of these roads linked Point Zero, the place where the bomb itself would be, and the observation bunkers placed at three of the four points of the

J. ROBERT OPPENHEIMER

compass, some ten thousand yards away. S.10,000, code-named Baker, was where the countdown would take place and from where Oppenheimer and the other VIPs would watch the test. It had its own telephone exchange of the type operated by cranking a generator, and was also in radio contact with scientists and military personnel out in the field. These radio contacts were to have been on a frequency which was unassigned to anyone else. However, after one or two strange occurrences, the scientists discovered that they were on the same frequency as a railway yard six hundred miles away at San Antonio, Texas, and could hear the railmen shunting their rolling stock. Presumably the railmen could also hear them preparing to test their atomic weapon – certainly the control tower at nearby Socorro airport could overhear their conversations. Again – so much for real security, because this lapse was never rectified in time for the test.

In March and April, the lonely MPs and scientists who had been the main occupants of the Trinity site had entertained themselves with movies, poker and occasional sallies out into the desert to hunt the roaming herds of antelope. Now everything had taken on a much more serious tone. Work had become the main occupation. The site sprang to life around five a.m. to make as much use of the cooler hours as possible, but work still went right on through the baking heat of the middle of the day. The sun scorched the sand and the temperatures rose to above 100°F. Alkali dust and sand got into the precision instrumentation and it stuck to the men's perspiring bodies. In spite of the heat few dared to strip off and when a wind got up many took to wearing protective goggles or handkerchiefs across their faces. The cold showers at Base Camp seemed only to replace one grimy deposit with another. The water, other than the drinking water which was brought in by truck, contained heavy concentrations of alkali and gypsum which left an irritant scaling on the skin and stiffened hair that was washed in it. The doctors at the Base Camp hospital faced increasing cases of skin disease and also diarrhoea brought on by the laxative properties of the gypsum.

The wildlife was yet another unpleasant factor to deal with. There were scorpions and tarantulas, which anyone working on the ground had to be aware of as well as other poisonous snakes and reptiles.

The fact that the Trinity site was at one corner of the Alamogordo Bombing Range was also a risk to be taken into account. Early on, a crew on a night-time training mission had mistaken Base Camp for one of their targets and had plastered it with practice bombs. One had been a direct hit on the stables, another on the carpentry shop – it was a miracle that no one had been hurt. Sometime later, in spite of remonstrances with the Commander of the Base, yet another incident occurred. A B-29 on an illegal hunting-shooting-fishing mission flew over a group of scientists out in the desert with a tail gunner blazing away at a nearby herd of long-suffering antelope. The group hugged the ground as bullets thudded round them.

In June, there came a heavy security clampdown. There were to be no more visits to nearby towns. There were to be no stop-offs at the one or two hotels on the road between Alamogordo and Trinity. Even the laundry had to be cleared through security. The build-up to the test was intensifying.

When the members of the Scientific Panel had left the Interim Committee meeting on 31 May, it had been agreed that they should meet as a group in mid-June to develop their own views on post-war policy. In the meantime, Oppenheimer returned to Los Alamos to a laboratory pre-occupied with the Trinity test, but Arthur Compton had returned to Chicago, to a laboratory in uproar. He was faced with the discrepancy between the views voiced at the Interim Committee meeting and the feelings of the project scientists and again, to pacify them, he set up a series of committees to study and report on the implications of the new weapon before the Scientific Panel's next meeting.

Without doubt the most important of these committees was the one chaired by Oppenheimer's old Göttingen professor, James Franck, which considered the social and political implications. Their report, given to Compton on 11 June, was a most thoughtful and perceptive study.

It predicted the almost limitless power of nuclear weapons. It also pointed up the futility of trying to prevent an arms race by throwing a cloak of secrecy over what were largely basic scientific facts or by trying to corner the supplies of raw materials. It saw the only hope for the future as lying in international control and it was concerned to recommend a course of action during the pressures of wartime which would help make such a system of control possible. One point the report made most clearly was that an *unannounced* attack on Japan was 'inadvisable' on any grounds, moral, political or diplomatic. Not only would the indiscriminate destruction wrought in such an attack sacrifice public goodwill for the US throughout the world, but it would 'precipitate the race for armaments, and prejudice the possibility of reaching an international agreement on the future control of such weapons.'

Thus, while the government advisers and the scientists on Franck's Committee were all agreed that an unannounced attack would be a shock, both to the Japanese and to the Russians, the scientists were concerned above all with the long term shock and the precipitation of an arms race. But yet again Oppenheimer did not seem to be one of them. At about this time, Szilard, who was a member of the Franck Committee, met Oppenheimer in Washington and conveyed this basic fear to him. Oppenheimer's reply gave the impression he had failed to grasp the long term issues. 'Don't you think, if we tell the Russians what we intend to do and then use the bomb in Japan, the Russians will understand it?' 'They'll understand it only too well,' was Szilard's reply.

Once the report was completed, its authors were determined that it was seen in Washington at the right levels. However, they were already suspicious of the usual channels of communication and so Franck himself took it into the capital and, with Compton, tried to see Stimson. Stimson, they were told, was out of town. He was not – but Compton and Franck believed what they were told.

Instead they left the report with a lieutenant in one of the offices there, along with a covering letter from Compton. That letter of Compton's was far more of a dissent from than an endorsement of the report. It stated that Franck had not mentioned the possible net saving of lives resulting from the use of the bomb nor the virtue of using the bomb in this war as a warning for wars in the future.

Four days later, Oppenheimer and the Scientific Panel had their meeting at Los Alamos and they gave detailed consideration to the Franck report. Compton described how he and the panel faced the dilemma it posed.

We thought of the fighting men who were set for an invasion that would be so very costly in both American and Japanese lives. We were determined to find, if we could, some effective way of demonstrating the power of an atomic bomb without loss of life that would impress Japan's warlords. If only this could be done!

During their troubled weekend at Los Alamos Oppenheimer's role seems to have been ambivalent. 'I set forth my anxieties and the arguments . . . against dropping [the bomb] . . . but I did not endorse them,' was how he himself recalled his attitude.

Indeed, the last person to hold out for some compromise measure was not

*Oppenheimer in mid-1945. In the period up to the test he had lost weight dramatically and, although more than six feet tall, weighed only 115 lbs*

Oppenheimer but Ernest Lawrence. In the end, however, even he gave in and the Panel reported that they could 'propose no technical demonstration likely to bring an end to the war . . . no acceptable alternative to direct military use.' They ended their report on a note which can be regarded as properly modest – or an act of moral cowardice.

It is true that we are among the few citizens who have had occasion to give thoughtful consideration to these problems during the past few years. We have, however, no claim to special competence in solving political, social and military problems which are presented by the advent of atomic power.

For all practical purposes the issue of whether the bomb should be used was now closed, but in retrospect it can hardly be said to have been opened. The scientists at Los Alamos still had their attention focused almost exclusively on making the bomb work. The efforts of the Franck Committee were nobbled by those who handled it – namely Compton and Stimson. The one who could, and perhaps should have seen the problem clearly was Oppenheimer, but for whatever reason he never, at this stage, was moved to argue from anything but a practical standpoint. He himself was to regret publicly the lack of farsightedness and political courage that the Scientific Panel had demonstrated during that crucial weekend meeting in June – his feeling of failure must have been compounded by the realisation that if he had taken the initiative, no one could have done more to change the course of events than he.

Edward Teller also became drawn directly into the debate on whether to use the weapon. Following the Scientific Panel's decision to use the bomb and its endorsement by the Interim Committee, Szilard had, as a last measure, circulated a petition. He had written to Teller asking for his support.

I was in absolute agreement [Teller has written], and prepared to circulate Szilard's petition among the scientists at Los Alamos. But it was my duty, first, to discuss the question with the director of the Los Alamos Laboratory, Dr J. Robert Oppenheimer . . . Oppenheimer told me, in a polite and convincing way that he thought it improper for a scientist to use his prestige as a platform for political pronouncements . . . I did not circulate Szilard's petition. Today [he wrote this in 1962] I regret that I did not.

This, Teller has implied, was one of the incidents which rankled with him for years and was eventually to form the basis for his split with Oppenheimer. However, there is a memo from Teller to Oppenheimer which puts another slant on Teller's position. In this memo he wrote about Szilard:

His [Szilard's] moral objections to what we are doing are, in my opinion, honest. After what he told me I should feel better if I could explain to him my point of view. This I am doing in the enclosed letter. What I say is, I believe, in agreement with your views. At least in the main points. I hope you will find it correct to send my letter to Szilard.

During the final months, the development of the bomb had gone through a series of nerve-racking cycles. April had been the good month. The juggling with the geometry of the explosive lenses had come to an end and Robert

Bacher had been able to report even better news of symmetry in the implosion shock wave. The work on the initiator, the source of neutrons used to help the chain reaction on its way, had gone well and the Theoretical Division were able to report on a series of designs which looked promising. Hans Bethe had also done one of his endless projections for the yield of the bomb and had come up with a yield of about five thousand tons equivalent of TNT – a good deal more than had previously been hoped for.

But May was a bad month: the work on the detonators failed to produce the reliability needed. It only required one of the hundreds of detonators around the surface of the bomb to fail and symmetry would be lost, and now only two months before the scheduled test, the new detonators began to fail in tests regularly, and inexplicably. In tandem with this, the contractor developing the firing circuits fell behind schedule in delivery and so the testing of the entire detonation package was delayed.

The effect of these shifts of fortune and the sheer weight of administration were now beginning to take their toll visibly on Oppenheimer. People remember him as looking drawn and preoccupied – forgetful of the normal courteousness which he showed to everyone at Los Alamos. Previously he had been able to escape on occasion with Kitty on riding expeditions into the mountains he knew so well, but in recent months this had not been possible. To complicate matters he had recently been stricken with, of all things, chickenpox, and since the spring he had lost more than two stones in weight. His was never the most robust of physiques but now he weighed a hundred and fifteen pounds – a little over eight stones for a man over six feet tall.

In early June, the contractors hired to build the tower at Point Zero arrived and began the erection of the hundred and ten feet-high lattice structure on which would sit Fat Man, housed in a small hut on the top. The height of the tower had been decided on after scaling up the results of the dress rehearsal shot in May, particularly with a view to minimising the problems of fall-out.

The stack of TNT used on that occasion had contained radioactive waste material which had been thrown up into the dust cloud that had been formed and provided a harmless simulation of fall-out. The results had been unsettling. The cloud had been swept by high altitude winds for hundreds of miles and it had been estimated that if that blast had been a full-scale explosion using a nuclear core, the radioactive dust produced would have deluged the small town of Carrizozo forty miles away.

The blast from Fat Man was projected to be many times larger, but by lifting the bomb that much higher from the ground it was hoped to reduce as much as possible the size of the lethal dust cloud. However, no one knew what would really happen. There were so many variables, from the size of the blast itself – still only an informed guess – to the precise weather conditions. It only needed a strong wind or an atmospheric phenomenon common in desert areas known as an inversion for the radioactive material to be trapped near the ground and then be blown for hundreds of miles.

In his book *Day of Trinity*, Lansing Lamont describes how Stafford Warren,

*The hundred feet steel tower erected at Point Zero. It was decided to detonate the bomb from the top of this tower to reduce the size of crater made and thus the amount of radioactive dust created*

the chief radiologist, and one of the army doctors, Captain James Nolan, drew up a set of evacuation plans and took them to Groves at Oak Ridge for his approval. Fall-out it seems had not been one of Groves' priorities and he baulked at the suggestion that troops and trucks be prepared for rapid evacuation of the Trinity site.

'What are you, a Hearst propagandist?' he asked Nolan.

By this Groves meant that any preparations for evacuation in nearby towns would jeopardise security and the test could find its way into the following day's headlines. Groves had already prepared a series of possible press releases depending on the size of the test. They ranged from 'A loud explosion was reported today. There was no property damage or loss of life,' to the cataclysmic 'A mammoth explosion today resulted in widespread destruction of property and great loss of life.' They did not include the comparatively subtle nuance provided by the fall-out risk and, to Nolan and Warren, Groves seemed genuinely annoyed by having to make allowances for it. Nevertheless, within a short space of time he had made arrangements with the Governor of New Mexico to declare martial law throughout the area and also to carry out mass evacuation, should it become necessary.

As to the fate of the scientists at Trinity, only five or ten miles from the blast, Bainbridge was asked to make a survey of the possible escape routes from the plateau. There were three: an old road running southwards, one of the new black top roads going northwards and an almost impassable track running through a gap in the surrounding mountains. That was all.

All sorts of rumours and fears circulated around the camp during those last weeks, not the least being that the bomb would set fire to the atmosphere. Earlier in the year Teller had tested all the calculations predicting the nature of the fission explosion and had reported that there was no possibility of atmospheric ignition occurring. Still, this did not end the stories which circulated in the mess halls of Trinity Base Camp on the hot evenings as the men sat round reading, drinking and playing poker. The tales passed from scientists to SEDs and on to eavesdropping MPs. The authorities were so concerned that they arranged for psychiatrists at Oak Ridge to be on standby ready to fly down to Trinity should any form of panic break out. Already, Stafford Warren had taken action on a number of people who had come to his notice as either rumour-mongers or abnormally affected by the tales they heard. He had returned them to Los Alamos.

At the end of June, the switchback in the fortunes of the technical programmers took a crucial upward turn. The workers in Frisch's critical assembly unit at Omega – the men 'tickling the dragon's tail' – had come up with a definitive figure, this time for the critical mass of plutonium. The Theoretical Division reported the production of a fully practical initiator unit and, perhaps most important of all, the contractors working on the detonator reported that they had produced entirely new designs, one hundred times more reliable than anything which had gone before.

On 30 June, Oppenheimer and the Cowpuncher Committee fixed the final date for the test – 16 July at four a.m. It was still believed that Bethe's estimate for the bomb – five thousand tons of TNT equivalent – was most likely.

In early July, Leo Szilard made one last effort to influence the course of events by preparing a petition to be sent direct to the President.

It was signed, though not without some soul-searching, by sixty-seven scientists at Chicago and urged Truman not to use the bomb unless Japan had been properly warned and still refused to surrender. Groves allowed it limited circulation but, throughout the project, let it be known that counter-petitions would not be frowned on. Truman himself never saw the petition. Groves carefully re-routed it so that it arrived in Washington after he had left for the Potsdam conference.

# CHAPTER 11  I AM BECOME DEATH

By early July the defeat of Japan was inevitable. Their navy was nearly destroyed, and with that the island had become vulnerable to a blockade. The cities had been devastated by the massed bombing raids by thousands of B-29s – indeed it was with some difficulty that Groves' Target Committee lighted on a city of sufficient size and military importance to serve as a target for the first bomb. Hiroshima was a city which had somehow escaped major damage during the war and its railway yards were of considerable military importance.

In spite of the fact that defeat was inevitable, there were two factors which more than anything dictated a swift use of the bomb. The first was the Russians. Did Stalin intend to join the final assault against Japan in time to save a significant number of American lives? If so, would he try to expand his expectations in the Far East? Could American-Soviet differences over Eastern Europe be resolved? How was Germany to be governed? Shortly after Truman had come to power he had tested the water through diplomatic channels to see whether another summit meeting with the Russians and the British, to discuss the future of the post-war world, would be worthwhile. On the basis of what he was told, he decided to suggest a meeting. The location chosen was at Potsdam, the seat of the Kaisers, twelve miles south of Berlin, and the date chosen after checking on the latest predictions from Los Alamos was 15 July. Truman had come to believe that, in a large measure, his success in resolving these questions depended on the results of the test at Alamogordo. He had no intention of using the bomb explicitly as some kind of instrument within the negotiations, but he did feel that, with the bomb behind him, he was not going to have to make any embarrassing diplomatic compromises.

*Churchill, Truman and Stalin at Potsdam. Truman believed that his success in dealing with the Russians depended in large part on the results of the Trinity test*

The second factor was Japan. In spite of the parlous state of their country and of their armed forces, the Japanese warlords were thought to be as far from surrender as ever and determined to fight to the end. Part of the reason for this was that the Americans had made it known that they intended to 'democratise' Japan, removing the Emperor and destroying the ruling class, and that they would only accept an unconditional surrender.

Yet by mid-July American Intelligence, which had broken the Japanese code before the war, knew of a telegram from the Japanese Foreign Minister to Ambassador Sato in Moscow. 'Unconditional surrender is the only obstacle to peace . . .' the telegram read. A little later the contents of the telegram were transmitted to the President, but it had no effect. The Americans were not prepared to accept peace until they had achieved this surrender. So the race to produce the bomb as quickly as possible went on. At the beginning of July, Oppenheimer was asked to bring the test forward to 14 July to fit the President's schedule at Potsdam.

On 2 July, Oppenheimer telephoned Groves describing a 'frantic' situation which meant that the earlier date would be quite impossible to meet.

What had happened was that the moulds for producing the explosive lenses had arrived in Kistiakowsky's Explosives Division and were found to be cracked and pitted – quite useless for the precise moulding needed for the implosion assembly. Kistiakowsky was desperate and organised his teams to work with him round the clock using dental tools to scrape and patch the defective castings.

Part of the difficulty [Kistiakowsky recalled] was that Oppenheimer insisted that we assemble two identical explosive facsimile bombs. One with the real core would go to Trinity, the other with a dummy core would be exploded twenty-four hours earlier at Los Alamos in a very sophisticated rig which was to tell us finally if we had the spherically symmetrical wave. It made more work at a time of crisis and I didn't think it was necessary. It was the beginning of problems between Oppy and me.

While Kistiakowsky struggled to put the castings right Oppenheimer was fighting a losing battle on the phone with Groves. Groves was insisting on the earlier date and he won the argument. But then the situation at Los Alamos again changed for the worse making 14 July out of the question. It was going to be 16 July.

Out at Trinity the metal tower was complete. Each day it was overflown by a B-29, making dry runs for its part in the test. Given the fact that the size of the blast was still unknown this was one of the most dangerous parts of the test. The crew were planning to fly close to the tower just before detonation, drop an instrument package in lieu of the real bomb, and then dive and bank furiously away to avoid being overwhelmed by the shock wave. It was to be a rehearsal for the drop over Japan.

But beneath the excitement and the feeling of being on the home-stretch there was still a feeling of uncertainty – a feeling which found expression for some in black humour. An example was this parody circulating in those tense weeks before Trinity:

> From this crude lab that spawned a dud
> Their necks to Truman's axe uncurled.
> Lo, the embattled savants stood
> And fired a flop heard around the world.

The mood of the scientists also found expression in an informal betting pool on just what the yield of the Trinity bomb would be. The bets ranged from the pessimistic to the cavalier. Edward Teller predictably made the most expansive estimate of forty-five thousand tons of TNT. Hans Bethe whose estimate of five thousand tons was the official prediction offered a slightly more optimistic estimate of eight thousand tons. George Kistiakowsky estimated one thousand,

*Isidor Rabi (r) talking to Ernest Lawrence and Enrico Fermi. Rabi was brought out to the Trinity site by Groves who felt Oppenheimer needed to be with his friends. Rabi arrived in the desert wearing a black homburg and sporting an umbrella*

four hundred tons and felt he was being far too optimistic.

Other scientists made still lower estimates, one taking the figure zero. Oppenheimer joined the pool at three hundred tons – hardly the prediction of a commander determined to encourage his troops, come what may. Indeed, you can think about that estimate and propose any number of theories about what Oppenheimer was thinking of when he made it.

Groves, certainly, was worried about Oppenheimer's condition, both physical and mental. With that hard-headed practicality which marked all his decisions, he had worked out a chain of command should Oppenheimer crack-up completely, but he had also taken steps to ensure that it did not happen. He felt that Oppenheimer needed the companionship of friends who had no definite commitment to the test. His brother Frank was already out at Trinity where he was working as an aide to Kenneth Bainbridge. Then, just a few days before the test, Groves had Isidor Rabi flown in from the east coast where he had been working on radar projects. Oppenheimer had been on close terms with Rabi for more than fifteen years now, ever since they had been students at Leiden.

'I was one of the few friends he had who could talk directly to him,' recalled

Rabi. 'I was not in awe of him but he knew that I liked him, and I appreciated his authority. He always knew he would get an honest answer from me.'

Rabi arrived at Trinity in early July dressed in a homburg, a dark suit and carrying an umbrella – his very incongruity seemed a reassurance.

On 5 July, Oppenheimer felt sufficient confidence with Kistiakowsky's progress on repairing the lenses to send the following telegram to Ernest Lawrence at Berkeley and Arthur Compton at Chicago.

ANY TIME AFTER THE 15TH WOULD BE A GOOD TIME FOR OUR FISHING TRIP. BECAUSE WE ARE NOT CERTAIN OF THE WEATHER WE MAY BE DELAYED SEVERAL DAYS. AS WE DO NOT HAVE ENOUGH SLEEPING BAGS TO GO AROUND, WE ASK YOU PLEASE DO NOT BRING ANYONE WITH YOU

Three days later the 'dummy' bomb at Los Alamos began a series of tests, each foreshadowing by a few days what would happen to the real bomb at Trinity. To start with, it was driven for miles over rock-strewn roads to simulate the journey down to Los Alamos. It came through this first experience unscathed.

On the evening of 11 July Oppenheimer collected one or two papers from his office and walked back to his home on Bathtub Row. There he said goodbye to his family. Kitty gave him a good luck charm, a four leaf clover that she had found in their own garden. They worked out a special message which Oppenheimer would send if the test was a success: 'You Can Change the Sheets'.

The next day, Thursday, at three p.m. Philip Morrison, accompanied by a guard and a radiologist, removed the fissionable plutonium core from the vault at Omega. The core had been separated into several sub-critical pieces which were fitted into two special valises for the journey down to Trinity.

Each one was protected against corrosion, against dropping into water [Morrison recalled], against overheating, against overcooking in every way we could think of. We regarded the test in the desert merely as an exercise for carrying out the same routines in the Pacific. But we were apprehensive about an automobile accident.

Morrison placed the special valises carefully next to him in the back seat of Robert Bacher's sedan and, with one security car ahead of them and one behind, they set off for Alamogordo.

I remember, when we were driving through Santa Fe, which was then quite a sleepy little town. I was just thinking about what an extraordinary thing it was to be driving along there in just an ordinary car and yet we were carrying the core of the first atomic bomb.

Later the same evening the unimpressive little procession turned off a dirt road and stopped outside the ranch-house abandoned by the MacDonald family. One of the rooms had been fitted out as an assembly room, and it was here that Morrison left his precious charges, ready for the critical assembly of the core the following morning.

*Philip Morrison, Oppenheimer's one-time student who sat with the core of the bomb as it was ferried in an ordinary sedan from Los Alamos to Trinity*

Just after midnight that same night, a much bigger convoy prepared to leave Los Alamos for Trinity. One truck carried the explosive assembly which would surround the core and was known as 'the gadget'.

For reasons of security we transported it at night [said Kistiakowsky], but to be whimsical I decided that I would start the trip at ten minutes after midnight, Friday the thirteenth.

One of the SEDs accompanying 'the gadget' was Leo Jercinovic.

We travelled accompanied by a very large entourage of security forces [he recalled], military police in front and behind us. I thought this was supposed to be a rather secret and quiet affair but every time we went through a town, why, they would turn on the sirens and the red lights and we would go through the town raising a raucous din – and of course this was early in the morning. They had hoped to warn off any drunken drivers who might drive into their path – which they succeeded in doing while waking up half the neighbourhood.

However, when they arrived at Base Camp after their long drive, Kistiakowsky's welcome was most unexpected.

I found the headquarters in a state of absolute uproar and poor Don Hornig told me that he had been up most of the night being quizzed by Oppenheimer and Groves, because the X Unit (the unit containing the firing mechanism) had failed after being used. So I went to see them and Oppie – he was very nervy – came down like a ton of bricks on me. So Hornig and I took the unit apart and we discovered that they had tested it so much that it had simply overheated and some of the solder joints had

J. ROBERT OPPENHEIMER

melted. After all, the thing had been designed only to be used once sitting on the bomb and it must have been tested hundreds of times. So, anyway, that minor storm passed.

At the same time at the MacDonald Ranch, a strange little ceremony was taking place. Robert Bacher, as the representative of the University of California, was handing over the core – and thus the bill for two billion dollars to General Thomas Farrell, Groves' aide. Before he signed the documents Farrell asked jokingly if he could see what he was buying. He was shown the core and given a pair of rubber gloves. Touching the smooth surface he found it was warm.

*General Thomas Farrell seen here with Groves after the war*

At nine a.m. the final assembly began. The team of eight scientists hovered round the table where the plutonium pieces lay. Louis Slotin, a Canadian, who had worked on some of the most dangerous of the experiments at the Critical Assembly Unit, sat before the pieces in deep concentration as he pushed them towards each other to the point where they were almost critical. The atmosphere in the room was extraordinary. A slight slip, a moment's criticality, and, not only would the core become unusable, but the assembly team could be condemned to a slow death from radiation exposure. Oppenheimer came to watch, but now everything was out of his hands. Like a producer just before the curtain rises he had no function to perform and his tenseness, Bacher felt, was affecting the others in the room. Quietly he was asked to leave until the assembly was done.

At the base of the tower, Kistiakowsky and his team had spent the day preparing 'the gadget' for the insertion of the core and at 3.18 p.m. he rang the MacDonald Ranch to say that they were ready. The core was laid on a litter and carried out of the assembly room to the waiting sedan. With Bacher again at the wheel, the device started for the tower.

To protect themselves from the dust and the sand the scientists at the base of the tower were working inside a tent which, after the heat and brilliance of the desert, had a cool ecclesiastical feel about it. In the gloom the core was attached to a manually operated hoist and raised above the explosive assembly before being slowly lowered into it. Yet again the atmosphere was extraordinary. Ticking geiger counters. The occasional instruction, nothing more. The subcritical parts of the core were held apart by so little that a knock could start a chain reaction. Oppenheimer again hovered round the operators as they guided the core downwards. As it was lowered into the heart of the bomb, the ticking of the geiger counters mounted to a crescendo. The operation was halted to make a check on the rising neutron count, then continued. The wind which had risen during the afternoon flapped the tent and threatened to swirl dust into the flimsy enclosure. Then suddenly the core stuck. Someone cursed quietly.

For a while it was not clear what had happened.

We knew it should fit because we'd tried it with dummies [said Robert Bacher], but then we realised this one was plutonium and was very hot and it was producing heat and had expanded a little. So, we decided to just wait to see whether the two pieces would arrive at some temperature equilibrium.

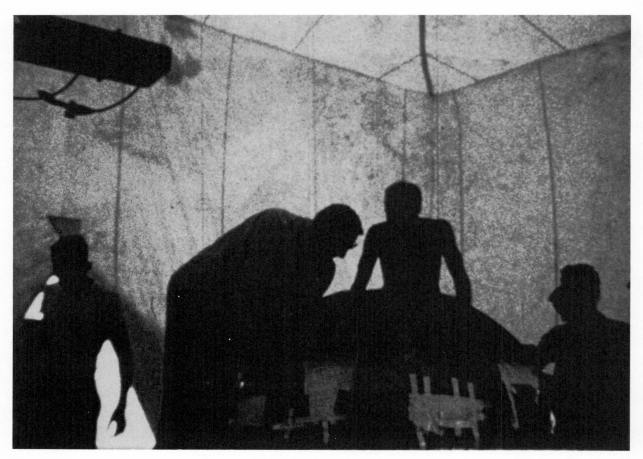

*Scientists working inside the tent set up underneath the tower at Point Zero. They are placing the core into the depths of the explosive assembly. This still is taken from recently declassified Los Alamos film*

More minutes of tension, while Oppenheimer, pipe in mouth, paced up and down outside the tent, then the insertion was tried again. It worked without a hitch. That particular ordeal was over. By ten p.m. the bomb assembly was complete and left in the flapping tent until morning.

The weather had now become another source of anxiety. After months of sweltering heat the pattern had been broken and a number of storms had been forecast. The team of weathermen under Jack Hubbard included the chief weatherman from the D–Day landings, and they became oracles whose every latest report was awaited with apprehension. They had access to service reports from all over the world. They floated weather balloons up over the site every few hours and once a day a small plane crammed with instruments flew northeastwards to try and predict the oncoming weather patterns. On Saturday morning, 14 July, there were storms throughout the area and Jack Hubbard forecast that they would continue for two more days at least.

On that same Saturday morning, Oppenheimer received a telephone call from Los Alamos. It told him that the test on the dummy rig that was foreshadowing the Trinity Bomb had been a failure. The explosive assembly had not produced a symmetrical shock wave but one which was completely disorganised. The team at Los Alamos told Oppenheimer that in their view the bomb was not going to work. After the weeks of strain and the tension and set-backs of the past few days, this was too much for Oppenheimer. Yet again Kistiakowsky was the butt of his attack.

I was accused this time of failing the project, of being the cause of embarrassment to everybody from Oppie upwards. I just said I didn't believe that that experiment is right, whereupon, I remember, my good friend Bob Bacher said to me, 'George, will you believe in Maxwell's equations?' I said, 'Bob, I do.' 'Well', he said, 'if you believe in Maxwell's equations then you must know that the results of that experiment are correct and the bomb won't go'.

Oppie was very angry, walking up and down desperately and so I said to him, 'look Oppie, I'll bet one month of my salary against $10 that this bomb will work.' Oppie took the bet but then I went away. I just couldn't take any more, just went out into the desert by myself.

A little later that morning Kistiakowsky returned to help with winding the bomb – if bomb it really was – slowly up the tower. The reliable Hans Bethe, who was still back at Los Alamos, had been asked to check on all aspects of the dummy test and report to Oppenheimer as soon as he could.

As the bomb, two billion dollars worth, was slowly winched away from the ground a very homely kind of precaution was brought into use.

We had ordered a very large number of mattresses which were in various trucks [remembers Leo Jercinovic, an SED working at Trinity], and as soon as the device was up that high off the ground we stopped the operation and came down and stacked about twenty feet of mattresses on the ground underneath the device. If it fell, at least it would have something soft to land on.

The bomb was going to take about two hours to raise to the top of the tower. The wind was strong and there was a real fear that the bomb would jar against

LEFT *Jumbo's fate was to be erected on a tower base less than three hundred yards from Point Zero as a somewhat crude evaluation of the force of the explosion. From Groves' point of view it was, no doubt, better than nothing*

BELOW *The explosive assembly arrives at the base of the tower at Point Zero after its hundred and fifty mile journey from Los Alamos. That day another assembly was tested at Los Alamos and reported as a dud*

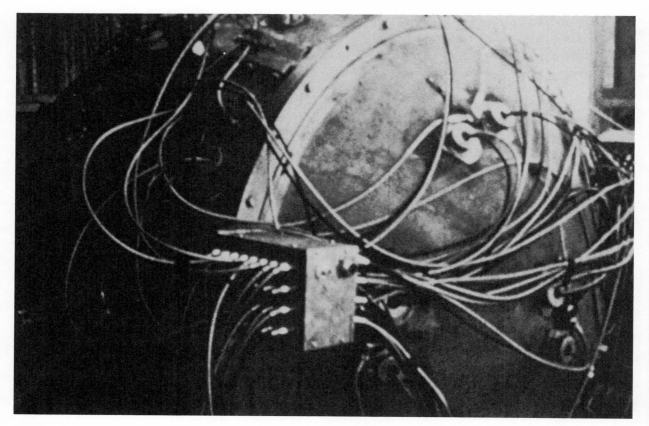

*The first atomic bomb,
complete with detonators at the
top of the tower at Point Zero,
a still from Los Alamos film*

the side of the tower. Slowly the hoist inched the bomb upwards, its cables running on skates over tracks along the outside of the tower. Suddenly one of the skates slipped and clattered down the side of the tower. The hoist jolted to a stop. Everyone held their breath – the bomb swayed in the narrow confines of the tower, but no damage was done. Eventually Jercinovic and another SED opened the trap at the top of the tower and eased the bomb into its final resting place in the galvanised iron shed a hundred feet from the ground.

That Saturday night, Oppenheimer slept very little. For part of the time he had been up discussing what could have gone wrong with the various tests, but even when he did eventually retire to the cubicle in one of the huts at base camp, he couldn't rest. Tom Farrell, who slept in the next cubicle could hear him tossing and turning in his bunk, coughing and coughing until it seemed he must make himself ill.

Early on Sunday morning a phone call came from Los Alamos. Oppenheimer took it. It was from Hans Bethe. He had checked the results of the test firing with the dummy rig and had found them to be meaningless. The experiments had been so designed that they did not really measure the true effectiveness of the implosion mechanism, only its side effects. Thus, while he could not say that the test had been a success he could at least assure Oppenheimer that it had not been a failure.

J. ROBERT OPPENHEIMER

It was therefore a buoyant Oppenheimer who, after a quick breakfast, set off on a tour of the site. It was a day for checking and rechecking the cameras, the electrical equipment, and the myriad experiments which were sprinkled over the desert around Point Zero. The weather was clear to start with, but, as the day wore on, the sky began to cloud over. By mid-afternoon thunder was audible and the weathermen were dotting the sky with their balloons trying to gauge some kind of pattern in the climatic turmoil that had descended on them.

At about four o'clock Oppenheimer visited the tower for the last time. He climbed to the top and there with the storm clouds scudding across the sky he stood by his laboratory's creation. Its outward appearance was brutish, belying the technical intricacies which lay within. It resembled nothing so much as a marine mine covered all over with the leads connecting the sixty-four detonators to the X assembly. Alone, Oppenheimer checked the assembly – alone, one hundred feet above the desert, with the wind rattling the corrugated iron, and the thunder rumbling in the distance.

Early that evening, Groves arrived at Base Camp, and immediately began to badger the weathermen for accurate predictions. Zero hour was only seven hours away and the weather had deteriorated markedly. It was drizzling and lightning flashes were now punctuating the growing gloom. The rain threatened the test by shorting the intricate electrical connections but it also focused all the fears of radioactive fall-out.

There were now groups of scientists spread throughout southern New Mexico preparing to monitor fall-out and with them were groups of military

*Oppenheimer out at the Trinity site mid-1945*

policemen whose job it would be to evacuate the population if the fall-out level became dangerously high. At that moment a group was sitting in a car park in Socorro, the nearest town of any size. How this handful of men would cope with the population of four thousand if the worst happened, no one really knew. Further away, three hundred miles from Alamogordo lay the city of Amarillo in Texas. There were no arrangements of any kind to evacuate its population of seventy thousand. Yet, with weather conditions as they were, it was possible that it could be inundated with material.

Together with the weathermen, Oppenheimer and Groves discussed the choices open to them. In the end they agreed that nothing could be decided at this stage and arranged to meet again at midnight. Groves retired and slept soundly. Oppenheimer sat, smoking endlessly, coughing, trying to read.

During that evening Bainbridge got wind of a rumour spreading like wildfire round the site. Some senior scientists had been overheard predicting that the bomb would ignite the atmosphere. They had been heard estimating how quickly the reaction would go and how far it would spread, and they had been inviting bets on the destruction first, of all human life, and second, just that of human life in New Mexico.

Bainbridge was furious and talked over the situation with Oppenheimer. The teams were already tired and near to breaking point and would in both men's view find it very difficult to cope with a postponement. This scare was yet one more reason why a delay in the test must be avoided at all costs.

In Berlin that same day, Truman and Churchill had arrived for the Potsdam conference. Only a mile or so away across the bomb-shattered city, Stalin was also preparing for the conference. Truman was relying heavily on the success of the test to support his negotiating position. It was for him essential that there should be no delay in testing the weapon.

At midnight Groves and Oppenheimer met to decide whether a delay was inevitable. By now the tower was shrouded in mist, the rain was continuing, and there were storms forecast to be moving towards the test site. Jack Hubbard had earlier that day predicted that the weather would clear in time but now his prediction was looking pretty silly. This uncertainty communicated itself to Groves who, during the meeting, decided to take matters into his own hands. 'Since it was obvious that they were completely upset by the failure of the long-range predictions, I soon excused them,' Groves has written. 'After that it was necessary for me to make my own weather predictions – a field in which I had no special competence.'

On that decision hung not only the fate of the test but possibly the lives of the people in the surrounding towns and cities. Although Oppenheimer and Groves between them agreed on a postponement for an hour

J. ROBERT OPPENHEIMER

Nearing the end of the
Potsdam conference. Churchill
had lost the General Election
in Britain and been replaced by
Attlee. When Truman had
eventually mentioned the
existence of the A-bomb, Stalin
showed little surprise. Standing
behind Truman is James
Byrnes who had decided
against including the Russians
in the Trinity test. He was
unaware that they already
knew all about it

or two, Oppenheimer continued to keep in contact with Hubbard.

Groves, in spite of his several hours' sleep, was very tense. Suddenly he decided that the tower was not properly secure.

You see, once the bomb had been fully assembled the military guards had been withdrawn [explains Kistiakowsky], so that if something went wrong, like a lightning strike, they wouldn't all get killed. The guards were scattered perhaps two miles away and Groves suddenly had this idea of saboteurs, even the Japanese, arriving by parachute. Military nightmares, that's what I called it, but he insisted on a guard being put on the tower.

Thus Kistiakowsky found himself spending the night in the company of several other scientists and some nervous military personnel, camped at the bottom of the tower armed with flashlights and a machine gun – waiting for an enemy they all felt quite sure would never arrive.

Having despatched this group, Groves turned elsewhere for problems to shoot and his attention lighted on Oppenheimer. Oppenheimer was in the Mess Hall at Base Camp talking with various scientists, drinking coffee and chain-smoking. He was in a reassuring conversation with Rabi when Fermi arrived, and presented Oppenheimer with an alarming prediction about fall-out. He was frightened that a sudden shift in the wind and a rain shower could deluge the test site itself with fall-out and he urged for a postponement.

To Groves, Oppenheimer seemed increasingly agitated and confused by the predictions of men whose opinion he valued; Groves intervened and suggested that he went with him to S.10,000 bunker. Again the scientific courtiers

Station South 10,000, the
main control point for the
Trinity test. It was from here
that Oppenheimer witnessed
the first explosion

intervened, expressing fears that Oppenheimer should not witness the explosion from such a short distance, but Groves insisted and the two drove off into the darkness towards the bunker.

There were pools of water everywhere around the bunker, [recalls Dick Watts, another SED who was at S.10,000] and I can remember watching Oppenheimer and Groves striding up and down, dodging these pools talking to each other intensely . . . trying to decide, well did we, or didn't we, shall we or shan't we, fire this thing off.

Oppenheimer had received Hubbard's latest forecast – they hoped for a lull in the storm before dawn and a north-easterly shift in the winds above twenty thousand feet which would sweep the fall-out away to the least populated areas around Trinity. But only minutes later the full force of the storm hit the tower. There were winds, driving rain and lightning striking all around, though as yet several miles from the tower itself. The scientists guarding the bomb sat counting seconds between flash and thunder. The lightning was moving closer.

Dawn was now only three hours away. They had to test the bomb in darkness to be able to observe it properly. So Groves and Oppenheimer took the only option left open to them – to delay up to five-thirty a.m. in the hope that the storm would clear. If it had not, then the arrival of dawn would determine a certain postponement.

At four a.m. the rain stopped. Hubbard waited another forty-five minutes and gave his final report: 'Winds aloft very light, variable to forty thousand, surface calm. Inversion about seventeen thousand feet. Conditions holding for next two hours. Sky now broken, becoming scattered.' The report was handed to Oppenheimer and it was agreed. The test would go ahead at five-thirty a.m.

At the base of the tower one of the young scientists in the arming party had managed to get some sleep.

I came to dreaming that Kistiakowsky had gotten a hose and was sprinkling the device down [remembers Joe McKibben], and then I came to and realised there were drops of water falling in my face off the tower and there was Ken Bainbridge leaning over me.

Bainbridge had been at the tower when the shot had finally been confirmed. Now the arming party, including Kistiakowsky and McKibben retreated from the tower for the last time, closing circuit switches as they went.

The nervous time for me was the last of those switches because prior to that you could not detonate the bomb from S.10,000 [explains Bainbridge], but this particular switch fed a power source to the detonating mechanism so that if somebody back there had done something wrong that would have been too bad. Kisty, McKibben and I left in my car and we travelled I think at thirty-five to forty miles an hour – the roads were such that it would have been foolish to have driven faster than that – and slower than that had no charm, no charm at all.

More than twenty miles to the north-west of the test site, on Compania Hill,

J. ROBERT OPPENHEIMER

the scientists not directly engaged in the test, the VIPs and the observers were gathering to watch the test in relative safety. They had all been issued with a plate of welder's glass through which to view the bomb. Edward Teller had even brought suntan cream with him to protect himself from the ultra-violet emission by the bomb. At five-ten a.m. a voice echoed across the desert from the loudspeakers set up on poles above them. 'It is now zero minus twenty minutes.' The countdown, conducted by Sam Allison, had begun.

The arming party arrived back at S.10,000 bunker to find it filled with physicists and army personnel – and one or two psychiatrists. Oppenheimer was there. He glanced at McKibben to see he was composed, then wandered away. As one of the last men to leave the tower, McKibben was the man to fire the bomb.

During the next few minutes Oppenheimer wandered in and out of the bunker, tense and withdrawn, as the processes of the countdown continued. At one point, one of the scientists who was sitting near McKibben and who had control of a panic switch to cut off McKibben's control panel should anything go wrong, tried to ease the tension with a wisecrack, 'What's likely to happen, Oppie, is that, at minus five seconds I'll panic and say – Gentlemen this can't go on – and then pull the switch.' Oppenheimer was not amused. 'Are you all right?' he asked coldly.

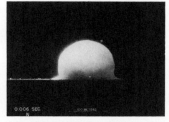

The countdown continued. Warning sirens sounded at Base Camp and the people remaining there had taken to trenches which had been dug nearby.

'Minus one minute... minus fifty-five seconds...' The countdown echoed from the loudspeakers across the deserted camp, accompanied now by music from a Voice of America station on the same frequency. They were transmitting Tchaikovsky's 'Serenade for Strings'.

At minus forty-five seconds McKibben threw the switch to introduce the automatic timing mechanism. 'At thirty seconds before the thing was due to go off,' says Bainbridge, 'I had a pretty good idea of what was going to happen because that was part of the job in planning the instrumentation.' At minus ten seconds McKibben threw the final manual switch.

Kistiakowsky rushed out of the shelter on top of the bunker. 'Ten... nine... eight... seven...' At the countdown point Allison suddenly thought the explosion would act like lightning and he might be electrocuted by the microphone he was holding. At minus one second he dropped the microphone and screamed as loud as he could 'Zero!'

Otto Frisch described the scene:

And then without a sound, the sun was shining; or so it looked. The sand hills at the edge of the desert were shimmering in a very bright light, almost colourless and shapeless. This light did not seem to change for a couple of seconds and then began to dim. I turned round, but that object on the horizon which looked like a small sun was still too bright to look at. I kept blinking and trying to take looks, and after another ten seconds or so it had grown and dimmed into something more like a huge oil fire, with a structure that made it look a bit like a strawberry. It was slowly rising into the sky from

the ground, with which it remained connected by a lengthening stem of swirling dust; incongruously, I thought of a red-hot elephant standing balanced on its trunk. Then, as the cloud of hot gas cooled and became less red, one could see a blue glow surrounding it, a glow of ionized air . . . It was an awesome spectacle; anybody who has ever seen an atomic explosion will never forget it. And all in complete silence; the bang came minutes later, quite loud though I had plugged my ears, and followed by a long rumble like heavy traffic very far away. I can still hear it.

'You felt the morning had come,' Phil Morrison was ten miles from Point Zero, 'although it was still night, because there your face felt the glow of this daylight – this desert sun in the midst of the night.'

Inside S.10,000 they had been aware of a dazzling bright light coming from the opening in the bunker behind them – an opening facing away from the explosion. For a few seconds there was silence then a thunderous roar.

'A few people laughed, a few people cried, most people were silent,' Oppenheimer has said. 'There floated through my mind a line from the *Bhagavad-Gita* in which Krishna is trying to persuade the Prince that he should do his duty: "I am become death, the shatterer of worlds".'

People congratulated him as he came out of the bunker to view the mighty rising fireball for the first time. There he met up with the frenziedly-excited Kistiakowsky.

I remember making a rather silly remark [says Kistiakowsky]. I suppose it was because of the tension of the last forty-eight hours . . . I slapped him on the back and I said 'Oppie, I won the bet.' In reply Oppenheimer, who was obviously at the height of emotional tension, couldn't do anything but pull out his bill folder and then he turned round and said, 'George, I don't have it.'

Shortly after this, Ken Bainbridge, solid, dependable, flushed with the success of his test, came up to Oppenheimer and grasped his hand. 'Oppie,' he said 'now we're all sons of bitches.'


Back at Base Camp, between the flash and the shock wave, Enrico Fermi had been constructing his own little experiment. In his hand he had been clasping some scraps of paper and as the shock wave hit the camp he let them fall to the ground. From the distance they had been displaced he had been able to calculate the yield of the new weapon – twenty thousand tons of TNT equivalent. His estimate proved amazing in its accuracy.

Isidor Rabi had also been at Base Camp and his observations had been personal ones. After a minute he had noticed gooseflesh on the back of his hands. 'The experience was hard to describe,' he says, 'I haven't got over it yet. It was awful, ominous, personally threatening. I couldn't tell why.'

A little later, as dawn was breaking, he saw Oppenheimer for the first time as he returned from the S.10,000 bunker. Something in his bearing brought Rabi's gooseflesh back again. In the half light he moved like a confident

stranger, at ease. 'I'll never forget his walk,' says Rabi, 'I'll never forget the way he stepped out of the car.'

*Oppenheimer returned to the Trinity site a month after the test. With him are (l) Kenneth Bainbridge, test director and (second from right) Robert Bacher; here they are testing the radioactivity levels of samples of sand*

News of the successful test reached President Truman in stages between 16 and 21 July, each new document filling in more details of that extraordinary event. Then on 21 July, Groves' full report of the test arrived and it made an enormous impact not only on Truman but on Churchill as well. Directly after the test, numbers of the scientists had left for the Pacific island of Tinian to make the final preparations to the Little Boy and Fat Man bombs which had been already delivered there.

Truman now knew that he no longer needed the Russians to help in finishing the war in the Far East. They might decide to join the war against Japan of their own accord, but Truman was 'still hoping for time, believing after the atomic bomb Japan will surrender and Russia will not get in so much on the kill. . . .' Thus a speedy and successful outcome for the first use of the bomb was of the greatest importance to him.

I AM BECOME DEATH          163

Eventually, Truman did decide to tell Stalin about the bomb and so he casually mentioned to Stalin after the plenary session on 24 July 'that we had a new weapon of unusual destructive force.' Stalin's reply was unexpectedly brief. He was glad to hear it and hoped we would make 'good use of it against the Japanese.'

Truman was puzzled by this cool reception from Stalin, but by that time Klaus Fuchs and the other spies had provided the Russians with a very detailed picture of the weapon that had recently been tested. The Soviets had already been working on a fission weapon of their own for almost two years.

It was shortly after this that Oppenheimer talked to his brother Frank about what had happened at Potsdam. 'I remember just how disappointed he was that the matter had not been laid forthrightly on the table before the Russians,' he said. 'It was our first realisation of how things would go after the war.'

# HIROSHIMA

## CHAPTER 12

At 02.45 hours on 6 August, the Enola Gay, a B29 bomber specially adapted to carry the uranium bomb, Little Boy, lined up for take-off from the air base on Tinian Island, near Guam in the Pacific. It took almost the entire length of the runway for the heavily laden aircraft to lumber into the air to begin its flight to Hiroshima.

Half an hour away from Tinian, Captain Parsons inserted the explosive charges and completed the final assembly of Little Boy.

In Washington it was mid-afternoon on a Sunday. General Groves had found it too much sitting in his office waiting for the news from Tinian, so, taking an officer with him, he set off for a game of tennis. Once at the courts, Groves rang into the duty office every few minutes for news. There was nothing to report.

At 06.05 hours the Enola Gay passed over Iwo Jima and headed on towards Japan. At 07.30 hours, Parsons inserted the red plugs that armed the bomb to detonate. Shortly after 09.00 hours (8 a.m. local time), Hiroshima came into sight.

That morning, just after 7 a.m. (local time), the air raid sirens sounded out over Hiroshima for the third time in a few hours. Planes had been sighted over Southern Japan and a little later a single B29 (the weather plane accompanying the Enola Gay) was seen approaching the city. However, since it quickly moved away, the all-clear was sounded at 7.30 and the city's rush hour began in earnest.

Shortly after 8 a.m. air defence spotters observed another flight of two or three B29s approaching, but no additional alert was sounded. The planes were mentioned on the radio with an instruction that people should take cover if they appeared over the city, but the announcer added reassuringly that they seemed to be only a reconnaissance mission. Most people continued on their way to work with the impression that any danger there was had passed.

At 09.14 hours (8.14 Japanese time), Major Thomas Ferebee dropped the bomb. Its sudden release made the Enola Gay lurch up into the air and at the same time the pilot, Colonel Paul Tibbets, threw the plane into a steep banking dive away from the dropping point.

A few minutes later, there was a brilliant flash, lighting up the interior of the Enola Gay, and a few seconds after that the plane was severely buffeted by two shock waves. However it was undamaged and remained on its course back to

Tinian. Fifteen minutes after the drop, Parsons was able to send back the following message: 'Clear cut results, exceeding TR test in visible effects, and in all respects successful. Normal conditions continued in aircraft after delivery was accomplished.'

Although the crew could see the mighty fireball rising and churning within itself to give rise in minutes to a mushroom cloud stretching to a height of 30,000 feet, they could have had little idea of the effect below them. These first-hand accounts from survivors of Hiroshima give some idea of the profound physical and mental shock of people who had no way of conceiving the dimensions of the weapon which had struck them.

A blinding flash cut sharply across the sky. I threw myself on the ground in a reflex movement. At the same moment as the flash, the skin over my body felt a burning heat. Then there was a blank in time . . . dead silence . . . probably a few seconds and then a huge 'boom', like the rumbling of distant thunder.

I worked in a factory with other students. We were out demolishing houses. At that moment I was hit by the bomb head-on from the left. I fell down instantly. I had a feeling that I was thrown into a blast furnace – and burned.

*The two pictures below show the devastation at Hiroshima. Estimates of the number killed vary between 78,000 and 200,000. The centre of the city was levelled and more than 60,000 buildings were destroyed*

I just could not understand why our surroundings had changed so greatly in one instant . . . I thought it might have been something which had nothing to do with the war – the collapse of the earth which it was said would take place at the end of the world, and which I had read about as a child . . .

Everything seemed dark, dark all over . . . Then I thought, 'the world is ending' . . .

There were dead bodies everywhere. There was practically no room for me to put my feet on the floor. At that time I couldn't figure out the reason why all these people were

J. ROBERT OPPENHEIMER

suffering or what illness it was that had struck them down . . . There was no light at all, and we were just like sleepwalkers . . .

My immediate thought was that this was like the hell I had always read about. I had never seen anything which resembled it before. But I thought that should there be a hell, this was it.

The number of deaths at Hiroshima either immediately or over a period of time will probably never be known accurately. The extreme confusion at the time made all assessments difficult, and each assessment could not help but be affected emotionally. The official figure is usually given as 78,000 but there are other figures. The city of Hiroshima estimates 200,000, a figure representing between 25 and 50 per cent of the whole daytime population. The centre of the city had been levelled and more than 60,000 buildings destroyed. Shortly after the bombing great fires swept across the city.

*Burns on the back of a victim of the Hiroshima bomb. Often such lesions would only be the precursor to the new and unexplained sickness, leading to death from radiation*

Back at Los Alamos, Oppenheimer read the message flashed by Parsons from the Enola Gay fifteen minutes after the drop, and called the whole staff of the laboratory together in one of the camp auditoria.

He entered that meeting like a prize fighter [recalls one scientist]. As he walked through the hall there were cheers and shouts and applause all round and he acknowledged them with the fighters' salute – clasping his hands together above his head as he came to the podium.

The United States campaign to end the war was going according to plan. The Japanese had been warned before Hiroshima, they had not agreed to unconditional surrender, so the bomb had been dropped. That same day, 6 August, another ultimatum to Japan was delivered by President Truman – surrender unconditionally or 'expect a rain of ruin from the air, the like of which has never been seen on this earth. . . .'

But Japan no longer possessed the ability to take quick decisions. The news that a single bomb had obliterated Hiroshima only reached Tokyo the following morning and then it seemed so incredible that an investigating team was sent to find out what had happened.

What they discovered was enough to produce a direct response from the Japanese, but two days had now passed since Truman's ultimatum. At 5 p.m. on the evening of 8 August, Ambassador Sato entered Foreign Minister Molotov's study in the Kremlin with a view to enlisting the Russians as mediators between the Anglo-American and Japanese governments. He was greeted with a stunning announcement: a state of war would exist between Japan and Russia the following day. The Russians had entered the war of their own volition, as Truman expected. Two hours later (1 a.m. 9 August Tokyo time), the Soviet forces crossed the Manchurian border driving back the depleted Japanese forces. This event coupled with the Hiroshima bomb two days earlier, according to one Japanese historian, provided the advocates for peace in the Japanese government with 'a supreme opportunity to turn the tide against the die-hards and to shake the government loose from the yoke of military oppression under which it had been labouring so long.' However, they needed time to act, time which a series of incidents 1500 miles out in the Pacific was going to deny them. The date chosen for the next attack was amazingly not to be decided by Washington but by the Commander on Tinian itself. This was how the sequence of events was described to Oppenheimer by Norman Ramsay, the senior scientist on Tinian.

Our original schedule called for take-off on the morning of the 11th August local time. However, on the evening of the 7th August, we concluded that we could safely advance the date to 10th August. When we proposed this to Tibbets [Commander of the bomber group] he said it was too bad we could not advance the date still another day since good weather was forecast for 9th August with at least five days of bad weather forecast to follow. . . . Finally, at 11 p.m. on 8th August, the unit was in the plane and completely and thoroughly checked out. Take-off was about 3 a.m. [a matter of 4 hours after Sato's meeting with Molotov]. We all aged ten years until the plane cleared the island. . . .

At 12.01 p.m. on 9 August, Fat Man, a duplicate of the implosion bomb tested at Trinity, was dropped on the city of Nagasaki. Had it not been for low cloud and fog over Kokura, the first choice as the target for this bomb, then Nagasaki would have survived. Instead, nearly 100,000 people were killed or maimed by the attack. The physical damage to the city was less than on Hiroshima but the number killed was probably greater. Twelve hours after the blast, Nagasaki was still a mass of flame visible to pilots more than two hundred miles away.

If the initiative for the scheduling of this sortie on Nagasaki had not been left

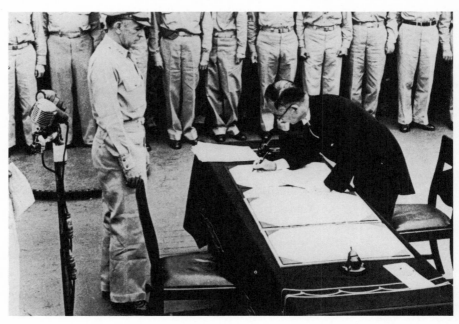

*General Douglas MacArthur watches as the Japanese Foreign Minister signs the surrender document aboard the US* Missouri *on 2 September 1945. In that document the future of the Japanese Imperial dynasty was assured*

J. ROBERT OPPENHEIMER

to the bomber command on Tinian, then the Japanese may well have had the time necessary to sue for peace. In the early morning hours of 10 August, in the Emperor's bomb shelter, the Japanese Premier Suzuki requested the Emperor's decision 'to accept the Allied Proclamation on the basis outlined by the Foreign Minister.' They still asked for one condition – that the United States guarantee the survival of the Emperor and his dynasty, and in the end they were given that guarantee. If that guarantee had been offered to the Japanese earlier, then there is a possibility, which even Secretary of War Stimson later recognised, that neither of the bombs dropped on Hiroshima and Nagasaki may have been necessary. With the future of their imperial dynasty assured, they might have surrendered anyway.

14 August was VJ Day and Los Alamos, like the rest of the world, celebrated with as much verve as it could muster. Sirens and klaxons sounded, there were parties all over the laboratory and a very drunk George Kistiakowsky was persuaded to lay on something special.

A whole damn bunch started wanting to arrange to fire 21 guns. We didn't have any guns and so I got hold of one of my young assistants and we drove to the explosive store and got out 21 cases, 50 pound cases of composite TNT, set them up in the field and exploded them. It was quite a show. Then I came back to the party and was told I'd exploded only 20.

The mood of jubilation was backed by the publicity that the laboratory was receiving from a grateful nation which believed it was being saved from the continuation of a grim and costly war. The President himself praised the laboratory publicly. 'What has been done,' he declared, 'is the greatest achievement of organised science in history. It was done under high pressure and without failure. We have spent two billion dollars on the greatest scientific gamble in history – and won.'

For some of the scientists there were medals and letters of merit and, now that their secret was out, men who, for the duration of the war, had been thought by friends and relatives to have ducked out of the war effort, found themselves treated as heroes. None of them had yet heard what one of their colleagues, Phil Morrison, would broadcast over the local Albuquerque radio station after his return from a mission to assess the bomb's damage.

We circled finally low over Hiroshima and stared in disbelief. There below was the flat level ground of what had been a city, scorched red . . . But no hundreds of planes had visited this town during a long night. One bomber and one bomb had, in the time it takes a bullet to cross the city, turned a city of three hundred thousand into a burning pyre. That was the new thing.

Even though this was not broadcast until a month or so after VJ Day, there were those who, even on that jubilant evening, felt that they were there celebrating a hollow victory. For years most of the men at Los Alamos had been

ABOVE *The revue staged by the British Mission at Los Alamos on VJ Day. The step ladder was part of their reconstruction of Trinity*

RIGHT *The Los Alamos library staff celebrating. Women and water were the great shortages at Los Alamos*

caught up in the excitement of the technical challenge and had given so little thought to the consequences of their action. Their celebration marked the profound relief that a monumental task had been achieved, but at the same time there was a realisation of the awfulness of what they had done. That night, as Oppenheimer walked away from the celebrations, he came across one of the younger scientists stone cold sober retching into the bushes.

Oppenheimer himself was one of the first men to voice doubts about what had been, in isolation, such a magnificent achievement. He admitted to one of the army of reporters now milling around the laboratory that he was a 'little scared of what I have made'. However, he then went on to say, 'A scientist cannot hold back progress because of fears of what the world will do with his discoveries.'

Someone might have added that this did not absolve them from voicing their misgivings and, over the next few weeks, as the projects began to wind down and the staff began to return to academic life, a profound depression settled over those who remained at Los Alamos.

On 21 August, Harry Daghlian, a young scientist working under Frisch, was assembling small bricks of uranium as a reflector around two very nearly critical hemispheres of plutonium. Each brick weighed about 12lbs and as the last one was being put into place it slipped and fell into the centre of the pile. Immediately the assembly went critical and a blue ionisation glow burst across the room, as Daghlian desperately tried to knock the brick off. In that instant, he had received a lethal dose of radiation. He rapidly developed second degree burns on hands and chest, a fever developed, and after two weeks the burns blistered and he lost his hair. He died twenty-eight days after the accident. His death was felt somehow to be a physical manifestation of the malaise which afflicted so many of those left on the Mesa – an intangible sickness which slowly corrupted all those who had been touched by it.

It was also a retribution, a means by which those who had created this new horror were at last confronted with the fruits of their labours.

Daghlian was to be described as the first radiation fatality, but he was not. In Hiroshima they had already been experiencing the dreadful 'poison' which followed in the wake of the atomic bomb.

My daughter . . . she had no burns and only minor external wounds [recalls a survivor]. She was quite all right for a while. But on the 4th of September, she suddenly became sick. She had spots all over her body. Her hair began to fall out. She vomited small clumps of blood many times . . . I felt this was a very strange and horrible disease. We were all afraid of it, and even the doctor didn't know what it was. After ten days of agony and torture, she died on September 14th . . . I thought it was very cruel that my daughter, who had nothing to do with the war, had to be killed in this way . . .

Oppenheimer was as much affected by the changes of mood at Los Alamos as anyone. He had written to Groves sometime earlier making it plain that he did not believe that Los Alamos should continue in its present form and that in particular 'the Director himself would very much like to know when he will be able to escape from these duties for which he is so ill qualified and which he has accepted only in an effort to serve the country during the war'.

Priscilla Duffield, his secretary for most of his period at Los Alamos, recalled how he felt at that time.

*16 October 1945. Oppenheimer making his speech accepting the Certificate of Appreciation presented to the laboratory by General Groves on behalf of the Army. After the ceremony Oppenheimer left Los Alamos to return to academic life*

I remember how pleased and excited he was to get a telegram from one university offering him a post although the stipend was a ridiculous $10,000 a year. It was a sum which a man of his reputation might well have considered insulting but he was so anxious to get away.

Oppenheimer arranged to leave his job immediately after a ceremony on 16 October when the laboratory was presented by the Army in the person of General Leslie Groves with a Certificate of Appreciation. The front of Fuller Lodge, one of the old Los Alamos School buildings, was decked in flags as Groves made a speech acknowledging the important work done by the laboratory. Then Oppenheimer replied in the quiet, low voice he often used when speaking publicly. First he expressed the hope that in the future everyone could look at the scroll that had been presented with pride, but then he went on,

If atomic bombs are to be added to the arsenals of a warring world, or to the arsenals of

J. ROBERT OPPENHEIMER

nations preparing for war, then the time will come when mankind will curse the name of Los Alamos and Hiroshima.

The peoples of this world must unite, or they will perish. This war, that has ravaged so much of the earth, has written these words. The atomic bomb has spelled them out for all men to understand. Other men have spoken them, in other times, in other wars, or other weapons. They have not prevailed. There are some, misled by a false sense of human history, who hold that they will not prevail today. It is not for us to believe that. By our works we are committed, committed to a world united, before this common peril, in law and in humanity.

Although he was returning to academic life at Cal. Tech., Oppenheimer knew all too well that he was not going to escape from this commitment even if he wanted to. A month or so previously he had sat in a barber's shop with Henry Stimson while the old man prepared for his last public appearance before leaving office. Stimson had asked to see him and they talked about their mutual experiences with the bomb that had affected them both so deeply. At the end, the old man rose from the chair and turned to Oppenheimer. 'Now it is in your hands', he said.

# CHAPTER 13    **THE MAN WHO WOULD BE GOD**

The year 1948 was very much a high point in Robert Oppenheimer's post-war career. He had become known widely as the 'father of the A-Bomb' and in that year achieved that accolade of pure fame, his portrait on the front cover of *Time* magazine. He was also widely quoted for a properly articulated expression of the feelings of guilt that had assailed him and so many of the other scientists involved on the Manhattan Project. 'In some sort of crude sense, which no vulgarity, no humour, no overstatement can quite extinguish,' he said, 'the physicists have known sin, and this is a knowledge which they cannot use.'

His popular acclaim, based as it was on his achievement at Los Alamos, and on his subsequent rise to prominence in government circles as an adviser, had in no way tainted the regard in which he was held by a large majority of the scientific community.

A new journal, *Physics Today*, was published for the first time that year and on the cover of its first edition there was a picture which was thought to need no word of explanation. A pork pie hat that was slung nonchalantly over a piece of complex industrial plumbing – in the mind of the editor, Sam Goudsmit, it could symbolise to his readers only one man. His reputation in the world of science was the basis for his influence in political circles and it gave him access to most of the top government officials. He served on numerous committees, was constantly in Washington, was always being called on for advice and seemed to be revelling in his new life style.

Phil Morrison, who had known Oppenheimer closely over more than ten years, found that they could no longer talk the same language. 'He moves in a different circle', he told Haakon Chevalier, continually referring to 'George thinks this . . .' and 'George says that . . .'. Finally Morrison was driven to ask who this George was – it was the then Secretary of State, George C. Marshall. At the same time as he occupied such a privileged and exposed position, Oppenheimer nevertheless had no fear in talking openly with *Time* about his left-wing past.

I became a real left winger, joined the teachers' union, had lots of Communist friends. It was what most people do in college or late high school. The Thomas (House Un-American Activities) Committee doesn't like this, but I'm not ashamed of it. I'm more ashamed of the lateness. Most of what I believed then, now seems complete nonsense, but it was an essential part of becoming a whole man. If it hadn't been for this late but indispensable education, I couldn't have done the job at Los Alamos at all.

*The first cover of the physics journal* Physics Today. *The fact that the photograph was uncaptioned was a tribute to Oppenheimer's international reputation*

# PHYSICS *today*

TRENDS IN AMERICAN SCIENCE by Vannevar Bush . . . . . . . . . . . . . . . . . . . . . . . . . *See Page*

VOL 1 NO 1 ● MAY 1948

So what had happened during those three years from the time when a depressed, emaciated, and exhausted Oppenheimer had left Los Alamos to take up a teaching position at Cal. Tech.? How had he, in spite of his initial heavy protestations of disinterest, become so much a part of the government's scientific establishment?

In the autumn of 1945, he returned to Pasadena and had begun once again to teach and to involve himself in research. He had gone back to working on cosmic rays, had shared in the work identifying the existence of mesons and had begun to develop an interest in the new research into other subatomic particles. But the phone calls from Washington never stopped coming. 'I was asked over and over both by the executive and the Congress for advice on atomic energy,' he said. 'I had a feeling of deep responsibility, interest and concern.'

But was this feeling simply the concern of a scientist with a personal sense of responsibility, or was it at least tinged with a growing interest in power? Certainly a number of his colleagues had begun to wonder.

One such group was the Association of Los Alamos Scientists, ALAS for short, which was founded at the end of August 1945 with the express purpose of influencing post-war nuclear policy. At their first meeting, they appointed a committee which included Hans Bethe, Edward Teller and Frank Oppenheimer, to draft a statement of their views. When it was done, they looked to Oppenheimer, who was already going to Washington regularly, to seek permission to release the document publicly. Oppenheimer agreed to do so and at first reported back optimistically on how their 'document' had been received. Then suddenly he wrote saying that the government had decided to make the ALAS paper a State document, thus barring its public release. He added, to everyone's surprise, that he agreed with this action, saying that he felt that a group statement was strongly inadvisable.

In spite of this view, most of the scientists – at least in Los Alamos –

maintained faith in Oppenheimer, but then only a few weeks later, in early October, they again had cause for dismay. This time it was a Bill put before Congress by two of its members, Representatives May and Johnson, with the object of putting the future administration of nuclear energy on a proper footing. Ever since the end of hostilities, the scientists had been campaigning to ensure that nuclear energy did not remain for ever in the hands of the military, and they were reassured that those framing the Bill were receiving the advice of Oppenheimer and his Interim Committee. However, when the 'May-Johnson' Bill was published they saw to their horror that it did not bar military officers from serving either as administrators or on the nine-man supervising committee.

It came as no surprise to learn that one of Representative May's collaborators was none other than General Leslie Groves, whom they saw as trying to legalise his wartime powers in a peacetime administration.

I must confess my confidence in our leaders, Oppenheimer, Lawrence, Compton, and Fermi . . . [wrote one disillusioned member of ALAS] who enjoined us to have faith in them and not influence this legislation, is shaken. I believe that these worthy men were duped – that they never had a chance to see this Bill.

*Members of a committee set up to formulate US policy on atomic energy: (l–r) Groves, Conant and Bush. Some people felt that Groves was out to legitimise his wartime control of the projects in peacetime*

But while this is probably true of other members of the panel, it does not seem to be true of Oppenheimer, who took positive action to try and quieten the voices of discontent around the project. He published a telegram from himself, Fermi and Lawrence, to the new Secretary of War which said:

WE WOULD MOST STRONGLY URGE THE PASSAGE OF THE LEGISLATION NOW BEFORE CONGRESS . . . WE ASSURE YOU THAT IN OUR OPINION THE LEGISLATION AS PRESENTED REPRESENTS THE FRUITS OF WELL-INFORMED AND EXPERIENCED CONSIDERATION.

In private, Oppenheimer had even discounted Leo Szilard's predictably critical reaction to the May-Johnson Bill as being unrepresentative. The project's scientists did not know this, but, even so, they were sufficiently incensed by the way the Bill was being handled for many of them to come to Washington to lobby for themselves. There they were dismayed yet again to see Oppenheimer confidently supporting the Bill before a Senate Committee. He urged its prompt passage, because, in his view, it would avoid further delays in both research and the pursuit of some international agreement on arms control, and instead of facing the objections of his fellow scientists head-on, he prompted them to think of the stature of those who had shaped it – Doctors Bush and Conant and Henry Stimson. 'I think if they liked the philosophy of this Bill,' he said, 'it is a very strong argument.'

Thus over this issue of military control of the atom, he seemed yet again to have flouted the trust placed in him by many of his fellow-scientists, and a number of them were never to forgive him for it. Oppenheimer was becoming what would, a few years hence, be called 'an inside scientist'. However, he did have clear reasons for what he was doing, even in these comparatively early days of political activity. He believed the bill was an interim measure that, at least, kept alive the Manhattan Project which he described at that time as 'without direction, without guidance, a burden to the people who are working on it,' and it also kept the momentum going for some system of international control.

His brother Frank was an active member of ALAS and describes himself as typical of those 'representing the idealistic outsiders' viewpoint.' He does not see his brother's actions as indicative of a different attitude to the basic objectives, but rather to how those objectives might be achieved.

Robert wanted to politicise more directly [he recalled] and work towards educating people both in the system and out. Right from the start he felt we hadn't much time to work towards the thing he felt most important, an international agreement on arms control, and that he must therefore concentrate on influencing the system from within.

Indeed, in so many ways Oppenheimer was behaving true to character. He had expected total loyalty and trust when he was teaching and the same when running Los Alamos. Yet again he wanted to do things his way and he was expecting the same level of trust, but now he was operating inside the hard world of American politics and such an approach was certain to be a difficult one.

Throughout that first post-war winter, Oppenheimer had continued to develop his own approach to international control of nuclear weapons. An initial breakthrough had come when the governments of the UK, the US, and Canada had announced their willingness to exchange information on nuclear matters with any nation which would reciprocate. They proposed a United Nations commission and everything seemed optimistic indeed when, in January 1946, the Russians voted along with everyone else to set up the United Nations Atomic Energy Commission.

*Under-Secretary of State, Dean Acheson, who headed the committee to formulate policy on international control of atomic energy*

To formulate American policy a special committee was appointed, headed by Dean Acheson with Groves, Bush and Conant as members. They in turn set up an advisory committee chaired by David Lilienthal, the boss of the Tennessee Valley Authority, the ambitious regional development scheme of the 30s and 40s, and with Oppenheimer as one of its members. Lilienthal and Oppenheimer were to meet for the first time through this committee and they took to each other immediately. Lilienthal in particular was adulatory of Oppenheimer. 'He is worth living a lifetime just to know that mankind has been able to produce such a being,' he said. 'We may have to wait another hundred years for the second one to come off the line.'

Groves, who found himself often at odds with the Lilienthal-Oppenheimer axis, was to view their relationship through jaundiced eyes. 'Everybody genuflected,' he complained, 'Lilienthal got so bad he would consult Oppie on what tie to wear in the morning.'

Certainly Oppenheimer was by far the most knowledgeable member of the advisory panel on nuclear matters and, during the early months of 1946, he did act as tutor and mentor to Lilienthal and others in the group. He also conferred

J. ROBERT OPPENHEIMER

at length with Isidor Rabi on the shape of US policy and Rabi recalls sitting in his living room on Riverside Drive, not far from where Oppenheimer grew up, watching the winter sun set over the Hudson as they talked airily of their international schemes.

At the end of their deliberations, they produced a report, described as the Acheson-Lilienthal report, but much of it was Oppenheimer's work. This extract conveys something of its essence.

International control implies an acceptance from the outset of the fact that our monopoly cannot last. . . . It is essential that a workable system of safeguards remove from individual nations or their citizens the legal right to engage in certain well-defined activities in respect to atomic energy which we believe will be generally agreed to be intrinsically dangerous because they are or could be made steps in a production of atomic bombs.

Nowadays, after thirty-five years of a continuous atoms race, the proposals of the Acheson-Lilienthal plan seem naïve and hopelessly optimistic, but Professor Rabi, very much a pragmatist, can recall the different atmosphere of those times.

There was a moment when our plans could have been realised, I am sure, and Oppenheimer was right to rush things, to try to push through a programme as quickly as possible. After all, think about the Union of the various states of America two hundred years ago. There must have been enormous vested interests in each of the individual states which would have preferred that they stay independent, but the call for unification came just at the right moment to overcome these interests. That was what we were looking towards with international control.

On New Year's Day 1946, the Oppenheimers were back in Berkeley and went to visit Frank and Jackie Oppenheimer, who were holding a party for friends. However, there seem to have been other guests in the house that day. From the very specific information available to the security officers about this party, one of them seems to have been a security agent. They knew that Robert and Kitty had slept in 'a sort of barn' on their visit and that Kitty had not been well that day.

Oppenheimer had gone to the party alone and there, it was alleged, met with two Communist Party members, David Adelson and Paul Pinsky. From their surveillance of Adelson, the FBI already knew that Adelson and Pinsky wanted 'to talk about the whole picture', presumably to find out where Oppenheimer stood, and also 'on the specific basis of getting J. Robert Oppenheimer to talk before those big meetings' that they were hoping to have. It seems that the 'big meetings' referred to were the forthcoming convention the Communist Party was holding in Sacramento.

However, the actual conversation between the two men and the Oppenheimer brothers was not recorded in any way, but an exchange between Frank and Robert, after the other two had left, was. According to the report, 'Frank remarked, "Didn't you think they were pretty political?" to which

Robert replied, "Well, to some extent they have to be but I think we just have to find out more about it. I am perfectly willing to believe they know what they're talking about, but I don't know," to which Frank replied that he did not know either.'

This report, although summarised by the FBI, was filed by Army Intelligence, but they were about to hand over responsibility for Oppenheimer to the FBI. Two days later another report, based on the surveillance of Adelson and his colleagues, went as follows:

On January 3rd, Barney Young told David Adelson that he and Paul Pinsky had had a talk with J. Robert Oppenheimer and that Oppenheimer had gone over some material that Paul Pinsky was to take up at the legislative convention in Sacramento, and that Oppenheimer had boiled it down for him.

This report is almost certainly by an FBI informant. From now on, for the next eight years, Oppenheimer was to be the subject of almost continuous Bureau surveillance by all the means at their disposal.

But what 'material' had Oppenheimer gone over? Above all, however trivial the essential content of the meeting, was it wise for a man in his position to be conferring with men known by the FBI to be active Party members? This was to be a question that would trouble many of those who read his file over the next few years.

*Bernard M. Baruch, the seventy-five-year-old financier who was appointed as the US's representative to the United Nations' Atomic Energy Commission. 'That was the day I gave up hope,' Oppenheimer said later*

On 16 March 1946, Truman's Secretary of State Byrnes appointed Bernard Baruch, the seventy-five-year-old financier, as US spokesman at the United Nations on the international control of atomic energy. 'That was the day I gave up hope,' said Oppenheimer years later, 'but that was not the day for me to say so publicly. Baruch asked me to be the scientific member of the delegation, but I said I couldn't.'

Because of his feelings about Baruch's appointment, Acheson took Oppenheimer to see Truman. There he was persuaded to go to San Francisco with Baruch, on the grounds that it would look bad if he did not, but he agreed unwillingly. At that meeting, Oppenheimer expressed his distress about the whole situation when suddenly he blurted out, 'Mr President, I have blood on my hands.' It was a statement which offended Truman greatly. 'Don't you bring that fellow around again,' Truman said to Acheson later. 'After all, all he did was make the bomb. I'm the guy who fired it off.'

The reason why Oppenheimer was so disappointed at the appointment of Baruch was that he saw Baruch as a conservative politician, without a particular vision in this area, who would not be able to resist all the concessions and changes that would be demanded by Congress and by the executive before he even approached the Russians. Oppenheimer was right.

We were optimistic, nevertheless, because we realised what a terrible state the world was going to get into if something like what we were proposing didn't happen [said Isidor Rabi]. I'm afraid we assumed the predicament was obvious to others and it was to most – even the military. Then the mood began to change, helped a bit by Mr Churchill and his Iron Curtain speech and that sort of thing. The Russians helped a great deal. They were suspicious of everything, though our manoeuvring was not very apt. – Yet when I think of the last thirty years or so, I wished they'd get some board of psychiatrists or physicians and find out what's wrong with the statesmen of the world. It's simply real madness what has happened.

For weeks Acheson and his camp, which included Oppenheimer, bickered with Baruch and his supporters. They were sure that Baruch was going to take too dogmatic and unrelenting a line with the Russians. In particular, they were concerned that the Russians would not accept Baruch's proposal that there would be no power of veto on the committee and that all decisions would be carried by majority vote. Oppenheimer's view was that such a proposal was unnecessary because, as he saw it, the penalty for serious abuse would automatically be war.

In the end, only days before the first meeting, Baruch went to Truman and presented an ultimatum – either he presented the case his way or he stood down.

This threat worked and it was Baruch who led the US delegation into the hastily converted gymnasium of Hunter College in the Bronx where the first meeting of the UN Atomic Energy Commission was taking place.

Oppenheimer sat with other members of the US section and sadly watched as the battle lines of self interest were drawn up with the Russians. Baruch proposed his abolition of the veto and his assurance that the US manufacture of

*The United Nations' Atomic Energy Commission in session. Baruch sits at the left end of the table*

bombs would cease but only when other conditions had been agreed on. The Russians retaliated by calling for the outlawing of all weapons first and refusing to consider the removal of the veto. The two sides were never to reach any rapprochement, but then the Russians knew how short lived the American monopoly would be.

Oppenheimer's vision which he believed had the irresistible appeal of sanity, he saw crushed there in Hunter College gymnasium.

One evening, Lilienthal encountered Oppenheimer in Washington, at the airport, looking depressed and unhappy. 'I am ready to go anywhere and do anything', Oppenheimer said to Lilienthal, 'but I am bankrupt of further ideas. And I find that physics and the teaching of physics, which is my life, now seems irrelevant.'

In June 1946, Haakon Chevalier was interviewed by the FBI. It was a marathon session lasting ten hours and revolved around what he knew about the English engineer George Eltenton, the man he had mentioned to Oppenheimer as the possible contact with the Soviet Embassy. Throughout the long interview, the interrogator broke off from time to time to go into the other room to make a series of telephone calls.

According to Chevalier, he avoided mentioning the 'kitchen conversation' with Oppenheimer more than three years previously, because he did not want to get either Oppenheimer or Eltenton into trouble. However, finally one of his interrogators produced a folder which, he said, contained 'three affidavits from three scientists on the atomic bomb project. Each of them testifies that you approached him on three separate occasions for the purpose of obtaining secret information on the atomic bomb on behalf of Russian agents'. The almost biblical use of the figure three bemused and puzzled Chevalier but it showed that they knew something about the approaches made to project scientists and so Chevalier eventually told them about the 'kitchen conversation'. To the very end of the interview, even after he had told them about this conversation, the FBI men were convinced that Chevalier was holding something back and Chevalier, intrigued to know how they got wind of the conversation, decided to make investigations of his own.

A chance meeting with Eltenton both eliminated him as the source and also explained the reason for the telephone calls – it transpired that he was being interviewed a few miles away across San Francisco Bay at the same time as Chevalier and the interrogators were cross checking with one another. A comparison of the information they gave the FBI, according to Chevalier, showed they had given the same information, so Chevalier decided to raise the matter with the only other possible source – Oppenheimer.

His chance came when he was invited to a cocktail party at the Oppenheimers'. He arrived early and went for a walk in the garden with Oppenheimer and told him about his interrogation by the FBI. He then raised the question of where the idea of approaches to *three* scientists would have come from, but, according to Chevalier, Oppenheimer, who was 'extremely nervous and tense' gave no answer to the question. Twice Kitty came to say that guests were arriving and on the second occasion Oppenheimer turned on Kitty and unleashed 'a flood of foul language'. Shortly afterwards their 'odd one-sided exchange' ended and they went in to join the other guests.

In September, three months after this conversation with Chevalier, Oppenheimer was himself interviewed by the FBI. This time the interview ranged beyond the 'kitchen conversation' to the activities of some of his past students like Lomanitz and Weinberg, and to meetings that he was alleged to have attended where Communists were present. His answers seemed to satisfy his questioners, but it was a pattern of questioning that was to become all too familiar over the next eight years.

In spite of the pessimism of so many of the scientists in those months after the war about the future of nuclear energy, within a year the project had indeed been moved out of the hands of the military. A senator from Connecticut, Brien McMahon, managed to push through Congress an act which set up the Atomic Energy Commission and emphasised civilian control and a high degree of freedom in research. The act still permitted a full military take-over in a time of national emergency, but that was a small price to pay for having the general development of atomic energy under civilian domination. Most people, moreover, approved of the appointment of David Lilienthal as the Commission's first Chairman. Serving with him as one of the five commissioners was Robert Bacher, who had headed the Theoretical Division at wartime Los Alamos. Bacher had been Oppenheimer's suggestion to Lilienthal.

Oppenheimer was also one of the natural choices for a nine-man General Advisory Committee to advise Lilienthal and the new AEC on scientific and technical matters. At the same time he was appointed director of the

LEFT *Senator Brien McMahon with Oppenheimer. McMahon successfully pushed the Bill through Congress which set up the Atomic Energy Commission and put atomic energy under civilian control*

BELOW *The first AEC Commissioners. In General Groves' view, the Chairman David Lilienthal was so much under Oppenheimer's influence that 'he would consult Oppy on what tie to wear in the morning.' (l–r) William Waymack, Lewis Strauss, David Lilienthal, Robert Bacher and Sumner Pike*

*The General Advisory Committee of the AEC visit Los Alamos in April 1947. (l–r) James Conant, Oppenheimer, General McCormack, Hartly Rowe, John H. Manley, Isidor Rabi and Roger S. Werner. Although not involved in the choice of members, Oppenheimer felt 'Truman has made an extremely good choice'*

prestigious Institute for Advanced Study at Princeton. Then at the first meeting of the GAC – for which he was a little late – he entered the room to find that his eight fellow members had already elected him chairman.

After the sad fiasco of the Baruch Plan, both these appointments were to provide him with a new lease of life.

Oppenheimer had not been involved in the choice of members for this Committee though, as he himself said, 'Truman had made an extremely good choice'. The nine members included Isidor Rabi, Enrico Fermi, James Conant, and Lee Du Bridge, a physicist who had been directing radar research during the war but whom Oppenheimer knew well. If Oppenheimer had chosen the Committee himself it is unlikely that its membership would have been very different. Its part-time secretary was another Los Alamos physicist, John Manley.

In a sense the General Advisory Committee was his committee [recalls Manley], though he never played boss to it, and the Atomic Energy Commission was the Committee's agency, though they never gave it orders. Aside from Bob Bacher and Walter Williams, this General Advisory Committee represented the only top-level people in the AEC who had had anything to do with the wartime project. So they had to take responsibility for decisions.

Many who know Oppenheimer's service to the nation at Los Alamos do not know it continued at the same magnificent level for the next four or five years after the war. This second time around, everything he did had to be done against selfish and short-sighted hysterical pressures. . . .

How Oppenheimer actually ran this Committee was, in the years ahead, to become an important question particularly as many of their decisions were to be the centre of controversy. In essence, the critics and victims of the Committee believed that Oppenheimer manipulated it to his own ends but, from within, this seemed to be anything but the case.

He was not an original [Isidor Rabi explained]. Most of the real ideas came from others but he could open doors and present them. Give Oppenheimer the glimmering of an idea and he'd present it most beautifully.

Far from bending us to his viewpoint, he took other people's views, absolutely. Then he'd make them more acceptable, more clear, more persuasive and this sort of thing made him a wonderful front.

There was a good deal of talk about how he had swayed or hypnotised or improperly influenced the General Advisory Committee [says John Manley]. I was there and I knew he didn't do any such thing. I can't imagine any nine people who'd be more insistent on each making up his own mind for himself. What happened was that he at all times had the national interest at heart and never did anything or wanted to do anything except in the national interest *as he saw it*, and they could tell this as well as I could.

Nobody was ever to disagree about the sincerity of Oppenheimer's actions, but there were to be many who would question his interpretation of the 'national interest'. Over the next few years Oppenheimer was going to learn the hard way the price of having an independent mind in the political world.

On Saturday 8 March 1947, a special messenger from the FBI appeared at the Washington offices of the AEC carrying a letter and a document for the Commission's Chairman, David Lilienthal. The document was from the FBI's director, J. Edgar Hoover, and was a summary of the files 'relative to Julius Robert Oppenheimer . . . and his brother Frank Friedman Oppenheimer.'

This summary document began with a straightforward account of Oppenheimer's life. Then it went on to itemise his 'Activities'. It referred to his membership of front organisations, and his employment of known communists at the Radiation Laboratory. It described his attendance at various Communist Party meetings before the war and mentioned that he was often referred to by 'high Communist Party functionaries' as the 'big shot' and as 'Oppie'. It wrote of his 1943 meeting with Jean Tatlock, and with Boris Pash in August of that year.

ABOVE *The Institute for Advanced Study at Princeton which provided facilities for some of the world's most renowned academics. Oppenheimer was appointed its director in 1947*

After the war, in late 1945, another conversation overheard between David Adelson and Paul Pinsky was reported.

'Isn't it nice that Oppenheimer is getting the credit he is,' said Adelson, referring to the reaction to the Hiroshima bomb.

'Yes,' replied Pinsky, 'shall we claim him as a member?'

Adelson laughed.

'Oppenheimer is the guy who originally gave me the push,' he said. 'Remember that session?'

'Yes,' Pinsky replied.

'As soon as they get the gestapo from around him,' Adelson went on, 'I am going to get hold of him and put the bee on him. The guy is so big now that no one can touch him, but he has got to consent and express some ideas.'

*Joseph Volpe, the AEC's Deputy General Counsel. He was to prove an invaluable ally in Oppenheimer's mounting security problems*

Other reports it contains of conversations among Party officials go on to underline that they certainly thought of him as 'one of our men' and then it alleges that early in the war, Oppenheimer had told Steve Nelson about the existence of the atomic bomb.

There is then a detailed account of Oppenheimer's various versions of the Chevalier incident and a brief account of what he had done since the war.

There are sections of the report which are still blanked out, but, without doubt, the major item in it is the account of the Chevalier incident.

Lilienthal had already been alerted at home personally by Hoover about the contents of the files, but when he read them over that weekend he was shocked enough to call a special meeting of his fellow Commissioners on Monday. The summary document had a similar effect on them, and they decided to call in people with long-standing personal experience of Oppenheimer to see what they felt. They tried to get hold of Groves who had, after all, finally ordered his clearance for Los Alamos, but he could not be contacted. So they brought in Vannevar Bush and James Conant, who both expressed the view that he had already 'clearly demonstrated his loyalty'.

This must have been some comfort at least for the Commissioners, but the

J. ROBERT OPPENHEIMER

AEC's own Security Division nevertheless began a detailed analysis of the FBI material. They added more material of their own to the file and this was then circulated by the AEC's Deputy General Counsel, Joseph Volpe, to the Commissioners. The one that seemed most concerned about what he read was Lewis Strauss and at the end of his scrutiny he asked Volpe his opinion of the material.

'Well,' said Volpe, '. . . his background is awful. But your responsibility is to determine whether this man is a security risk now, and except for the Chevalier incident, I don't see anything in this file to establish that he might be.'

This was the view that Strauss must ultimately have agreed with because there was no dissent to the clearance which those Commissioners were soon to vote

## THE WEATHER

# Times Herald

VOL. IX, NO. 162 — WASHINGTON, D.C. — SATURDAY, JULY 12, 1947 — PRICE SINGLE COPY 5¢

AVERAGE NET PAID CIRCULATION For the Last Three Months EXCEEDED 250,000 DAILY and SUNDAY *The LARGEST Circulation in Washington*

# U. S. ATOM SCIENTIST'S BROTHER EXPOSED AS COMMUNIST WHO WORKED ON A-BOMB

### U.S. Speeds Arms To Greece on Eve of Paris Parley on Aid

**Russia Expected To Start Own Plan**

**Military Equipment On Way to Athens**

### Navy Granted Over 4 Billion By Conferees

**Fund Is 200 Millions Less Than Requested**

### —And How's Business?:
### Goal of 60 Million U.S. Jobs Reached First Time in History

**Census Bureau Reports 60,055,000 Employed, With 1,730,000 Gain in June**

### Morse Delays Senate Vote On Tax Cut

**Holds Floor to Seek Eight Amendments**

### Frank Oppenheimer Was at Oak Ridge, Los Alamos Plants

**Participation in Red Activities Known To U.S. Security Officials for Months**

By JAMES WALTER

**Was Party Member in 1937**

### Rep. Jones Wins Senate Approval

**Ohioan Confirmed After Brief Debate**

### Georgia Guards Kill 5 Convicts

**8 Other Unarmed Prisoners Wounded**

### No A-Theft Proof, Says Hickenlooper

By SIDNEY EPSTEIN

### Marshall Sees Europe Split

### Rep. Mansfield Dead; Oldest Congressman

### Bulb Thief Leaves Police in the Dark

### Li'l Abner's Creator For Pershing Medal

### Medical School Gets $1,000,000 Clayton Gift

### Aga Khan's Condition Reported 'Very Weak'

### Slip of the Tongue:
### Wife's Courtroom Outburst Saves Convict From Prison

### Design Is Selected

### No Ghost Writing, Either:
### Unpublished 'Sherlock Holmes' Found in Old Cardboard Box

### Today to Be Sunny And a Bit Warmer

**Index of Today's News and Features**

for Oppenheimer. Even Hoover, when the Commissioners consulted him, agreed that, apart from the 'Chevalier incident' and Oppenheimer's failure to report 'what must have seemed to him an attempt at espionage at Berkeley', Oppenheimer had now moved away from his pro-Communist sympathies.

Indeed, in a memorandum to Hoover dated 27 June 1947, it was recommended that 'in view of the fact that our investigation of Oppenheimer has been negative, it is recommended that the technical surveillance on him not be re-installed . . .' The surveillance was duly removed and, for a time at least, Oppenheimer and his family were free from the FBI's attentions.

In spite of this official clearance by the AEC and the FBI, there was still no telling when some item concerning the past of anyone with one-time left-wing associations might break into the press. The Cold War was intensifying and, in parallel with this, anti-Communist feeling was running high. On 12 July 1947, the Washington *Times Herald* carried the following story:

Amid official revelation that security of some of this nation's atom secrets has been jeopardised, this newspaper today can reveal that Dr Frank Oppenheimer, brother of the American scientist who directed development of the atomic bomb at Los Alamos, was a card-carrying member of the Communist Party who worked on the Manhattan project and was aware of many secrets of the bomb from the start.

The article included the following italicised disclaimer:

*The Times Herald wishes to emphasise that the official report on Frank Oppenheimer in no way reflects on the loyalty or ability of his brother, Dr J. Robert Oppenheimer.*

*Oppenheimer at the Argonne National Laboratory, one of the new laboratories set up under the aegis of the GAC. Although resisting certain kinds of weapon development during its early days, the GAC revitalised atomic energy research*

While the paper was still rolling off the presses, Frank was contacted for his comments on the story. Frank was at that time teaching in Minnesota but the paper eventually spoke to him at one-thirty a.m. at the lakeside cottage where his family was spending the summer.

They wanted a statement [he recalls]. The story was full of implications that I had given away secrets, that I had met Communists in New Mexico, and a number of other things apart from my Party membership. I was in no position to analyse the story. I should have said 'No comment', but I said it was all untrue. I had no reason to lie about my past Communist membership since I had been a very open Communist.

Frank was also reported to have denied his Party membership. When Oppenheimer was told by a friend what Frank had said, he replied, 'I'm afraid he lied.'

In those first months of its existence, the General Advisory Committee was a very real revitalising force for the whole atomic energy programme. It revived the reactors at Hanford, which had burned out and stopped producing plutonium. At Oak Ridge the immensely costly electromagnetic separation plants which had served a valuable function in the wartime race against time were shut down. Los Alamos was relieved of its routine production line work so that the physicists there could concentrate on the sophistication of the bomb design. Two new laboratories, at Brookhaven and Argonne, joined Los Alamos

J. ROBERT OPPENHEIMER

in this basic research and under the watchful eye of the GAC grew in size and prestige to match Los Alamos.

For physics at least, this period under Oppenheimer and his Committee was something of an age of enlightenment. There was money, there was equipment, and there was an atmosphere of expansionism. The United States monopoly of nuclear power seemed set to last for years if not decades; in 1948 even Oppenheimer himself had predicted that it would last well into the fifties.

*Oppenheimer with Albert Einstein at Princeton. Einstein was on the Institute staff. Oppenheimer professed great admiration for him and described his personal qualities as 'the counterpart of great work: selflessness, humour and a deep kindness'*

In the meantime, he was still working towards the increasingly unattainable ideal of international control. Acting as an adviser to both the Departments of State and Defense, Oppenheimer watched the propaganda war with the Russians bloom in the United Nations. He voiced strongly his concern that such propagandising might lead over-zealous politicians into commitments that could not be kept. For someone whose left-wing sympathies were at that very moment under close scrutiny, he had surprisingly scathing opinions about the Soviets and the fruitlessness of negotiating with them. He despaired of any hope of nuclear accord with them, citing their belief 'in the inevitability of conflict – and not in ideas alone, but in force'.

With the brutal take-over of Czechoslovakia in February 1948, and the beginning of the Berlin blockade in April, the threat of Communism was becoming a reality, and the United States reacted accordingly. In that election year, anti-Communism became a political issue, with Republican presidential candidate Thomas Dewey promising a clean-up in government, and Truman replying that if anyone thought him soft on Communists in the government they were lying.

So when Truman was surprisingly returned for a second term, the whole anti-Communist movement which had been fanned to the proportions of a witch hunt by the election campaign went on unabated. The hunt was brought even closer to Oppenheimer when in early 1949 the House Un-American Activities Committee (HUAC) turned its attention to the alleged Communist penetration of the Berkeley Radiation Laboratory in the early days of the war.

# THE PLAGUE OF THEBES CHAPTER 14

Rossi Lomanitz, last mentioned when he disappeared as Private Lomanitz into the Army in 1943, had been teaching physics since the war in Nashville, Tennessee. In the spring of 1949, he was called as a witness before HUAC and on his way to testify he stopped off at Princeton to talk with David Bohm, another ex-student of Oppenheimer's who was also due to testify. Bohm had been brought to Princeton by Oppenheimer and as he and Lomanitz walked down Nassau Street they met their old professor returning from a visit to the barber's. The question of the HUAC hearings arose and Oppenheimer advised them both to tell the truth. However, when he later saw the transcripts of their interviews he found that when asked whether they had known Steve Nelson, they both pleaded the Fifth Amendment. This worried Oppenheimer. He didn't like it, he recalled, when people he knew had to plead the Fifth Amendment. It could also be that he saw how a suspicious mind would interpret their action.

Some months later, in early June of 1949, Oppenheimer himself appeared before HUAC. They were still investigating the Radiation Laboratory and began, very politely, by questioning him about both Joseph Weinberg and Lomanitz. His answers were protective of them.

He was then asked about another ex-student, Bernard Peters, whom he had years ago described to the security officer at Los Alamos as 'quite a Red' and a 'crazy person'. He did not back away from these remarks but instead underwrote them firmly. In so doing, he was to anger a sizeable section of the scientific community.

Next he was asked about Eltenton and Chevalier and the 'kitchen conversation', and in his reply he absolved Chevalier of any deliberate motive. 'Dr Chevalier was clearly embarrassed and confused, and I, in violent terms, told him not to be confused and to have no connection with it. *He did not ask me for information.*'

Later that morning, he was asked a question by Congressman Velde, which touched on his own behaviour in the matter: 'Did you report [the conversation] to the security officers?' To which he replied, 'I did, first, to the security officers at Berkeley; second to Colonel Lansdale; and third, to General Groves.' No mention was made of the eight-month delay before the security officers were first approached, but his reply seemed to have satisfied the Committee.

They moved on to ask about Frank's Communist Party membership. Oppenheimer happily furnished a negative reply to questions about his present membership but when asked about his brother's membership in the past, he tried a reply which can only be described as brazen.

Mr Chairman – I ask you not to press these questions about my brother. If they are important to you, you can ask him. I will answer, if asked, but I beg you not to ask me these questions.

It is a measure of Oppenheimer's power of persuasion that the Counsel replied, 'I withdraw the question'. Jo Volpe, the AEC's Counsel, who sat beside Oppenheimer during these hearings, has said that Oppenheimer 'seemed to have made up his mind to charm these Congressmen out of their seats'. Sure enough, at the end of his testimony, they all came forward to shake his hand. One of the committee members made a short speech of appreciation.

Before we adjourn, I would like to say – and I am sure this is the sense of all who are here – I have noted for some time the work done by Dr Oppenheimer and I think we all have been tremendously impressed with him and are mighty happy we have him in the position he has in our program.

The committee member was Congressman Richard M. Nixon, from California.

Only six days later, on 13 June 1949, Oppenheimer appeared before yet another hearing, this time the Joint Committee on Atomic Energy, which was investigating a charge that the infant Atomic Energy Commission was guilty of 'incredible mismanagement'. He was about to be drawn into a political battle of considerable proportions.

It had all begun following the previous year's elections and Truman's amalgamation of the separate armed services departments into one Defense Department. At the same time the new Secretary of Defense, Louis Johnson, was carrying out big economies in the armed services. Over three years the defence budget had shrunk from $48 billion to $15 billion and the three services were now competing desperately against one another to obtain a larger share of that budget. In particular, there was fierce competition between the Navy and Air Force over their particular roles in the long-range atomic strike strategy. In Johnson's cuts the Navy had lost their super carrier from which to launch atom bombers so they, in turn, openly criticised the Air Force's strategic warfare doctrines, even going so far as to criticise the morality of what they were doing. Thus the services were enormously sensitive to any moves or suggestions which could threaten their role and they resented the way in which the AEC under Lilienthal had control of the testing and deployment of all nuclear weaponry. Behind Lilienthal stood the GAC and at the head of the GAC was Oppenheimer.

But the armed forces were not the only vested interests moving against the AEC at that time. The AEC were very hard taskmasters. The contractors working for them were kept tightly under control and they resented this. It broke the pattern of the military industrial complex. How could the rich remain patriotic if one did not keep them rich? So Congress had voted for an

investigation to be headed by Senator Bourke B. Hickenlooper which was to look into, among other things, alleged waste of money on community projects at Hanford, Los Alamos and Oak Ridge; the loss of large quantities of U-235 at Argonne laboratory; and an inadequate security clearance system. But these specific charges were only a front for all the pressure groups from both industry and the armed services which gathered behind Hickenlooper, and, inevitably it now seems, the issue of security, with all the opportunities it afforded for generalised and unsubstantiated attacks, became the main battlefield.

The issue that Oppenheimer found himself facing was the exporting of radioactive isotopes to foreign researchers who might have dubious political credentials, and it was an issue which had already brought him into conflict with one of the Commissioners, Lewis Strauss.

Somehow Lewis Strauss stood apart from his colleagues on the Commission. He was a self-made man with a quick mind and enormous ambition. As a young naval officer in the First World War, he had caught the attention of Herbert Hoover, and had then seen high politics at first hand when

*AEC Commissioner Lewis Strauss. A self-made man, he had made a personal fortune on Wall Street between the wars and then risen to the rank of Rear-Admiral during World War II*

he had served as Hoover's personal assistant. Between the wars, he made a personal fortune on Wall Street, but at the beginning of the war he had joined the Navy again, where as Chief of their Ordnance Division he had become a Rear Admiral. Everybody who met him was struck by his charm and his urbanity, but those attributes cloaked a complex, impatient and far from scrupulous character. A young lawyer who knew him at the AEC, Harold Green, remembers how, on one occasion, he invited Strauss to come as his guest to a social occasion at his synagogue.

He walked into my house and kissed my wife who he'd never seen before and he said, 'I understand you have children, may I see them?' And he heard them and without waiting for an answer he was in there playing with the children and changing the diapers of the baby. Later, I learned from my friend in division security that, before he accepted the invitation he had a very quick security check done on the Rabbi. After dinner was over, he stood up and began helping clear the table and wanted to help wash the dishes. He was a very human kind of person.

However, that same evening, Green experienced an example of Strauss's other side. Just beforehand, Green had heard that J. Edgar Hoover had got Strauss to remove a senior security officer from within the AEC and so during the evening Green raised the point with him. 'I said to him, "I understand my good friend X is leaving the Commission?" And Strauss replied, almost with tears in his eyes, "Yes, what a tragedy. You know I got that job for him, but I'm afraid my enemies will crucify him after I'm gone because of his loyalty to me."'

Strauss was also known to have an almost paranoid distrust of the staff

*Oppenheimer on 13 June 1949 testifying before the Joint Congressional Committee on Atomic Energy on the exportation of radioactive isotopes. It was his dismissive comments on this occasion that so angered Lewis Strauss*

members of the AEC and of anyone who opposed him. There was no room for differences of opinion with Strauss. People were either for him or against him. Indeed, he had not forgotten that he had been outvoted two years earlier on the isotope issue and he was now using the Joint Committee as a way of getting back at his colleagues.

In particular he had latched on to the 2001st request to the Commission for a millicurie of Iron 59, from the Norwegian Royal Defence Research Establishment who wanted it to trace its movement through molten steel. It was a straightforward request, but Strauss had discovered that one of the members of the research team could be described as a Communist.

When Oppenheimer took the witness stand, he must have known of Strauss's feelings and he knew Strauss was present in the room. Nevertheless, when asked about the possible military applications of these isotopes this was his answer:

No one can force me to say you cannot use these isotopes for atomic energy. You can use a shovel for atomic energy. In fact you do. You can use a bottle of beer for atomic energy. In fact you do. But to get some perspective, the fact is that during the war and after the war these materials have played no significant part and in my knowledge no part at all.

A ripple of laughter ran through the hearing room. Even to outsiders it was apparent that Oppenheimer was making a fool of someone, but to anyone with knowledge of Strauss's continuing campaign on this issue, Oppenheimer's satire was intentionally wounding. Joseph Volpe, who was sitting next to Oppenheimer, looked at Strauss. His eyes had narrowed, the muscles of his jaws began to work visibly and the colour had risen in his cheeks.

Then Senator Knowland of California asked a question: 'Is it not true, Doctor, that the over-all national defence of a country rests on more than secret military development alone?'

'Of course it does,' replied Oppenheimer. '. . . My own rating of the importance of isotopes in this broad sense is that they are far less important than electronic devices, but far more important than, let us say, vitamins, somewhere in between.'

Again there was laughter. But later in the same session Oppenheimer took a serious line on questioning about giving more authority to security personnel. This he described as 'morbid'.

'The best guarding is simply to lock everything up and not let anybody in,' he told them, but he wanted to show that this was impossible and that there was only one natural projection to the efforts to improve security. 'The best security is in the grave', he said.

At the end of the hearing, Oppenheimer turned to Joseph Volpe and said, 'Well Joe, how did I do?'

With Strauss's face clearly imprinted on his memory, Volpe replied, 'Too well, Robert. Much too well.'

Seventeen years afterwards, Lilienthal could also remember Strauss's face that day. 'There was a look of hatred there that you don't see very often in a man's face.'

The next day, 14 June 1949, Frank Oppenheimer appeared before the House Un-American Activities Committee and he and his wife Jackie admitted to having been members of the Party. However they stated that they had left it 'long before' Frank had become involved in nuclear research.

Less than an hour after appearing before these hearings, Frank learned – by chance from one of the Washington newsmen reporting his appearance – that he was no longer Assistant Professor of Physics at the University of Minnesota. The University were asking him to resign.

Unable to get another college job, Frank retired to a piece of land he had bought in Colorado to raise cattle. His was a promising career in physics which had been ruined. His membership of the Communist Party had ended in 1940. He had done valuable work at the Radiation Laboratory during the War at the end of which Groves had written him a personal letter expressing 'grateful thanks for your indispensable part' in the project. He had entered research after the war but had been forced to leave in 1947 and now, after two years as a teacher, he was being driven out of that profession. Oppenheimer cannot have been insensitive to the implications for him of his brother's fate, but nevertheless he could not avoid feeling just a little envy. 'Absolutely away from this nightmare which has been going on for many, many years,' said Oppenheimer.

Oppenheimer spent the summer teaching in Pasadena, then early in September 1949 he returned to Princeton. 'I had just got into the house,' he said, 'when I heard the phone ringing. It was to tell me that our surveillance network had picked up evidence that the Russians had detonated an A-bomb.'

The information on the Russian bomb was fragmented and, to non-scientists particularly, far from totally convincing. An Air Force B-29 flying over Japan detected unexpected amounts of radioactivity in air samples it was collecting and when these samples were analysed, the kind of radioactivity they contained certainly indicated an atomic bomb. At the same time a scientist working for the Navy carried out a routine analysis of rainwater samples collected for him on ships and bases all over the world. Evidence of 'Joe I' came to him as tell-tale signs of fission products – cerium 141 and yttrium 91 – in the water.

But the belief in the US monopoly of atomic power was so deep-rooted that the Government was simply incredulous. Truman himself did not believe the evidence. He called Oppenheimer to Blair House and asked him if he thought it was true. Oppenheimer said yes, but even he failed totally to convince Truman, who went on for years believing that it could have been a mistake.

Next Oppenheimer was called as a witness in front of a secret session of the JCAE where again he had to try to convince the incredulous members of the committee. At one point, Senator Arthur H. Vandenberg asked, 'Doctor, what shall we do now?'

'Stay strong and hold on to our friends,' Oppenheimer replied. Right from the beginning he was afraid of a panic reaction which would mean new policies being devised without proper thought, but he was perhaps being unrealistic in his hope that people would follow his advice. When Truman, on Oppenheimer's advice, decided to pre-empt any Russian announcement of their test, by telling the nation about it himself on 23 September there was an 'almost hysterical reaction both in government circles and in the country'.

On the evening of the day of the announcement, Oppenheimer received a phone call from Edward Teller who was now working on the Super at Los Alamos again. 'What shall we do? What shall I do?' Teller asked excitedly. 'Just go back to Los Alamos and keep working,' was Oppenheimer's answer, then, after a long pause he added, 'Keep your shirt on.'

This was advice which Teller certainly did not heed. Within days he was talking to Ernest Lawrence and Luis Alvarez about the possibility of a crash programme on the Super. Inspired to action, Alvarez and Lawrence decided to come east to Washington and on 6 October they started on the first leg of their journey – to Los Alamos for a meeting with Teller.

Just before he left Berkeley, Lawrence had spoken to Lewis Strauss on the phone and, as a result, the next day Strauss wrote a memo to his fellow AEC Commissioners calling for a 'quantum jump in American planning'. By this he meant

*Ever since the war Edward Teller had suffered continual frustrations in his efforts to develop the thermonuclear weapon. The news that the Russians had broken the US atomic weapons monopoly gave him renewed hope of support for the new weapon*

that we should now make an intensive effort to get ahead with the Super. By intensive effort, I am thinking of a commitment in talent and money comparable, if necessary, to that which produced the first atomic bomb. That is the way to stay ahead.

He also proposed that the GAC should be consulted as soon as possible to 'ascertain their views as to how we can proceed with expedition'. Thus with Lawrence and Alvarez on their way to Washington and Strauss pushing for action, the pressure for the Super was mounting.

The history of the Super and the career of Edward Teller had been intertwined since the conferences in 1942 back at Le Conte Hall, Berkeley.

Teller was among those scientists who had seen the potential for using the fission reaction to produce enough heat to initiate the fusion between two atoms of deuterium. This fusion itself produced enormous quantities of energy and so a massive explosion would result.

In 1942, although everyone realised the Super was dependent first on achieving a successful fission weapon, there were thought to be no major problems in the way of such a weapon.

In 1943, however, it was discovered that tritium, another form of hydrogen, would be needed for a successful thermonuclear reaction. It required less energy to trigger its fusion than deuterium but at that stage of the war, building a plant to produce tritium in sufficient quantities for a weapon was just not feasible. This put the weapon out, at least for the duration of the war, but Teller and his own small team continued to work on it. Indeed, it was Teller's proprietary interest in this new weapon that had brought him into direct conflict first with Bethe, then with Oppenheimer.

By the time the war ended, the work done by Teller's team had complicated rather than simplified the problems of the weapon. They had not worked out a reasonable way of holding the two gases deuterium and tritium around the bomb's fission core. They had thought of combining them chemically with lithium to produce a solid compound and of impregnating paraffin wax with the gases, but neither of these had so far proved practicable. Their only hope seemed to lie in freezing the gases solid but this meant that the bomb had to become one enormous refrigeration plant. Indeed it would be so cumbersome that if it was ever to be used in combat it would have to be arranged that the enemy would not only allow it to be delivered but also provide workshops where frozen deuterium and tritium could be shaped and moulded for use. It was, at this point of development, impracticable, and Teller had found himself fighting an unsympathetic laboratory director at Los Alamos to try and get the resources to continue research. By 1949, the picture was still substantially the same, but it was Teller's belief that if work had been allowed to proceed he could have already cracked the basic problems. He was embittered and frustrated but now, following the Russian bomb, it looked as if, at last, things would go his way.

David Lilienthal responded more slowly and cautiously to Strauss's memo than Strauss had expected. But like Oppenheimer he knew of technical developments which made him question any headlong rush towards a completely new weapon. In recent months, the work in the AEC's various laboratories had led to the production of a conventional fission weapon which would produce a blast of 500,000 tons of TNT equivalent – twenty-five times as powerful as the bomb that destroyed Hiroshima. It was reckoned that it would 'take out' any target in the world, so why was a Super needed at all?

Nevertheless, Lilienthal agreed to call a special meeting of the GAC and in his letter to Oppenheimer he said he would welcome the group's 'advice and assistance on as broad a basis as possible.' This brief was to prove of considerable significance in later developments. A meeting was agreed for the weekend of the 29 and 30 October.

In the meantime, the lobbyists for the Super, Alvarez and Lawrence, arrived in Washington and began their efforts to whip up support for their project. They lunched with members of the Joint Committee, met with Department of Defense advisers, and lobbied each one of the AEC Commissioners. In New York, they stopped off to talk with GAC member Isidor Rabi. Lawrence, and Alvarez, significantly, found him 'very happy at our plans'.

By the 14 October, Lawrence was satisfied with the results of his efforts and left Washington to return west. At almost the same time, Teller arrived on the East Coast proposing to do his own lobbying and even, thinking ahead, his own recruiting. He went to see Hans Bethe at Cornell appealing to him to give up his job there, to come and work on the Super at Los Alamos. He had just succeeded in persuading him when the phone rang. It was Oppenheimer who wanted to invite Bethe to a conference in Princeton. Fearing the worst, Teller went with him. 'He'll change your mind for you,' Teller warned Bethe.

However, after their meeting with Oppenheimer, Teller recalls Bethe turning to him and saying, 'You see, you can be quite satisfied. I am still coming.'

But two days later, Teller heard that Bethe had indeed changed his mind and was not coming to Los Alamos after all. Bethe says that it was discussions with two friends that changed his mind, but Teller did not know that. He was convinced that it was Oppenheimer's doing.

In Princeton, Oppenheimer was well aware of the lobbying that had been going on and on 21 October wrote a letter to his fellow GAC member, James Conant, which spelt out clearly how he felt.

First he pointed to the fact that effectively the Super was

not very different from what it was . . . more than seven years ago: a weapon of unknown design, cost, deliverability, and military value. But a very great change has taken place in the climate of opinion. On the one hand, two experienced promoters have been at work, i.e., Ernest Lawrence and Edward Teller.

After elucidating the attitudes of the Joint Congressional Committee and the scientists such as Bethe who were all seriously considering the H-bomb, he went on to discuss his real concern.

What concerns me is really not the technical problem. I am not sure the miserable thing will work, nor that it can be gotten to a target except by ox cart. It seems likely to me even further to worsen the unbalance of our present war plans. What does worry me is that this thing appears to have caught the imagination both of the Congressional and of military people, as the answer to the problem posed by the Russian advance. It would be folly to oppose the exploration of this weapon. We have always known it had to be done; and it does have to be done, though it appears singularly proof against any form of experimental approach. But that we become committed to it as the way to save the country and the peace appears to me full of dangers.

Whether one agrees with these views of Oppenheimer's or not, it has to be admitted that they are rooted in a careful analysis of the situation and that they have a clear unemotional logic. It is very difficult to see in them the schemings of an underground Communist trying to manipulate the whole American war machine to give the Soviets an advantage as some were later to suggest. Quite simply, he was stating that the Super was not necessarily going to work and that there were feasible alternatives which must not be forgotten.

\*　　\*　　\*　　\*　　\*

The morning of Saturday, 29 October was grey and wet as the eight members of the General Advisory Committee met with their Commissioners and a number of expert advisers in a room at the Atomic Energy Commission's headquarters in Washington's Constitution Avenue.

In the hall outside the committee room, watching the comings and goings of such war heroes as General Omar Bradley for the Army and General Norstad for the Air Force, was Luis Alvarez. He was waiting in the hope of getting a first hand report of the Committee's deliberations.

During the morning, the Committee heard assessments of the Soviet explosion and its implications. Bradley did most of the talking for the Armed Services. He took the line that there was no choice but to build the Super, but when he was asked by Oppenheimer what military advantages he could see for such a weapon over the largest of the fission bombs, Bradley answered, 'Only psychological'.

After their briefing, the members of the Committee broke for lunch before going into closed session. Down in the lobby Alvarez and Oppenheimer met and the two of them went to lunch together where they discussed the likely outcome of the meeting. Even though Oppenheimer knew of Alvarez's lobbying tactics a week or so earlier, he still seemed prepared to talk openly with him and even at this early stage of the meeting to give him a fairly clear idea of what he thought the Committee's answers to a crash programme would be. After lunch, Alvarez did not wait for the final outcome to the meeting but set off to California. He was depressed, convinced by his conversation with Oppenheimer that the Committee would not recommend a crash programme.

The afternoon's closed session began with Fermi providing a technical summary of the prospects for the weapon. In essence, his view was that the chances of successfully building a deliverable weapon with such a programme were little better than even. Given this assessment, Oppenheimer then went round the table asking each of the Committee members in turn to give their views as to what the country should do.

Their comments ranged over the weapon's technical feasibility and whether the weapon would add substantially to the military strength of the US. They raised such questions as whether there would not be a greater chance of reaching the enemy targets using several bombers carrying smaller weapons, rather than one or two aircraft bearing Supers. They talked about the political risks of the United States being seen to embark on producing a weapon of such unlimited power and they also addressed themselves to the moral question.

They were concerned, as Oppenheimer later put it, by 'the employment of these weapons on a massive scale against civilisation and cities. . . .' There was no chance of selecting a militarily justifiable target with this weapon.

Oppenheimer was the last to give his views. He found that 'there was a surprising unanimity – to me very surprising – that the United States ought not to take the initiative at that time in an all-out programme.' Then he went on to say, 'I am glad you feel this way, for if it had not come out this way, I would have had to resign as Chairman.'

The GAC spent much of the time during the next two days drafting their report to the AEC and their agreement was such that they were able to produce a report from the whole group on the fission as well as the thermonuclear programme.

We all hope that by one means or another, the development of these weapons can be avoided. We are all reluctant to see the United States take the initiative in precipitating this development. We are all agreed that it would be wrong at the present moment to commit ourselves to an all-out effort towards its development.

Two of the Committee's members, Isidor Rabi and Enrico Fermi, also produced a minority report condemning the weapon on moral and ethical grounds.

The fact that no limits exist to the destructiveness of this weapon makes its very existence and the knowledge of its construction a danger to humanity, as a whole. It is necessarily an evil thing considered in any light. For these reasons, we believe it important for the President of the United States to tell the American public and the world that we think it is wrong on fundamental ethical principles to initiate the development of such a weapon.

Fermi and Rabi also expressed the view that one last effort should be made to produce an agreement on international control, but if such an effort failed, then the US 'should with considerable regret, go ahead'.

The other six members produced an appendix of their own, written not by Oppenheimer but by James Conant.

We believe a super bomb should never be produced. Mankind would be far better off not to have a demonstration of the feasibility of such a weapon until the present climate of world opinion changes . . .

In determining not to proceed to develop the super bomb, we see a unique opportunity of providing by example some limitations on the totality of war and thus of eliminating the fear and arousing the hope of mankind.

Perhaps it was a pity that the GAC did err from straightforward technical considerations of the Super to produce statements with such a large element of wishful thinking. Who was going to follow their 'example'? Did they really believe that the Russians would not continue to develop atomic weaponry?

The day after the GAC meeting, Oppenheimer stayed on in Washington and conferred with Secretary of State, Dean Acheson. Acheson was deeply troubled by Oppenheimer's line of argument. 'You know, I listened as carefully as I knew how,' he told an adviser, 'but I don't understand what Oppie is trying to say. How can you really persuade a hostile adversary to disarm "by example"?' He was to be the first of many to criticise this part of Oppenheimer's and the GAC's thinking but others were not to be so charitable in their analysis of the motives that lay behind it.

Not that the Committee was totally unanimous. One member, the Berkeley chemist Glenn Seaborg, who, nearly ten years before, had discovered

*Cyril Smith, the metallurgist and the one member of the GAC who recalled that Oppenheimer read out the Seaborg letter to the Committee at their meeting of 29 October 1949*

plutonium, could not attend the meeting because of a long-standing engagement in Sweden. In something of a rush just before he left on his trip, however, he wrote a letter to Oppenheimer setting out his views on the question of a crash programme.

Although I deplore the prospects of our country putting a tremendous effort into this, I must confess that I have been unable to come to the conclusion that we should not. . . . My present feeling would perhaps be best summarised by saying that I would have to hear some good arguments before I could take on sufficient courage to recommend not going towards such a program.

He had begun his letter somewhat diffidently. 'I will try and give you my thoughts for what they may be worth,' and he had ended in much the same vein, '. . . I am afraid that it is the best that I can do at this time.' Nevertheless his views, however tentative, could be seen as departing from the final verdict of the Committee. Yet Oppenheimer himself was to admit later that he could not recall ever having read that letter out to the Committee. One Committee member, the metallurgist Cyril Smith, was to disagree with Oppenheimer over this, recalling that he had seen the letter, but it was Oppenheimer's own recollection which was to be used by his enemies against him.

Ten days after the GAC's weekend meeting on the Super, the AEC's five Commissioners failed to arrive at a consensus of opinion over the question of a crash programme on the Super and decided to report individually to the President. Lilienthal and one other Commissioner, Sumner Pike, were flatly against the crash programme. Dr Henry De Wolf Smyth, now the only Commissioner who was a scientist, favoured trying to strike an agreement with the Soviets before going ahead with the programme. Gordon Dean, the newest Commissioner, felt much the same as Smyth. Only Lewis Strauss said categorically that the Americans must proceed with the Super without delay and he made his views known as widely as possible. He went to see Louis Johnson, the Secretary of Defense, whom he managed to persuade to the belief that 'the Russians were building an H-Bomb, that the US were being sold down the river, and that the US must proceed with an H-Bomb programme. . . .'

*Henry De Wolf Smyth, an AEC Commissioner, who favoured trying to strike an agreement with the Russians on arms control before going ahead to develop the Super*

In a matter of days the balance of opinions amongst the other Commissioners had also been changed. Gordon Dean had joined Strauss. Smyth had shifted in that direction too and only Lilienthal, who was resigning shortly anyway, and Sumner Pike stood firm against the crash programme.

I think Oppenheimer underestimated the effect of the continuing low-level attacks on Commission Policy [the GAC Secretary John Manley is reported as saying]. I think he overestimated his strength to resist the pressures exerted in Washington. Partly the pressures had taken the form of those damned Congressional hearings. Partly the pressures were exerted more quietly by the military. . . .

Certainly the Air Force were angry with the GAC's decision. As General Roscoe Wilson was to put it some years later:

The approach to the thermonuclear weapons also caused some concern. Dr Oppenheimer, as far as I know, had technical objections, or, let me say, approached this with conservatism for technical reasons, more conservatism than the Air Force would have liked. The sum total of this to my mind was adding up to that we were not exploiting the full military potential in this field.

Given the statement of one senior military adviser at the time that, 'it's a fundamental law of defence that you always have to use the most powerful weapons you can produce', and coupling this with the sensitivity provoked by the severe cut backs in defence spending, it is possible to see the kind of pressure that the Air Force would start to apply on the AEC. They had no wish to be limited by the balanced-force concept that Oppenheimer, through the AEC, was promoting. They wanted to develop the full potential of Strategic Air Command, albeit at the expense of the other possibilities.

*John Manley who served as secretary to the GAC*

But, although the pressure groups were working behind the scenes, for those two months at the end of 1949, the US Government took the official position that it would not develop the Super. Back in 1945, Oppenheimer had been a prime witness to a situation where each participating group in the development of the A-bomb – the army, the government, and the scientific community – had simply played out their roles. The scientists, including Oppenheimer, had been the idiot savants who had expected the government to make a proper decision while the government seemed to expect that the military would take upon itself the crucial decision on the value of using the bomb. In their turn, the military saw their function as finishing the Japanese as quickly as possible. Because of this, the greatest decision of all, whether to use atomic weapons at all, had not been faced by anyone. This time, however, Oppenheimer and his Committee had faced that decision and for those two months one major strand in the arms race came to a standstill. It was a real achievement, one that it is easy to lose sight of. How long the decision would have held it is difficult to guess, but then the US Government received a jolt from which it was never to recover.

On Friday, 27 January 1950, Sir Frederick Hoyer Millar, atomic expert at the British Embassy in Washington, paid an urgent visit on Under Secretary of State, Robert Murphy. There he told Murphy that they had arrested Klaus Fuchs in London, and that Fuchs had confessed to passing information over to the Russians throughout the war and afterwards.

All those who had worked with Fuchs at Los Alamos, and had known the depth of his involvement with the project, his work on the Patents Committee logging all new work for possible claims after the War, realised that the Russians must know practically everything of importance both about the fission bomb and the Super.

Edward Teller, for one, realised that all his ideas on the Super including his most recent had been written into a top secret *Disclosure of Invention* paper prepared by Fuchs and von Neumann and the Russians must now understand it fully and might even be laughing at its lack of elegance. In his anger, he moved quickly and on 30 January, the first working day after the announcement of Fuchs's arrest, he and Lawrence addressed the Joint Committee on Atomic Energy. They made it quite clear that there was now no choice but to move ahead on the Super as rapidly as possible. Their plea was so strong that the Committee also acted promptly. That same day, members of the Committee saw the President and told him, 'You have got to overrule this [the decision of the GAC]. Mr Teller says there is a possibility here.'

A little earlier that same day, Oppenheimer had also seen the President and had told him just how much Fuchs knew. Truman had then convened a meeting with Johnson, the Secretary of Defense, Secretary of State Acheson, and Lilienthal. With Lilienthal still opposing them, these three advisers voted two to one to inaugurate the crash programme on the Super.

A few minutes before one o'clock the next day, the White House press corps were read the following statement from the President:

It is part of my responsibility as Commander-in-Chief of the Armed Forces to see to it that our country is able to defend itself against any possible aggressor.

Accordingly, I have directed the Atomic Energy Commission to continue its work on all forms of atomic weapons, including the so-called hydrogen or super-bomb.

The pause in the arms race which Oppenheimer had helped to achieve had been brutally ended. With Truman's decision not only had the Thermonuclear Age begun, but there was a dramatic shift in the balance of power within the Government.

That very same day, 31 January 1950, Lewis Strauss was celebrating his fifty-fourth birthday. For him the President's announcement had been a great triumph against his four fellow Commissioners. That day he had already been to the White House, and feeling the weight of opinion behind him now, had resigned as a protest over the Commission's delaying actions. He had then gone to the Shoreham Hotel to celebrate both his birthday and the President's decision to pursue the Super.

Amongst the company of politicians, government officials, and military men who were his guests on this occasion was Oppenheimer. What must have been going through his mind as he stood there watching a celebration of the decision to make the most deadly weapon ever created we can only guess at.

There is one clue, however. Ernest K. Lindley, the newspaper columnist, was also a guest at the party and he spotted Oppenheimer standing alone and morose on the sidelines of the celebration.

'You don't look jubilant,' Lindley said. After a pause, so long that Lindley thought he had lost track of the question, Oppenheimer finally replied:

'This is the plague of Thebes.'

# THE NET TIGHTENS CHAPTER 15

The fact that the Russians had an atomic bomb and that in all probability they had details of the most up-to-date workings on the Super had a profound effect on the whole fabric of American society.

Just nine days after the Presidential announcement, on 9 February 1950, Joseph R. McCarthy made a speech in Wheeling, West Virginia, in which he was reported to have said:

> While I cannot take the time to name all of the men in the State Department who have been named as members of the Communist Party and members of a spy ring, I have here in my hand a list of 205 that were known to the Secretary of State as being members of the Communist Party and who nevertheless are still working and shaping the policy of the State Department.

Within days, following a telegram from the State Department requesting information, McCarthy had panicked and had reduced his total to 'fifty-seven card carrying Communists', but by the time McCarthy was back in Washington on 20 February the figure had grown again to eighty-one. Even though he steadfastly refused to put names to any of the number, the Government and the President were sufficiently nervous to dignify his charges with a Foreign Relations Committee investigation of them. McCarthy and the full-blooded persecution of 'communists' were on the move.

*LEFT Senator Joseph R. McCarthy (l) who was the focus of the anti-Communist witch hunt which so severely disrupted America in the early fifties. Oppenheimer was one of many whose past left-wing associations came under McCarthy's scrutiny*

*BELOW Paul Crouch and his wife Sylvia, 'paid consultants' of the Justice Department who provided damning evidence at a number of HUAC hearings. It was Sylvia who named Oppenheimer as host to 'a session of top drawer Communists' back in 1941*

In May 1950, a Mrs Sylvia Crouch appeared before the California Committee on Un-American Activities and, in her evidence, named Oppenheimer as the host, back in 1941, to a 'session of a top drawer Communist group known as a special section, a group so important that its make-up was kept secret from ordinary Communists'. She knew this, she said, because she and her husband, Paul, had been there. In the next few years, Crouch, who had become a 'paid consultant' of the Justice Department, was to provide damning evidence at many of these hearings.

As a consequence of what was alleged on this occasion, the FBI went to interview Oppenheimer – twice within a week. According to the report of those interviews,

Oppenheimer stated that he held a number of social functions at this address [10 Kenilworth Court, his Berkeley home in 1941] but that none of them were ever closed meetings of a Communist group. In addition, he pointed out that his son, Peter, was born May 12, 1941; that in July 1941, his wife was still ill, and that he also was quite worn out physically. He stated that the condition of his wife and himself practically excluded them from having attended any meetings at that time. He said he does recall attending a gathering as such at which William Schneiderman, whom he knew to be a leading Communist Party functionary speaker . . . that he believes the gathering took place at the home of his [Oppenheimer's] friend, Haakon Chevalier . . . that there were people present who he knew had no affiliation with the Communist Party.

In a summary of this report sent by Hoover to the Assistant Attorney General, Oppenheimer had during the interview said 'that he was greatly concerned with the allegations against him due to their possible effect on his reputation.'

He was to deny continually the Crouch charges. This was a period when he remembered taking a holiday with Kitty in New Mexico and the Chevaliers had looked after Peter. However there is evidence, which, while it does not confirm his attendance at this particular meeting, supports the general assertion that Oppenheimer was a member of a Communist Party group.

It comes from none other than Haakon Chevalier.

In a letter to Oppenheimer dated 23 July 1964, Chevalier wrote about information he wished to include in his forthcoming book on their friendship:

The reason for my writing to you is that an important part of the story concerns your and my membership in the same unit of the CP from 1938 to 1942. I should like to deal with this in its proper perspective, telling the facts as I remember them. As this is one of the things in your life which, in my opinion, you have least to be ashamed of, and as your commitment, attested among other things by your 'Reports to our Colleagues' which today make impressive reading, was a deep and genuine one, I consider that it would be a grave omission not to give it its due prominence.

Before going ahead, however, I think it only fair to give you an opportunity to say whether you would have any objections.

Oppenheimer had. In a curt business-like reply, he said,

Your letter asks whether I would have any objections. Indeed I do. What you say of yourself I find surprising. Surely in one respect what you say of me is not true. I have never been a member of the Communist Party, and thus have never been a member of a Communist Party Unit. I, of course, have always known this. I thought you did too. I have said so officially time and time again. I said so publicly in response to what Crouch said in 1950. I said so in the AEC hearings ten years ago.

As ever,
Robert Oppenheimer.

The phrasing of this note is somewhat strange. In the sentence, 'What you say of yourself I find surprising,' Oppenheimer is no doubt referring to Chevalier's admission of his membership in the '. . . CP from 1938 to 1942.' Is his surprise that Chevalier was a member of the Party or that he was now going to admit it? He then denies his own membership. 'I, of course, have always known this. I thought you did too.' Is he simply correcting a friend's wrongheadedness or is he obliquely directing him to the line he must take?

One thing remains certain. Although he honoured his old friend's objections in his book, Chevalier has never retracted his view that he and Oppenheimer were indeed members of the same unit of the Communist Party.

On 25 June 1950, the Korean War began, and the attention of Oppenheimer and the other members of the GAC was turned towards producing nuclear weaponry small enough for use on the battlefield. In spite of the President's directive, the work on the Super was given little priority and was overall at a low ebb.

Edward Teller was near to despairing at this time. His current approach to the weapon had undergone scrutiny at Los Alamos by the mathematician Stanislaw Ulam and his initial calculations showed that Teller's idea of using a deuterium/tritium mix to lower the energy threshold required to produce the fusion was likely to produce a fizzle. Teller reacted angrily. He did not trust Ulam and refused to believe his results.

His anger and frustration, however, were compounded by reading the report of a special panel charged with looking at the long range future of the atomic weapons programme. The panel was chaired by Oppenheimer. Teller interpreted its findings when he read it as stating that the Super was interfering with the small weapons programme. Certainly he found that the report caused him additional problems in the already disturbed waters of Los Alamos.

What annoyed and concerned Teller even more was the fact that one of the members of the panel and a signatory of its report was Luis Alvarez, who was very much in favour of the development of the Super for personal reasons. How had Alvarez gone along with the panel's decision? Was it not yet another example of Oppenheimer's seemingly hypnotic power over his committees?

When Alvarez himself cast his mind back over the sequence of events on the panel, he remembered that he had very strongly resisted some early statements by Oppenheimer against the H-bomb programme. However, when the panel

*Luis Alvarez, a member of the panel chaired by Oppenheimer which was studying the long-term future of atomic weapons. In agreeing to the panel's report which was unfavourable to the Super, Alvarez incurred the wrath of Edward Teller*

held its final meeting to draft its report, he recollected that he may have been in some haste to catch a flight back to California and may have rushed his consideration of the draft. However, a little while later he was contacted by Oppenheimer and asked to go to Pasadena to peruse a copy of the final report. This he did and, after studying it along with Robert Bacher and Charles Lauritsen, as well as Oppenheimer, he signed it.

Only afterwards, when he became the target of Teller's fury, did he see the implications of the report in a new light.

Its conclusion read as follows:

In fact we believe that only a timely recognition of the *long range* character of the thermonuclear program will tend to make available for the basic studies of the fission weapon program the resources of the Los Alamos laboratory.

In other words, Los Alamos should for the immediate future concentrate on fission weapons. So how had Alvarez missed this? Had he been duped or hypnotised or what? Alvarez's explanation was that he had been a victim of Oppenheimer's skilled politicising. He had been asked – and agreed – to go to Pasadena where he had considered the report in Bacher and Lauritsen's company. If the report had been sent to him at Berkeley, then he may have consulted Lawrence and may have had much more opportunity to see the report in a different light.

As it was, he believed himself to have been out-manoeuvred. 'Oppenheimer was in effect practising Political Science 4 B,' he said, 'on the post-graduate level, while I was still on Political Science 1 A, the freshman course'.

However, while he saw nothing sinister in this, Teller did. So did increasing numbers of other people who stood to be affected adversely by Oppenheimer's actions.

William Liscum Borden was thirty years old, and already the Executive Director of the Joint Congressional Committee on Atomic Energy which had been investigating the charges of mismanagement at the AEC and, in particular, the security clearance procedures which the Commission used. In November 1950, he asked the AEC to provide him with the files of ten or a dozen of the employees they considered among their most difficult 'security cases'. One of the files he was given was Robert Oppenheimer's.

*William Liscum Borden, the Executive Director of the Joint Congressional Committee on Atomic Energy. His investigations of Oppenheimer's security files were to lead him to charge that Oppenheimer was an 'espionage agent' and acted under 'a Soviet Directive'*

The early months of 1951 were very difficult for Edward Teller who, in spite of Ulam's pessimistic calculations, was going ahead to test a crude thermonuclear device on Eniwetok Atoll. It was an experiment intended only to demonstrate that deuterium and tritium would indeed fuse when subjected to the heat of an atomic explosion. It was not a hydrogen bomb.

Yet even as the plans for this particular test were being finalised in mid-January 1951, Teller was beginning to see his way forward to the next stage – translating the tritium and deuterium fusion into the form of a practical weapon.

J. ROBERT OPPENHEIMER

This basic step of Teller's has recently (late 1979) been declassified and it is now possible to describe in general terms the problem he faced and how it was overcome.

The problem had its parallels in the pre-detonation problem the Los Alamos scientists faced with the plutonium bomb. Unless the fusion reaction could be made to occur with sufficient speed, the fission bomb trigger would blow it apart before the fusion was properly under way. Indeed the catalysing energy from the fission bomb trigger had to be delivered to the bulk of the tritium/deuterium mixture at very nearly the speed of light to achieve this.

It seemed an almost impossible condition to fulfil because it was thought that most of the energy from the fission reaction would be transmitted in the form of heat which, relatively speaking, moves slowly.

It had then occurred to Teller, perhaps prompted by Ulam, that at the extremely high temperatures of the fission trigger, temperatures never experienced and examined before on earth, the energy might be emitted, not as heat, but as X-rays. And X-rays travel at the speed of light.

So Teller and one of his young co-workers, Freddie de Hoffmann, tried to work out a configuration of the fission trigger and the fusion mixture which would best ensure that the X-rays would permeate the mass of fusion material instantaneously. De Hoffmann recalls how the calculations went.

I then remember working a good portion of the night on it, and when Edward came in in the morning, we looked at it and – it's vivid in my memory – somehow the thing didn't quite go the way either of us expected it to be. And Edward, with his usual insight, simply looked at it . . . I mean one factor was off – you know it was a quick calculation overnight – and as soon as we had rectified that, the thing [seemed] solved.

So over a short period in the spring of 1951, the hydrogen bomb was born. The next step was to prove that fusion would indeed occur and this was the function of the test on Eniwetok (codenamed Greenhouse). It was scheduled for 8 May. In Teller's view it was not just a test but 'a great scientific experiment. If it is a success,' he said 'it could mean that mankind has achieved a new means of obtaining energy, just as Fermi proved in 1942.'

In fact Greenhouse was a considerable success, but in his moment of triumph, Teller was unaware that his test was not the first experimental proof of the possibility of a fusion reaction. Late in 1950, some six months before Greenhouse, the Russians had tested some kind of thermonuclear device.

Furthermore the existence of this bomb was known about by certain Air Force scientists and officers who passed the information on to the President and to Secretary of State, Dean Acheson. But was the AEC or either Teller or Oppenheimer informed about this test? This question was asked of Robert Le Baron, who, at this time, was chairman of the Military Liaison Committee, the link between the Pentagon and the AEC. His reply is astonishing.

'No, they were not notified. It was top secret. Any letter of transmittal would have gone over my desk and I did not sign such a letter.'

There is something bizarre, and deeply troubling, in a security system so rigid that it denies information of such importance to the very agency and the very scientists engaged in the country's race for survival. As a result, the damaging struggle between the various factions over weapons strategy was to continue. A report on the successful Greenhouse test was produced and circulated in the AEC and it was with pleasurable anticipation that Teller looked forward to a meeting at Princeton where the strategic implications of Greenhouse were to be discussed. Amazingly, however, Teller was not included among those due to speak and, as the meeting got under way, it became apparent to Teller that his new ideas described in the Greenhouse report were being ignored.

My amazement multiplied when Gordon Dean, still Chairman of the AEC spoke without mentioning the . . . report which I had explained to him two months earlier. My amazement approached anger as other scientists and officials who knew of the report spoke without referring to it.

Finally I could contain myself no longer. I insisted on being heard. My demand was met with spirited debate, but it was decided that I should be allowed to speak.

So Teller made his way to the blackboard and, with the help of two of his colleagues, began an impromptu explanation of his theories. At the end of the debate, which was to last for two days, Teller seemed to have won the grudging admiration of most of those present.

At the end of those two days [recalled Gordon Dean], we were convinced, everyone in the room, that at least we had something for the first time that looked feasible in the way of an idea. I remember leaving the meeting impressed with this fact, that everyone around the table without exception – and this included Dr Oppenheimer – was enthusiastic. . . .

Indeed, even Teller was to admit that Oppenheimer seemed to have changed his point of view and now 'warmly supported this new approach.' And Oppenheimer later held that if a weapon of this kind had been suggested initially, he would never have opposed it. He described Teller's new development as 'technically so sweet that you could not argue about that' and now he could see only one possible course of action. 'You go ahead and do it and you argue about what to do about it only after you have had your technical success.'

This is a strange remark, seemingly ignoring the experience with the atom bomb where the momentum of the 'technical success' carried everyone on to the brink with hardly a moment for thought. Certainly it is not a comment to be expected from anyone who entertained strong moral scruples about the development of this weapon of mass annihilation. It would seem that, whatever his own feelings were and the goals he eventually hoped to attain, Oppenheimer's actions were in the end governed by an appreciation of the political and technical realities of the time. Such behaviour can seem cynical but in his defence it can be said that few people achieved more in the fight to avert the arms race than he did.

However, one thing did continue to bother Edward Teller about both Dean and Oppenheimer's reaction to his new development. He had talked to them both about it before the Princeton meeting and yet they reacted as if Princeton was the first time they had ever heard of it. Bearing in mind his difficulty in obtaining a hearing, it is not surprising that Teller felt that only as a last resort had they admitted the value of his new ideas.


On 3 August 1951, Lewis Strauss and William Borden met and spent most of the time talking about Oppenheimer. They found that they had a number of misgivings in common and after discussing their mutual anxiety over Oppenheimer's loyalty, they agreed that they were unlikely now to confirm or dispel their fears through surveillance as Oppenheimer certainly knew by now that his phone was tapped.

From the anecdotes Strauss told at that meeting about Oppenheimer's automatic election as Chairman of the GAC, and his seeming effect on Bethe's decision to join Teller at Los Alamos, it was clear that he too now held the same generalised fears about Oppenheimer's influence on his fellow scientists and committee members.

In spite of having given his approval to the development of the new Teller hydrogen weapon, Oppenheimer still persisted with his efforts to develop small nuclear weapons for battlefield use. Yet again, it brought him into direct conflict with the Air Force and Strategic Air Command.

The Air Force continued to view any attempt to diversify into other forms of nuclear weaponry as a threat to the future of Strategic Air Command and their virtual monopoly as the purveyors of the new weaponry. This was despite the fact that nuclear weapons could now be made from lower-grade ores which were cheaper and more plentiful. There was in fact no longer the pressure on raw materials which demanded an either/or decision between tactical battlefield weaponry and strategic weapons, but so far this fact seemed not to have permeated Air Force thinking. In other quarters, however, the new possibilities were being investigated seriously and in the summer of 1951, a study group had been set up at Cal. Tech. as part of Project Vista, to look at the kind of nuclear weapons needed for the battlefield and how they might be used. Oppenheimer was not part of this study group, but when they ran into problems in drafting their final report they called in Oppenheimer to help them. It is a measure of the high regard he was held in as politician and scientist that he was then asked to rewrite the crucial fifth chapter of the Vista Report.

But rumours of what had been going on in Pasadena permeated through to the Pentagon and to Air Force Secretary, Thomas K. Finletter. From the slogan being bandied about out there: 'Let's bring the battle back to the battlefield' he was concerned that the report might be threatening the Air Force's position. So he sent the Air Force's Chief Scientist, David Griggs, out to investigate. He was shown the newly-drafted chapter five of the Report and was horrified to see that not only did it recommend a restriction on use of the

H-bomb to a purely retaliatory role against the Russians, but it also advocated a three-way split of the American supply of fissionable raw material. He was told that Oppenheimer had been responsible for the drafting of the report, and this was to be the first in a chain of events that led Griggs to join the growing ranks of people who entertained 'a serious question as to the loyalty of Dr Oppenheimer'.

The next event in the chain was the following spring when Griggs was involved in a recriminatory lunch with Rabi and Lee DuBridge, during which he accused the GAC of not doing enough to promote the H-Bomb. Angrily, Rabi said that Griggs could only accurately assess GAC's role if he had seen the minutes of the meeting and how the arguments had developed, but to do this, Rabi added, Griggs would need Oppenheimer's permission.

So on 23 May 1952, Griggs and Oppenheimer met in Oppenheimer's Princeton office. Oppenheimer did not show him the minutes but instead he let him read a summary of the October 1949 meeting of the GAC. He then assured him that, since then, the GAC had done all in their power to promote the H-Bomb.

Then their conversation turned to another topic – a story circulating about Finletter in which he was quoted as saying that if the US had a number of H-Bombs it would rule the world. Griggs asked Oppenheimer if he had anything to do with propagating the story and Oppenheimer replied that he had heard the story as a first-hand account. Griggs retaliated that he had been at the meeting where Finletter was said to have made the remark and that no such comment had actually been made. Oppenheimer remained firm, citing his version of the meeting, saying that it came from a totally reliable source.

As their conversation grew more personal and more difficult, Oppenheimer then asked Griggs if he thought he was pro-Russian or merely confused. Griggs responded that he wished he knew. Oppenheimer then asked if Griggs had expressed doubts about him to other people in the Defense Department, and Griggs replied that he had heard such doubts expressed and had even discussed them himself with Finletter.

At which point, Oppenheimer called David Griggs 'a paranoid' and their exchange came to a heated and unsatisfactory conclusion.

This was not the end of the sequence, however, because only a few weeks later Griggs and Oppenheimer were to meet again, at a lunch arranged by Finletter to see if he and Oppenheimer could not come to some sort of understanding.

According to one of the participants, this lunch was one of the most uncomfortable occasions he had ever been party to. Oppenheimer was late and as the meal progressed he systematically froze all of Finletter's attempts to be friendly and open. His whole manner was arrogant and as the meal progressed he became 'rude beyond belief'.

After the disastrous meal was over, Finletter reacted with amazing good humour. He laughed out loud, then told his aides, 'I don't think you fellows have convinced me I should feel any more positively about Dr Oppenheimer.'

In alienating so many influential men, to little avail, Oppenheimer had become his own worst enemy. He had now managed to alienate Strauss, Teller, Griggs, various senior members of the Air Force Staff, and now the Air Force Secretary. But if this behaviour was not excusable at least it was understandable. Oppenheimer knew that, daily, his every action was under round-the-clock surveillance, and he could never have been certain what kind of conspiracy was being mounted against him and when it would eventually come to a head. Indeed, earlier that year, one of the AEC Commissioners, Thomas E. Murray, had publicly declared that Oppenheimer was a security risk and should be removed. In the spring, the AEC's own director of research had made allegations about Oppenheimer to the FBI and the FBI had then seen fit to leak these allegations to the press.

*AEC Commissioner Thomas E. Murray who in 1952 publicly declared that Oppenheimer was a security risk*

Then in June, only a week or two after the disastrous lunch with Finletter, Oppenheimer came up for re-election as Chairman of the GAC. How much he may have known about the backstage politics is difficult to assess, but an FBI report of 29 May 1952 shows the lengths to which Senator Brien McMahon, the same McMahon who had helped free the AEC from military domination in 1946, was prepared to go to ensure he was not reappointed.

McMahon states he is personally going to talk to the President. He is opposed to Oppenheimer's reappointment. He has worked out a plan whereby Oppenheimer would take the initiative and decline to serve another term by an exchange of letters and everybody will be happy. McMahon is still fearful of the influence Oppenheimer might have on other scientists in the event there is any open rupture.

But Oppenheimer had, for whatever reason, decided that he had chaired this committee for long enough and on 25 June he informed the AEC chairman, Gordon Dean, of his decision. So Oppenheimer was not reappointed to the GAC and nor were his two friends and colleagues, James Conant and Lee DuBridge. But although this represented a dramatic reduction in his influence, those who were opposed to him were not, it seems, going to be content until they had ousted him completely from power and even publicly disgraced him.

Francis Cotter had been an FBI agent and at one time he was attached to Los Alamos, but in July 1952 he became the security officer of the Joint Committee on Atomic Energy. In briefing him for his first assignment, his director William Borden told him that there was now evidence from the interviews with Klaus Fuchs in London that Fuchs had an accomplice while working at Los Alamos. He then instructed Cotter to look into the security file of Robert Oppenheimer to see if Oppenheimer was that accomplice.

As Oppenheimer's star seemed to wane, then another was on the ascendant. After years of frustration, it looked as if Edward Teller's dream was about to be realised. In spite of resistance from the AEC, and from the GAC and Oppenheimer in particular, the Air Force decided to try to set up another laboratory where Teller and his colleagues could proceed freely to develop the Super.

Then at the last minute, when it became apparent that the Air Force were in earnest, the AEC stepped in and offered Teller the facilities at Livermore, just outside San Francisco. The GAC had endorsed the decision and, as Oppenheimer put it, only eight months after they had voted out a similar proposal by eight to one, 'This we liked and this we endorsed.'

In May 1952, as the Livermore laboratories were nearing completion, Teller was interviewed on two occasions by the FBI. Following their earlier encounters with men like Commissioner Murray, the FBI were now following up all those people who were known to be critical of Oppenheimer, and Teller was one of them.

Teller's theme was a familar one. He told his interviewers about scientists he had approached to see if they would work for him on the Super at Los Alamos and who did not come. In Teller's view, Oppenheimer 'might have had something to do' with their declining his invitation. He referred to one of the AEC Commissioners, Henry Smyth, who opposed the H-bomb and 'that he, Teller, believes Smyth has done so through the influence of Oppenheimer.'

He implied that Hans Bethe had been sent by Oppenheimer to Los Alamos to see whether the H-Bomb was really feasible after all.

He then moved on to discussing Oppenheimer himself and he described him as 'a very complicated person, even though an outstanding man.' According to the report he then went into an aspect of Oppenheimer's past which had, so far, remained untouched.

'In his youth, Oppenheimer was troubled with some sort of physical or mental attacks which may have permanently affected him.'

This perhaps refers to Oppenheimer's fits of depression. Teller himself seemed very uncomfortable about the course the interrogation was taking – or amazingly devious – because after each statement he made he asked that they should 'not be included in a report for dissemination' because it could prove 'embarrassing' or would 'merely add fuel to an already smouldering fire.'

Toward the end of the interview, the matter of Oppenheimer's loyalty came up and, according to the report, Teller said that 'in all of his dealings with Oppenheimer he has never had the slightest reason or indication to believe that Oppenheimer is in any way disloyal to the United States.'

Teller did not want this view included in a report for dissemination either because, according to the report, he felt it would be 'subject to considerable cross-examination'.


Throughout the protracted negotiations over the new laboratory for the Super, the scientists at Los Alamos had been making preparations for the next test of the thermonuclear principle, codenamed Mike. By the autumn of 1952, the vast, cylindrical housing that contained the fuel and the refrigeration apparatus was being set up on the small island of Elugelab in Eniwetok Atoll. It still needed the vast refrigeration plant for the tritium/deuterium mixture and was thus described as 'the 65 ton monster', but it also incorporated the basic configuration that had been worked out for an actual weapon. The tritium/deuterium mixture was at the centre surrounded by the fission material. This in turn was encased in conventional explosive. When Mike was detonated, the conventional explosive drove the fissionable material inward, compressing it into a critical mass, and creating the atomic explosion which in its turn compressed and heated the fusion mixture to produce a thermonuclear reaction.

Teller had by now left Los Alamos and played no part in the test. He was to witness it in front of a seismograph in the basement room at Berkeley. The theoretical expectation for the device was a few megatons – in other words several hundred times the yield of the Hiroshima bomb. However, the massive fireball spread so far that it terrified observers who had seen many other tests before. The whole island of Elugelab, one mile in diameter, disappeared. It so unnerved the director of Los Alamos, Norris Bradbury, that for a time he considered keeping secret the magnitude of what happened. The yield of Mike was estimated to be ten megatons, five hundred times greater than the Hiroshima bomb. In many ways its massive fireball symbolised the ascendancy of Teller over Oppenheimer, except that it was not going to be that simple.


When Eisenhower's Republican administration took over the government in January 1953, there were three main changes which were to affect Oppenheimer most directly. The first was the elevation of Republican Joseph

McCarthy, from being merely the ranking minority member of the Senate's Investigations Subcommittee, to become its Chairman with powers which extended to the selection of their investigative targets.

The second was the appointment, in March, of Lewis Strauss as the President's special assistant on atomic energy matters.

The third was a new presidential security order, a continuation of the reaction to the Communist threat. Under its terms, a government employee had not only to be judged as 'loyal' to serve his country, he also had to have a background which meant that employment by the government was 'clearly consistent with the interests of national security'.

All three boded ill for Oppenheimer and now his critics were bold enough to come out into the open – or almost. In May, an unsigned article was published in the business magazine, *Fortune*, entitled 'The Hidden Struggle for the H-Bomb: The Story of Dr Oppenheimer's Persistent Campaign to Reverse US Military Strategy.'

The article recounted the events of the last four years in which the military establishment was pitted against 'a highly influential group of American scientists' who were determined to discredit the Strategic Air Command and whose 'prime mover' was Oppenheimer.

As an illustration of Oppenheimer's influence, the article picked on the 'change of atmosphere' in the Vista study group after consulting with Oppenheimer. His draft of Chapter Five had 'produced an explosion in the Air Force' because among other things it has contained a 'veiled suggestion that Air Force doctrine was based on the slaughter of civilians' and suggested that a substantial part of the atomic stockpile 'should be diverted from Strategic Air Command'.

In conclusion, the article raised the 'serious question of the propriety of scientists trying to settle such grave national issues alone, in as much as they bear no responsibility for the successful execution of war plans'.

This article immediately prompted discussion among members of McCarthy's Senate Investigations Subcommittee, and Lewis Strauss got wind of their deliberations and immediately went to see Hoover. According to Hoover's account of the meeting in an FBI memorandum,

while, he, the Admiral, felt that inquiry into Oppenheimer's activities might be well worth while, he hoped it would not be done prematurely or by a group that did not thoroughly prepare itself for the investigation. I told Admiral Strauss that I certainly shared his views as to this and outlined to him briefly the visit which Senator McCarthy had made to my office concerning the contemplated investigation of Dr Oppenheimer. I told Admiral Strauss that I had advised Senator McCarthy that I felt that he should see that there was a great deal of staff work done before embarking upon any investigation of Oppenheimer. . . . I stated (to McCarthy) I felt this was not a case which should be prematurely gone into solely for the purpose of headlines. Admiral Strauss said he shared those views completely. . . .

McCarthy had decided to heed Hoover's advice and on receiving what one

OPPOSITE *The 1952 test of 'Mike' the American thermo-nuclear device. Its yield, five hundred times greater than the Hiroshima bomb, far outstripped expectations and so unnerved the director of Los Alamos that he considered keeping results of the test secret*

*J. Edgar Hoover, Director of the FBI. The reports made by his Bureau, recently released under the Freedom of Information Act, underline the level of surveillance used on Oppenheimer*

member of his committee described as 'some pretty high assurances that it would not be neglected', he decided not to pursue the Oppenheimer case, at least for the time being. But both Hoover and Strauss knew that it would only be a matter of time before McCarthy would take matters into his own hands.

Perhaps Strauss hoped that when Oppenheimer's contract with the AEC came up for renewal at the end of June, it would be allowed to lapse and the Oppenheimer problem would fade with it. However, the end of June also marked the end of Gordon Dean's term as Chairman of the AEC and one of his last acts as Chairman was to extend Oppenheimer's contract as consultant for another year. He did this without any consultation with his successor, Admiral Lewis Strauss.

On taking over, however, Strauss acted with great speed. On his first working day in office, 7 July, Strauss arranged for the removal of whatever classified documents still remained in Oppenheimer's files. Strauss's own explanation, years later, was that there was a twenty-four hour guard to protect Oppenheimer's documents, and that he had moved the documents to another AEC building within the Princeton area both as an economy measure and a way of improving security. It was an ingenious explanation but one which, given the background tone of conversations between Strauss and Hoover, can be dismissed.

The fact that Strauss was out to get rid of Oppenheimer is confirmed by an FBI report of a conversation between Strauss and liaison man Bates.

Strauss stated ... that he was still extremely concerned about Oppenheimer's influence in the atomic energy program; and was watching the matter closely and hoped to be able in the future to terminate all AEC dealings with Oppenheimer.

But Oppenheimer knew how to fight back. Over the years he had fostered special relationships with certain influential journalists such as the Alsop brothers and James 'Scottie' Reston of the *New York Times* and with influential specialist journals like *Foreign Affairs*. Over the next few months, Oppenheimer was to use all these in his fight back against his opponents. The first was an article he himself wrote for *Foreign Affairs* in July.

It was in this article that Oppenheimer likened the two great Powers, Russia and America, to 'two scorpions in a bottle, each capable of killing the other, but only at the risk of its own life.' In it he also provoked the Air Force by telling how 'a high ranking officer in the Air Defense Command' had said 'that it was not really our policy' to attempt to protect American civilians against atomic attack, 'for that is so big a job that it would interfere with our retaliatory capabilities'. Oppenheimer then continued 'Such follies can occur only when even the men who know the facts can find no one to talk to about them, when the facts are too secret for discussion, and thus, for thought.'

A response to the piece appeared in the August edition of *Fortune* and the identity of their mystery author was revealed – it was the editor himself, Charles Murphy, an Air Force reservist who had recently spent some time with some of the highest-ranking officers in the service. The response was critical of almost every aspect of Oppenheimer's thinking and commented that the 'fatal flaw' in his ideas was that they failed 'to allow for the terrible consequences that could ensue if the Kremlin leaders declined to act reasonably.'

In his *Foreign Affairs* article, Oppenheimer had expressed the view that the Soviet Union were about 'four years behind us'. A month later, in early August, the Russians tested their first deliverable thermonuclear weapon. It was not until the following February that the Americans were to test Bravo, their first deliverable weapon. In that terrible race which Oppenheimer had predicted and had tried at various stages and in various ways to halt, the Russians now had an advantage – they were not four years behind but six months ahead. Ironically, the scientist who had directed their project and had therefore done more than any other to give them that advantage and the strength to allow the Kremlin to pursue its particular repressive vision of the Communist State was the physicist and latter-day dissident, Andrei Sakharov.


While Oppenheimer spent the summer months lecturing in South America, William Borden spent them fretting over a final analysis of his case against the physicist. He had left his job with the Joint Committee and was about to join Westinghouse but was determined, before going, to put all his thoughts into a letter to the FBI director, J. Edgar Hoover.

On Saturday night, 7 November, Borden went to the main post office in Pittsburgh and mailed two copies of his letter, one to Hoover and the other to the Joint Committee on Atomic Energy. To ensure that his letters, which contained his grave charges against Oppenheimer in detail, did not go astray, both were sent registered mail, return receipt requested.


That November, Oppenheimer went to London to deliver the BBC's Reith Lectures – an assignment which he counted as one of the most important in his life. He had picked as his theme 'to elucidate what there is new in atomic physics that is relevant, helpful and inspiriting for men to know'.

The lectures were a great success, though one critic's comments bring to mind the frequent observation made about Oppenheimer that some personal magnetism gave even the most ordinary exchange, the most threadbare platitude, an extraordinary and original quality.

'His glittering rhetoric held his listeners in a web of absorption that was often less attentive than trance-like', commented the critic, while another said, 'It is incantation not exposition.'

Certainly, reading the text of those lectures now, much of it seems full of rhetoric and impressive generalisations which seem neither prescient nor very original. However, in one of the lectures he expresses very clearly his political and philosophical view of 'communism'.

It is a cruel and humourless sort of pun that so powerful a present form of modern tyranny should call itself by the very name of a belief in community, by a word 'communism' which in other times evoked memories of villages and village inns and of artisans concerting their skills, and of men of learning content with anonymity.

But perhaps only a malignant end can follow the systematic belief that all communities are one community; that all truth is one truth; that all experience is compatible with all other; that total knowledge is possible; that all that is potential can exist as actual.

This is not man's fate; this is not his path; to force him on it makes him resemble not that divine image of the all-knowing and all-powerful but the helpless, iron-bound prisoner of a dying world.

*Kenneth Nichols, Groves' wartime aide who was appointed General Manager of the AEC in late 1953 and became deeply involved in preparing the case against Oppenheimer. So thorough was Nichols' preparation that there were those who believed him to have a personal grudge against Oppenheimer*

J. ROBERT OPPENHEIMER

Whatever his hopes for communism had been fifteen years earlier, there is little doubt that in these words he was expressing the strongest rejection of a dogma which sought to limit what he described as 'the open society, the unrestricted access to knowledge, the unplanned and uninhibited association of men for its furtherance. . . .'

When the lectures were over, Oppenheimer and Kitty went on to visit friends in Europe and, on the evening of 7 December 1953, they left the elegant Hotel George V for Montmartre, for a dinner appointment with Haakon Chevalier and his new wife Carol at their flat.

It was, according to Chevalier's later recollections, a happy reunion, with a salad from a salad bowl which was a present to the newly married couple from the Oppenheimers, and champagne and toasts over the dessert with Robert and Kitty writing their names on the champagne cork afterwards. That night, however, as he was leaving the apartment, Oppenheimer seemed to Chevalier uneasy, with considerable misgivings about his return to the US. 'I certainly don't look forward to the next few months,' Chevalier recalled him saying.

That visit, the last time Oppenheimer and Chevalier were to see each other, had been made under continuous FBI scrutiny. When the reports of the meeting got back to Washington, it was seen, at least by some, as yet another example of Oppenheimer's erratic behaviour.

Kenneth Nichols, the newly-appointed General Manager of the AEC said:

You know just before going to Europe, Oppie had gone out to Los Alamos. He hadn't been out there for over a year but he went and got a thorough briefing on all that was going on, then took off for Europe and made contact with Chevalier. I thought it was either arrogance or darned poor judgement, but one of our Commissioners thought it was more than that, that it was disloyalty to a trust.

# CHAPTER 16  **INDICTED**

The letter William Borden sent to FBI director Hoover was a remarkable document, thoroughly researched and taking a hard, not to say extreme, line in interpreting the fruits of that research. The letter was organised into four main sections:

1 Oppenheimer's pre-war activities and associations, with evidence indicating that:
   a. He had contributed substantial monthly sums to the Communist Party;
   b. His ties with Communism had survived the Nazi-Soviet Pact and the Soviet attack on Finland;
   c. His wife and younger brother were Communists;
   d. He had no close friends except Communists;
   e. He had at least one Communist mistress [a reference to Jean Tatlock];
   f. He belonged only to Communist organisations apart from professional affiliations;
   g. The people whom he recruited into the early wartime Berkeley project were exclusively Communists;
   h. He had been instrumental in securing recruits for the Communist Party; and
   i. He was in frequent contact with Soviet espionage agents.

2 The circumstances of his 1942 entry into government service, with evidence indicating that:
   a. In May 1942, he either stopped contributing funds to the Communist Party or else made his contributions through a new channel not yet discovered;
   b. In April 1942, his name was formally submitted for security clearance;
   c. He himself was aware at the time that his name had been so submitted; and
   d. He thereafter repeatedly gave false information to General Groves, the Manhattan District, and the FBI concerning the 1939–April 1942 period.

3 His conduct during the war, with evidence indicating that:
   a. He was responsible for employing a number of Communists, some of them non-technical, at wartime Los Alamos;
   b. He selected one such individual to write the official Los Alamos history [a reference to an ex-student, David Hawkins];
   c. He was a vigorous supporter of the H-Bomb program until August 6, 1945 [Hiroshima], on which day he personally urged each senior individual working in this field to desist; and
   d. He was an enthusiastic sponsor of the A-Bomb program until the war ended,

when he immediately and outspokenly advocated that the Los Alamos laboratory be disbanded.

4 His conduct following the war especially regarding the H-Bomb, with evidence that:
   a. He was remarkably instrumental in influencing the military authorities and the Atomic Energy Commission essentially to suspend H-Bomb development from mid-1946 through January 31, 1950;
   b. He has worked tirelessly, from January 31, 1950 [the date of Truman's announcement of an all out program on the H-Bomb], onward, to retard the United States H-Bomb program;
   c. He has used his potent influence against every post-war effort to expend capacity for producing A-Bomb material;
   d. He has used his potent influence against every post-war effort directed at obtaining larger supplies of uranium raw material; and
   e. He has used his potent influence against every major post-war effort toward atomic power development, including the nuclear-powered submarine and aircraft programs as well as industrial power projects.

It was a powerful case, not so much a presentation of new facts to show his guilt as a convincing re-interpretation of well-known incidents in Oppenheimer's life, to conform to the overview of Oppenheimer as a Soviet agent. In his conclusions, Borden expressed his overview thus:

1 Between 1939 and 1942, more probably than not, J. Robert Oppenheimer was a sufficiently hardened Communist that he either volunteered espionage information to the Soviets, or complied with a request for such information. (This includes the possibility that when he singled out the weapons aspect of atomic development as his personal specialty, he was acting under Soviet instructions.)
2 More probably than not, he has since been functioning as an espionage agent; and
3 More probably than not, he has since acted under a Soviet directive in influencing United States military, atomic energy, intelligence and diplomatic policy.
   It is to be noted that these conclusions correlate with information furnished by Klaus Fuchs, indicating that the Soviets had acquired an agent in Berkeley who informed them about electromagnetic separation research during 1942 or earlier.

The same day that Borden posted his letter to Hoover, Herbert Brownell the Attorney General had attacked the previous Truman regime for promoting a suspected Russian spy back in 1946. Now even Eisenhower felt threatened by the activities of McCarthy and the other anti-Communist witch-hunting groups that had sprung up, and in this political climate, these charges against Oppenheimer were bound to cause a sensation.

First Hoover and Brownell went to forewarn the President of the charges in Borden's letter, then the FBI spent the next three weeks substantiating the charges. Their inch-thick report, along with the Borden letter, was despatched to the White House at the end of November.

At a meeting in the Oval Office late in the afternoon of 3 December, the President put in motion a chain of events which were to lead to what effectively

*On 3 December 1953, after receiving a full report from the FBI on Borden's charges against Oppenheimer, Eisenhower, pictured here with Hoover, ordered a 'blank wall' to be placed between Oppenheimer and any further access to secret information until his case could be considered by a Personnel Security Board*

*Harold Green in 1978, outside the Watergate Building which houses the offices of his law firm*

was a trial for treason. After consulting with Strauss, Eisenhower ordered a 'blank wall' placed between Oppenheimer and any further access to secret information until his case had been properly investigated.

The following week, the AEC Commissioners agreed 'unanimously to institute the regular procedures of the Commission to determine the veracity or falsity of the charges'. These 'regular procedures' were the Personnel Security Boards appointed by the General Manager to inquire into an employee's suitability for one of the various grades of security clearance. Hundreds of these Boards were held by the AEC all over the country every year, and normally they were little more than a formality involving an hour or two's examination of the subject by the four-man Board. Only very exceptionally were either parties represented by counsel and, when they were, the normal rules of evidence which controlled the activities in a court of law did not apply. This was to be of crucial importance for Oppenheimer.

As the first step in the procedure of setting up the Board, the charges against Oppenheimer had to be properly framed – a task normally performed by the AEC's General Counsel. However, the present incumbent, William Mitchell, had only recently been appointed so the task was handed to a young lawyer working in his office, Harold P. Green. Green was given his brief late in the evening on Friday, 11 December.

I was told that I had to have the charges drafted in time for the Commission to see it on Monday morning [Green said]. As I recall, I came in about 4 o'clock on the Saturday morning to the AEC's offices and the first thing I did was to go systematically through all the files and I was told that the General Manager's personal secretary would be available over the weekend when I needed her.

What Green had not expected was that the General Manager himself would come into the office. However, right from the start, Kenneth Nichols was to be deeply involved in mounting the case against Oppenheimer.

It wasn't very much past seven o'clock when my phone started ringing [Green recalls] and Nichols at the other end said, 'C'mon down, I want to talk to you', which he did five or six times during the day, which was a damned nuisance because every time he called me down, I had to take all these files and lock them in the office safe. Then when I got back, I had to bring them all out again – it was quite something. Anyhow, when I got down to his office, there he was, the classic military officer, like a bantam game cock, tense, intense. 'Have you seen that yet?' he would ask, or 'At last I've got that bastard.' That kind of thing firing me up to perform great deeds. I never liked him much and I could not help being conscious of the fact that here is the guy who was going to be deciding the case and I already know how he's going to decide it. You see under the Commission's rules he had the final decision of authority.

So why was Nichols seemingly so anxious to make the charges against Oppenheimer stick? Had he during those years with Groves on the Manhattan Project been a victim of Oppenheimer's sharp tongue or had he been appalled by what he had seen of Oppenheimer's attitudes after the war? Nichols himself maintains that any suggestion that he had any kind of personal grudge against Oppenheimer 'is completely wrong, because my contacts with Oppie were always most pleasant. I had no trouble with him and I always enjoyed working with him.' As to the implications in Green's comments that he was trying to ensure that the charges against Oppenheimer were as strong as possible, Nichols again demurs. 'My own feeling on this was that Oppie had a better than four to one chance of being cleared. That was why we tried so damned hard to keep the hearings secret – because we thought he would be cleared.'

Not all the evidence, from the FBI files and elsewhere, supports this view, however. Perhaps the view of Nichols as the 'ultimate professional' is one way of resolving the dichotomy between his professed personal warmth towards Oppenheimer and his zeal in pursuing the charges against him, but over the ensuing months Nichols was to play an important part in the events leading to the hearings.

As Green worked on alone through that December weekend, he was shocked by much of what he read in the files.

I have rarely seen a case in which there was so much devastating derogatory information about the individual, but on the other hand, I kept on thinking to myself, 'How can we be so stupid, after all these years, to do this to this kind of man.' Certainly I felt that I wouldn't have initiated these proceedings particularly as so much of the derogatory information was so old – except that is for the H-Bomb stuff – and that it was like locking the barn door after the horse is gone.

This 'H-Bomb stuff' was to provide the substance for one of the most important moments in the whole Oppenheimer case. On Sunday, 13 December, Harold Green finished his work on framing the charges. It was earlier than he expected and he had two hours to fill before he was due to meet the General Counsel, William Mitchell, to go over them. Sitting alone in the empty AEC headquarters, Green's mind roamed over the question of Oppenheimer's attitude to the H–Bomb. He had been told when he started work that he could not include these in the charges as it would appear that Oppenheimer was being tried for his policy opinions. However, it occurred to Green that perhaps it would be possible to frame the H–Bomb charges in such a way as to provide a test of Oppenheimer's veracity – his truthfulness. So with nothing better to do, Green decided to try out a draft in this vein. When Mitchell arrived for their meeting that afternoon, he reviewed and accepted the charges in full, including those Green had drafted on the H–Bomb. Thus Oppenheimer was to be faced with allegations about his attitude to the H–Bomb which were to 'raise questions as to your veracity, conduct and loyalty'.

At three p.m. on 21 December, just a few days after his return from Europe, Oppenheimer met with Lewis Strauss and Kenneth Nichols in Strauss's office. Oppenheimer had not been told the reason of the meeting, so it began with an exchange of pleasantries. After a while, however, Strauss cut these short and told Oppenheimer that a review of his file, together with the information from Borden's letter had cast doubt upon his security clearance and that the AEC had drafted a letter of charges, which explained why his clearance was in question. According to the FBI report on the meeting,

Strauss let Oppenheimer read the statement of charges prepared by the AEC. Oppenheimer then commented that some of the charges were incorrectly stated; some he, Oppenheimer, could deny; while others were correct. According to General Manager Nichols the meeting was amiable; Oppenheimer did not seem greatly surprised, but did not indicate he was previously aware of the AEC contemplated action.

It would seem that the FBI had received their account of the meeting from Nichols through a new character on the scene, Liaison Supervisor Charles Bates. Years later, Bates was to become well known for his conduct of the Patti Hearst case, but for the next few months he was to provide a firm link directly between FBI chief Hoover and Lewis Strauss.

Even though Oppenheimer had now seen the list of charges, Nichols still did not sign the letter.

We hoped at this stage that Oppie would take the option of resigning, but we were absolutely determined that we weren't going to suggest it in case we were accused of forcing him out by listing these charges. Anyway, eventually he said, 'Would resignation eliminate all that?' I answered, 'Yes it would, because we have no basis for any hearing if you're not an employee on the government payroll. But it's up to you if you want to do that.'

Strauss gave Oppenheimer a day to make up his mind whether he would resign or face a hearing and so the fateful meeting came to an end. Oppenheimer left, saying he was going to see attorney Herbert Marks, and was given the use of Strauss's Cadillac to make the visit. On the way he was tailed by FBI agent Charles Lyons, who at four forty-five p.m. called to say that Oppenheimer was at that moment 'closeted with Volpe' – Joe Volpe, the former General Counsel to the AEC. But it seems that the surveillance might not have ended here because Harold Green recalls that shortly afterwards a report arrived on his desk describing Oppenheimer's visit to Volpe.

Then there was a detailed account of what transpired in his conversation with Volpe [says Green]. How they got to know about it, I don't know, presumably by some form of bugging, but whether they had something planted in anticipation that he would go there or whether they had equipment which enabled them to bug it instantaneously or what I don't know. Anyway, then there was a similar thing when he left Volpe's office and went to Herb Marks' office – there was a similar account of that conversation.

If what Harold Green alleges is true, then the FBI and the officials of the AEC were breaking one of the great codes of legal practice, the bond of privacy between counsel and client. Certainly, throughout the case, the AEC, through the FBI, were always very well informed of Oppenheimer's intentions and indeed on one occasion Strauss was reported to have commented to Liaison Agent Bates 'that the Bureau's [the FBI] technical coverage on Oppenheimer at Princeton [his home] had been most helpful to the AEC in that they were *aware beforehand of the moves he was contemplating*'.

Oppenheimer did not spend long with either Volpe or Marks and these visits did not provide him with the final answer to the decision facing him – whether to resign or whether to face the charges. Indeed Oppenheimer delayed contacting the AEC for a day longer while he wrestled with the options. If he did not face these hearings, what chance was there that McCarthy might pick him as a target anyway? If he resigned, would that be the end of the matter or would his resignation and the charges be leaked to the press, with his resignation becoming, in effect, an admission of guilt?

In the end, Oppenheimer, along with Kitty, took the train down from Princeton to Washington on the evening of 22 December and at nine o'clock the following morning went to Strauss's office where he told Nichols and Strauss in person that he would submit to a hearing.

Later that day, the Oppenheimers returned to Princeton, hoping to enjoy the enforced lull of Christmas and the New Year, but on Christmas Eve they received a visit from two AEC representatives. They were carrying a letter which stated peremptorily that Oppenheimer was 'hereby directed to deliver' all the remaining AEC documents in his possession. Until the documents were catalogued by his secretary and then removed, Oppenheimer was refused access to his own vaults.

Immediately after the New Year, Oppenheimer went in search of a counsel to help him. He very much relied on Herbert Marks for advice on this question. Marks's own previous involvement with the AEC as one of its General Counsels prevented him from accepting this role. Nevertheless, he did take a strong lead in shaping the case and indeed in the early weeks of January created a certain amount of friction in the Oppenheimer camp. Marks felt very strongly that Oppenheimer should be represented by someone who was as distinguished in the legal field as his client was in the scientific, but Joseph Volpe who was also being consulted by Oppenheimer felt that above all the counsel must be a thoroughly skilled trial lawyer – the American equivalent of a barrister. Kitty sided with Volpe and indeed one of their conversations was noted by the FBI who on 5 January stated that 'Volpe expressed his dislike of Marks. He feels that Marks is insisting upon handling the case or running it, to a point where his judgement seems more influenced by that end than other factors.'

Nevertheless, it was Marks's view that held sway and he went with Oppenheimer to consult with various eminent legal figures before ending up in the offices of Paul, Weiss, Rifkind, Wharton and Garrison in Madison Avenue. Yet again, the content of the discussions in those offices was known in detail to the FBI who reported that, on 12 January,

fourteen members of the firm had a meeting, at which it was agreed that the firm ought to and would accept Dr Oppenheimer's case if he so desired. Two conditions were discussed: one relating to the fact that some of the firm members were currently under attack; the second was the extent to which former Judge Rifkind would participate.

In the end it was decided that the case would be taken by Lloyd Garrison and that the firm would forgo any fees for their work. It was a generous act and a bold one, as all kinds of pressures could be brought to bear on anyone seen to be supporting 'Left Wing' causes, but it was very much in the firm's liberal tradition. Garrison himself had been a pioneering activist in government labour relations work, a leader in the American Civil Liberties Union, and had earned a reputation for unimpeachable integrity and a devotion to public causes. He was tall and Lincolnesque in appearance, gentle in manner, and devoted what spare time he had to bird-watching and reading philosophy and Greek literature. However, much to Volpe's chagrin, he had very little courtroom experience, but at this stage, this did not really matter as Garrison was looking for a leading counsel actually to present the case.

There was a great deal of work to be done, and so Garrison, Marks and Oppenheimer met for discussions. After Garrison had read the AEC's letter of charges, Oppenheimer said to him, 'It looks pretty bad, doesn't it?' Garrison agreed that it did.

From the beginning he had a quality of desperation about him – in his appearance and in his manners [Garrison recalls]. I think we all felt oppressed by the atmosphere of the time but Oppenheimer particularly so . . . I found him enigmatic, fascinating of course, with those most beautiful blue eyes, but he was hard to be intimate with. We saw so much of each other that it was always a little surprising to me that we didn't have any of that feeling of comradeship you might have expected from sharing an ordeal of this sort. Cold is too strong a word, he wasn't cold but he kept his distance.

Right from the start, however, there was agreement that they should take the

*Lloyd Garrison, Oppenheimer's defending lawyer. A one-time Dean of the Law School at the University of Wisconsin, he had a reputation as a pioneering activist in Labour Relations work. At the time he was chosen his lack of trial experience was not considered particularly important*

J. ROBERT OPPENHEIMER

'whole man' approach to mounting their case.

We felt there was no way of arriving at a final conclusion about whether this fellow should be entrusted with atomic secrets or not other than the combined judgement of men of the highest integrity and reputation of what they felt about him. This seemed to us much more conclusive than the dredging up of all these little incidents from his past which in the extraordinary atmosphere of the time were magnified in importance, you know, a hundred fold.

So Garrison and his team began to marshal as much support for Oppenheimer as they could. Their every move was followed by the FBI and then relayed to an increasingly nervous Lewis Strauss. Their report to him for the last week in January showed that Oppenheimer himself had managed to see Groves, who looked like supporting him, and Ed Condon, and a number of scientists at a Conference on High Energy Physics held at Rochester, New York.

Among the scientists Oppenheimer conferred with there was Edward Teller.

When he saw me, he asked me, 'I suppose, I hope, that you don't think that anything I did has sinister implications?' I said I did not think that – after all, the word 'sinister' was pretty harsh. Then he asked if I would speak to his lawyer, and I said I would.

I went and saw Mr Garrison who trotted up something of a defence for Oppenheimer. I forget what the defence was, but since it consisted of things that I already knew, it left me entirely unimpressed. I did not make a point of it, but as far as I was concerned it was irrelevant. It did not change my mind.

Teller, it seems, was set against Oppenheimer. In the same week Lloyd Garrison himself had made contact with Allen Dulles of the CIA and Herb Marks had met with Robert Bacher.

During the same period, 'Scottie' Reston of the *New York Times* had tried to contact Oppenheimer but, according to the FBI, Garrison had initially advised that it would be best not to talk to him. However, by the end of the month, the FBI knew that Garrison and Reston had made contact and that Reston had been told all about the AEC charges. Furthermore, they reported to Strauss that 'he intended to print a story, but he did not wish to do so until he had discussed the matter with Oppenheimer'.

Oppenheimer's legal collaborators were not the only group taking action on his behalf. Early in January, Isidor Rabi, who had succeeded Oppenheimer as Chairman of the GAC, had gone to see Strauss and had suggested the appointment of a Board to hear Oppenheimer's case which, according to the FBI report, Rabi hoped 'would whitewash Oppenheimer'. Strauss had replied that he did not intend to be pressured into any action of this kind, but that was not the end of the matter. On 26 January, Rabi again went to see Strauss, this time with a draft of a letter being prepared to Strauss. It stated that a resolution had been passed by the GAC that all of its members as individuals were willing to testify on Oppenheimer's behalf. Strauss told Rabi he considered this blackmail and that he could not be swayed by such action.

Strauss must have felt very much as if he was sitting on a volcano. One of the most eminent of newspaper columnists could publish an article about the charges at any time, and the scientific community was aligning itself against him. He knew also that McCarthy was waiting in the wings and that if he took over the case against Oppenheimer it would be difficult to know where it might end. Strauss's own career might well be jeopardised.

So Strauss decided to use every means at his disposal to make his case against Oppenheimer stick. He pushed the FBI as hard as he could for the most complete surveillance of Oppenheimer possible. Indeed, not only were his movements being monitored around the clock, but it appears from detailed reports of conversations at dinner parties in other people's houses, that the FBI were bugging him almost everywhere he went. On 2 February an addendum to an FBI report stated,

We do feel that Strauss should be again cautioned concerning the use of the information we furnish him which was obtained from the technical surveillance because if information should leak from AEC that the Bureau has such coverage, Oppenheimer and his attorneys will undoubtedly use it for propaganda purposes.

In the margins of the report are two handwritten comments. One says, 'I concur. H.' The other, 'Strauss so advised 2-4-54 CMB'. But Oppenheimer was to remain under surveillance nevertheless.

The AEC also had to find a counsel to present the material to the Security Board and Strauss took the advice of the Attorney General's office. They came up with one of the most robust Washington trial lawyers, Roger Robb. Robb had a reputation for obtaining 'an unusually high percentage of convictions'. He had acted as attorney for a journalist called Fulton Lewis Jr who was very much attached to the McCarthyist groups, but he had also successfully defended the Communist leader, Earl Browder. When he took on the case he had no prior knowledge and no strong commitment to it, so his first task was to start reading through the enormous quantity of material that had been marshalled. His lack of commitment disappeared rapidly.

There were so many things in those files that didn't add up [Robb explains] unless you applied a theory to them which was that Oppenheimer was a Communist and a Russian sympathiser, and that's the only way I could add it up. . . .

It was inconceivable to me, having the general knowledge of this kind of case that I did, that the way the Communist Party operated and having this man in their grasp today, and having this man join this top-secret project tomorrow, they'd just drop him like a hot cake, but they didn't do it. I'm sure they didn't, it just doesn't make sense.

Robb obtained his 'Q' clearance, which he needed to read the Oppenheimer files, almost immediately. He spent the best part of the next two months closeted in his office with his assistant, Art Rolander, chain-smoking Havana cigars and carefully sifting and tagging the material. He did so much reading that some way through his preparation he had to go to the optician's for new glasses.

After a while, Robb felt the time was right to go and interview some of the

*Roger Robb, the counsel chosen by the AEC to present the material to the Security Board. Unlike Garrison he had a reputation as a robust trial lawyer who obtained 'an unusually high percentage of convictions'*

other personalities in the case. He flew out to the West Coast where he met Teller, 'one of the finest gentlemen I ever knew', and they talked in particular about Oppenheimer's role on the development of the H-Bomb programme. 'Talked' is perhaps a misnomer, because Teller had that morning just been to the dentist and initially was able only to communicate by signs and jottings on his office blackboard. Then Robb met one or two other scientists on the West Coast before returning, via some discouraging meetings with the staff at Los Alamos, to the East Coast and more detailed consideration of the evidence.

Having begun to pull all these strings together [recalls Robb], I had been told that you can't get anywhere cross-examining Oppenheimer, he's too smart. He's too fast and he's too slippery. So I said, 'Maybe so, but then he's not been cross-examined by me before.' Anyway, I sat down and planned my cross-examination most carefully, the sequences to it and the references to the FBI reports and so on, and my theory was that if I could shake Oppenheimer at the beginning, he would be apt to be more communicative thereafter.

As I was going through, I kept reading about the interviews he had with Pash and with Lansdale, back in 1943, about the Chevalier incident – the report said they were recorded and I said 'Where are those recordings?' and I was told they were probably over at the FBI. So I said, 'Well, let's get them, I think they ought to be found before they end up at the bottom of a bin!'

The tapes of those ten-year-old interviews were eventually unearthed and Robb was now able to compare in detail the recordings of Oppenheimer's description of the 'Chevalier incident' given to Pash and Lansdale all those years ago with his more recent description. Oppenheimer was to have no knowledge of the existence of those tapes until he was confronted with them at the hearing.


While Roger Robb was immersing himself in the Oppenheimer files, Lloyd Garrison had run up against a serious problem. In mid-January, he had applied for 'Q' clearance as Robb had done, but while the AEC was prepared to clear Garrison, they were not prepared to clear Marks and a junior colleague of Garrison's, Sam Silverman, whose clearance was also requested. Oppenheimer's legal advisers met and decided that unless all of them were cleared then none of them should be. Therefore they faced the possibility of the Board being privy to all sorts of information which they did not know about, but nevertheless they persisted in their stance.

We thought that if we had clearance [Garrison has written], the Personnel Security Board might more readily be drawn into an examination of the technical pros and cons of proceeding with H-Bomb development and with other aspects of defense related to it. They could thereby lose the main point, which is that if Dr Oppenheimer's motives were honorable, his technical recommendations were irrelevant.

They hoped the Commission would co-operate – with the declassification of documents and such like – but as time went by, they became more and more fearful that secret matters could be raised unexpectedly and they would be forced to leave Oppenheimer 'unrepresented and alone' in the Hearing Room. Accordingly a fortnight or so before the hearing, Garrison changed his mind and did write asking for clearance for himself. It was never to arrive.

In addition, when Garrison and Marks asked for as many relevant documents as possible, they were told over the telephone by Kenneth Nichols that with two exceptions, every single one of their requests was to be denied.

As the hearing approached, it seemed to be developing into a lopsided contest between the Commission's fully-documented version of the case and Oppenheimer's ability to recall, in detail, events that had occurred twelve or more years previously.

In spite of their enormous potential advantage, the Commission were taking no chances in establishing their case against Oppenheimer. Throughout February and March, the FBI were following up every possible lead they could, which might produce hard information on Oppenheimer's pro-Communist, pro-Russian activities. They interviewed a security guard at Los Alamos who had been Oppenheimer's chauffeur. This revealed very little of value. They interviewed another fairly lowly employee at Los Alamos, Henry Nieber, who had emptied Oppenheimer's trash can, and remembered finding amongst the rubbish copies of the *Daily Worker* and the *New Masses*.

They spent an enormous amount of time and effort trying finally to prove the testimony of the 'consultant', Paul Crouch, who said that he had been present at a Communist meeting at 10 Kenilworth Court in July or August 1941, which Oppenheimer had also attended. They took him on drives around the Berkeley hills, trying to identify the house, and tried to confirm his description of the layout of the apartment where the meeting took place, but in spite of all these efforts, Crouch's reputation as a paid informer had to be taken into account.

I read all of Crouch's statements very carefully [Robb recalls], and I concluded that if I call him and he testifies, and then the Board should find against Oppenheimer, then the Communists and the Oppenheimer people are going to say Oppenheimer was condemned at the testimony of Paul Crouch, so why not keep him out of it entirely?

Though the FBI's investigations were never to be introduced into the record as evidence, they were nevertheless sitting in the files that the Board was to spend a week perusing in detail in the company of the AEC counsel Roger Robb.

Oppenheimer and his advisers were also doing their best to check out incidents as Oppenheimer recalled them. They too were devoting some time to Paul Crouch's claims about the meeting in the summer of 1941 and Oppenheimer set out to prove that he was in New Mexico at the ranch at the time. Hans Bethe was used as one of the witnesses. He remembered that it was his first visit to the ranch and how Oppenheimer had been kicked by a horse. He was also able to pinpoint the date of that visit. Another helper was Dorothy McKibbin who had run the reception office for Los Alamos in Santa Fe throughout the war. Still living in Santa Fe, she went around the town trying to root out old grocery bills, even records of visits to the dentist, to prove that the Oppenheimers had been there at that time. In the end because Crouch was not called, Oppenheimer's alibi was not tested, but the Board still had Crouch's deposition in front of them.

On 4 March, after two months' research and redrafting, Oppenheimer completed his written reply to Nichols' letter of charges and despatched it to the AEC. In tune with the 'whole man' approach his team had adopted, it was more an autobiography than a point-by-point rebuttal of the charges. 'The items of so-called derogatory information set forth in your letter,' he wrote, 'cannot be fairly understood except in the context of my life and my work'. Some short extracts will give some idea of its tone.

I was born in New York in 1904. My father had come to this country at the age of 17 from Germany. He was a successful businessman and quite active in community affairs. . . . I studied and read Sanskrit (in California in the early Thirties) . . . I read very widely, mostly classics, novels, plays and poetry. . . . Beginning in late 1936, my interests began to change. . . . I can discern in retrospect more than one reason for these changes. I had had a continuing smoldering fury about the treatment of Jews in Germany. I had relatives there . . .

This final version was bland, perhaps to a fault. Even the early drafts are carefully phrased but by the final draft Oppenheimer has eliminated anything but the safest material. Take for example his various versions of how Jean Tatlock introduced him to left-wing contacts. The following quote, in its entirety, represents his early draft for this section. Those sections enclosed in the square brackets were excised in the final draft sent to Nichols.

I should not give the impression that it was wholly because of Jean Tatlock that I made left wing friends, or felt sympathy for causes which hitherto would have seemed so remote from me, like the Loyalist cause in Spain, and the organisation of migratory workers [and in general virtues of trade unions]. I have mentioned some of the other contributing causes. [But Jean Tatlock opened the door, and I found many friends to welcome me.] I liked the new sense of companionship, and for the first time felt that I was a part of the life of my time and country. [I found too that my new sympathies – it would be wrong to call them interests because I was never that well informed despite my subscription to the *People's World* – were already shared in some measure by a good many of my students and older friends.]

It seems all the time Oppenheimer was wary of giving even the slightest opportunity for misrepresentation and in the end produced a document which, while providing an adequate summary of his remarkable career, did not really explain him or his motives.

The date fixed for the hearing was 12 April. Ever since early January, the

AEC had been involved in casting for their three-man Board. Hal Green was asked his advice by General Counsel, William Mitchell, and he suggested that they should simply recruit three members from the Chicago Board because they were 'very, very tough, very, very fair, with lots of experience'. However, he soon heard that the Commission was set on looking for a Board of standing equal to Oppenheimer's own.

'It was also perfectly clear to me from the conversations I'd had that they were really interested in more of a hanging jury,' says Green, 'one susceptible at least to subtle pressures, to bring in a verdict denying clearance.'

The first member to be chosen was the Chairman, Gordon Gray, a former Secretary of the Army and president of the University of North Carolina. There was no doubt about his distinction, but he seemed to be totally unaware of the venom lying just beneath the surface, and suggested as another possible member of the Board, David Lilienthal. Bearing in mind Lilienthal's close ties with Oppenheimer and the enemies he had made during his time with the Commission, it was quite clear to the Commission that they had a 'naïve' Chairman. Needless to say, Gray's suggestion was not followed up.

As the second member of the Board, Strauss finally settled on sixty-six-year-old Thomas Morgan, the one-time Chairman of the Sperry Corporation and a prominent Democrat. He was to distinguish himself by his almost total silence during the four weeks of the hearing. The choice of the third member of the Board presented particular problems because he had to be a scientist, and one who did not feel some strong professional allegiance to Oppenheimer.

J. ROBERT OPPENHEIMER

They had the idea of going to the Boards throughout the country to see who they could come up with [recalls Hal Green]. So all over the country, the AEC officers were given the assignment of taking out all the records of all the old cases, studying which scientist – usually there was a scientist on every Board – seeing which one was on the Board, then analysing the transcript to see what kind of questions he asked and then analysing their voting records. And the best they came up with was Ward Evans, a professor of chemistry at North Western University in Chicago. He was an arch-reactionary, a hard nosed, security zealot, who almost always voted in denying clearance.

*Dr Ward V. Evans, the scientist on the Personnel Security Board, a professor of chemistry at North Western University, Chicago. He had considerable experience of these Boards and was known as an arch-reactionary who almost always voted for denying clearance*

Oppenheimer did have the right to challenge the Board, so the casting had to be precise; the Commission must have been greatly relieved when he had no fault to find.

Not only were Oppenheimer and his team suffering from enormous disadvantages over security clearance, admittedly partly of their own making, but they were facing a Board which had been chosen as likely to produce a verdict against them. Before the hearing opened, another major disadvantage emerged.

If Oppenheimer was being tried in a court of law for treason, then he would have been protected by the rules of that court, and in particular by what some lawyers called the 'blank pad rule'. By this they mean that when judge and jury start a trial, they have in front of them what is in effect a blank pad on which no evidence has yet been written. Then in court, the only information that can be recorded on that 'pad' and used in deciding the case is that permitted by the judge in open court, under strict rules of evidence.

Some hearings not heard by court of law were also covered by this rule but not the AEC's Personnel Security Hearings. Indeed, as already pointed out, the Board in security hearings such as these would have already seen all the material in the investigative file whether that information was to be tested or not. However unfair this may seem, there was nothing unusual about it. What was unusual was the way in which the absence of those rules was exploited to the full by the AEC's counsel, Roger Robb. In the week before the hearings, he spent much of the time closeted with the three Board members going through with them the investigative files on the case. It was as if in a court of law the judge had met with the prosecuting counsel before the trial and then, when asked if the defence counsel would share the same privilege, refused him. This actually did happen: when Garrison asked if he too could spend some time with the Board, his request was refused.

# CHAPTER 17  OPPENHEIMER 'ON TRIAL'

The Atomic Energy Commission's Building T-3 was one of those depressing 'temporary' government buildings that has long since passed its intended life-span. Its Room 2022 was a standard Government Issue executive's office once occupied by the AEC's Director of Research but now prepared to act as miniature courtroom.

In the room there was a sort of 'U' shaped arrangement of tables [recalls Lloyd Garrison]. The Board sat across the bottom of the 'U' while Robb was at the left hand corner and I was at the lower right hand corner. The witness chair was at the open end space at the bottom, and the stenographer was at the right hand corner just in front of the Board in the hollow of the 'U', but that was about it. All very bare. Oh yes, and there was a sofa behind the witness stand where Robert sat when he was not on the witness stand.

It was in this bare utilitarian setting that Robert Oppenheimer would spend four weeks listening to the details of his life being dissected and painfully torn apart.

The morning of Monday, 12 April, was clear and bright, when just before

*The Atomic Energy Commission's Building T-3 in Washington where the month-long Oppenheimer hearing was held*

ten a.m. the various parties began to assemble in Room 2022. For Oppenheimer's party, things got off to a poor start.

We were discussing various things right up to the last minute, and that made us late [says Garrison]. And when we did arrive we made a pretty bedraggled kind of spectacle. Kitty had had the misfortune to fall down some stairs just before and she had her leg in a cast and was on crutches and her appearance didn't add much to the smoothness of things. The Board was pretty irritated with us anyway.

'The hearing will come to order.' With these words, Chairman Gordon Gray opened the proceeding, 'in the matter of J. Robert Oppenheimer.'

*Kitty and Robert Oppenheimer in 1948*

For nearly an hour, those in the Hearing Room heard nothing but the soft North Carolina voice of Gordon Gray as he read into the record the three thousand word AEC letter of charges and Oppenheimer's reply. Then he ventured some opening remarks and after stating that in his view 'this proceeding is an inquiry, and not in the nature of a trial' he then went on to state that the proceedings were to be 'regarded as strictly confidential'.

That very morning, Garrison and the rest of Oppenheimer's team had been discussing whether to make the charges against him public – indeed it was this discussion that had made them late. They were still in close touch with 'Scottie' Reston of the *New York Times*, who so far had published nothing about the hearings, in spite of what he had said to Garrison back in January. Now he was anxious lest the story break anyway and had been putting pressure on Garrison and Oppenheimer to allow him to publish his prepared pieces on the case. That lunch time, in spite of Gray's recent admonition on confidentiality, Garrison rang Reston and authorised him to go ahead with his story.

That afternoon, guided by Garrison, Oppenheimer talked about his career. Easily and confidently, he went into how he had formulated the Acheson-Lilienthal report on international control of atomic energy, how Strauss had hired him for the Institute of Advanced Study. Right up to the adjournment at five o'clock Oppenheimer acted as if he were presiding over a friendly meeting.

The next morning, the *Times* published Reston's story under the following headline:

DR OPPENHEIMER SUSPENDED BY A.E.C. IN SECURITY REVIEW; SCIENTIST DEFENDS RECORD; HEARINGS STARTED: ACCESS TO SECRET DATA DENIED NUCLEAR EXPERT – RED TIES ALLEGED.

*Gordon Gray, the Chairman of the Personnel Security Board. He had been Secretary of the Army and President of the University of North Carolina*

Accompanying this story was a very full account of episodes from Oppenheimer's career – quite obviously the piece had been prepared well in advance. It was picked up by agencies, newspapers, and radio stations right across America and elsewhere in the world as well. This was just what the AEC and Strauss had been fearing for months, because now they were as much a victim of a frightened Administration as Oppenheimer himself.

Trapped right in the middle of this storm was Gordon Gray, who found that the whole nature of the inquiry had been dramatically re-interpreted by the

*Mervin Kelly, President of the Bell Telephone Company and the first of the thirty-one distinguished pro-Oppenheimer witnesses*

outside world. When the Board recommenced at nine-thirty a.m., Gray was clearly irritated, particularly with Garrison who, he said, had failed to 'indicate to me in any way' that he had handed documents to Reston. This was a considerable setback for Garrison and his strategy, since his choice of witnesses, his unaggressive approach, had all been tuned to impress the urbane Gordon Gray, and yet here Gray was, on the second day of the hearing, truly annoyed at what Garrison had done.

Tempers calmed as Dr Mervin Kelly, President of the Bell Telephone Laboratory in New York and the first of thirty-one pro-Oppenheimer witnesses, was sworn in. He talked of his defence research work with Oppenheimer and of Oppenheimer's 'accuracy of thought and cleanness of expression'. When Robb began his cross-examination, Garrison and Oppenheimer saw him use the technique that they had been dreading. After discussing with Kelly whether the H-Bomb was on the agenda of a long-range planning committee Kelly had served on in 1950, he turned to Gray and said, 'Mr Chairman, I would like to read the witness something from the report which is classified.' For the next few minutes, Oppenheimer was to remain in the Hearing Room alone, unrepresented, his counsel dismissed from the room. Whatever the practical outcome of this incident, and in retrospect it appears to be quite small, the psychological impact, the demonstration of power Robb had, which stemmed from his superior knowledge and his privileged security position, must have been unnerving.

Later that second day, Oppenheimer resumed the stand – Kelly had been squeezed into his monologue for convenience – and continued to talk about his relationship with the US government. His address extended on into the third day, when he talked of his fondness for his brother Frank, and how his relationship with him was less intimate after Frank had married Jackie in 1936. It was Jackie who had interested Frank in politics and together they had joined the Communist Party. However, Oppenheimer observed that Frank had so many other interests – physics, music, art and so on – that 'he couldn't have been a very hard-working communist'. Indeed Oppenheimer went on for so long about his brother that Robb began to show signs of impatience. Then late in the morning, Garrison finished his leading and Robb took over with a cross-examination which was to last for twelve hours over three days.

From the start, Robb was laying the traps which might only bear fruit after hours of careful questioning. First he pinned Oppenheimer to an admission that his letter to Nichols answering the charges was 'the whole truth and nothing but the truth'.

Then he asked him why, during World War II, Oppenheimer had considered current (as distinct from past) Communist Party membership as incompatible with secret war work. Was it because party members were expected, if so ordered, to commit espionage? 'I was never told that,' replied Oppenheimer, but Robb persisted.

Q: Doctor, let me ask you a blunt question. Don't you know, and didn't you know certainly by 1943, that the Communist Party was an instrument or a vehicle of espionage in this country?

A: I was not clear about it.

Q: Didn't you suspect it?

A: No.

Q: Wasn't that the reason why you felt that membership in the party was inconsistent with the work on a secret war project?

A: I think I have stated the reason about right.

Q: I am asking you now, if your fear of espionage wasn't one of the reasons why you felt that association with the Communist Party was inconsistent with work on a secret war project?

A: ˙ Yes.

Q: Your answer is that it was?

A: Yes.

After this success in making Oppenheimer admit to a fear of espionage by those associated with the Communist Party, he was to follow up this particular line of questioning not immediately but half an hour later.

The subject at hand was Oppenheimer's letter to Colonel Lansdale in 1943, asking whether the newly drafted Rossi Lomanitz could not be assigned to the Radiation Laboratory in Berkeley.

Q: Of course you would not have written that letter if you had known Lomanitz was a Communist, would you?

A: No.

At the back of this pattern of questions was the knowledge of what Oppenheimer had said in those tape-recorded interviews with Pash and Lansdale back in 1943, recordings that were made before he wrote the letter about Lomanitz. In it he had said: 'I know for a fact, I know, I learned on my last visit to Berkeley, that both Lomanitz and Weinberg were members of the Communist Party.'

Carefully, over a period of time, Robb had led Oppenheimer straight into a trap and he was to do it twice more on that first morning. Each time, Oppenheimer contradicted the material in those ten-year-old interviews. Was he lying deliberately to the Board, or was he a victim of a shaky memory and carefully planned questioning?

Certainly it must have been a horrifying experience for him, as he faced a man who was rapidly showing himself to be a skilled attorney. How much does Robb really know? . . . What is he going to ask next? . . . That question seems harmless enough but what might he be getting at? . . . Is he leading me into a trap?

After the lunch recess, Robb turned to the most sensitive matter of all, the 'Chevalier incident'. Again the pattern was to be much the same – establish the current version of the 'incident' which Oppenheimer had recited on so many occasions and then juxtapose it with the very different and more detailed version on the tapes of the Pash interview. In his current version no mention was made of the way the information would be transmitted to the Russians, so Robb began here:

Q: Did Chevalier in that conversation say anything to you about the use of microfilm as a means of transmitting this information?

A: No.

Q: Did he say anything about the possibility that the information would be transmitted through a man at the Soviet consulate?

A: No, he did not.

Q: Did he tell you or indicate to you in anyway that he had talked to anyone but you about this matter?

A: No.

Q: Did you learn from anybody else or hear that Chevalier had approached anybody but you about this matter?

A: No.

The last negative was almost inaudible. Gradually during this part of the cross-examination Oppenheimer had visibly slumped in the witness chair. The gaps between question and answer had grown longer and longer. There was a feeling of impending revelation.

Q: Now let us go back to your interview with Colonel Pash. Did you tell Pash the truth about this thing?

A: No.

Q: You lied to him?

A: Yes.

The informal conversation of ten years ago, which even at the time Oppenheimer could only suspect to have been recorded, was now being inflated into a place where the scientist perjured himself.

Q: So that we may be clear, did you discuss with or disclose to Pash the identity of Chevalier?

A: No.

Q: Let us refer then, for the time being, to Chevalier as X.

A: All right.

Q: Did you tell Pash that X had approached three persons on the project?

A: I am not clear whether I said there were three X's or that X approached three people.

Q: Didn't you say that X had approached three people?

For the first time, Oppenheimer had no quick parry for this question, but after a long and painful pause gave his answer.

A: Probably.

Q: Why did you do that, Doctor?

A: Because I was an idiot.

Everyone in the hearing room seemed to realise that this was a turning point in the inquiry.

His statements to Pash were completely at odds with his testimony at the hearing [recalls Robb]. Oppenheimer was smart enough to know that that was a serious discrepancy, and I remember him sitting there with his hands between his knees, washing his hands between his knees, head bowed, white as a sheet. I felt sick.

On the side lines, Lloyd Garrison had been watching helplessly while his client struggled.

Until the end he never did stop to think 'How could I best put this'. Whether this was because he felt he was so right that he didn't need to pause or that he was contemptuously lording it over the other fellow by spitting the answer out immediately I don't know, but this endless cross-examination simply wore him down, bit by bit.

In spite of his misgivings, Robb still went on to make the final kill. He confronted him with section after section of the old recordings. Time after time he made him go back over the various details that made up what he had made Oppenheimer admit was a 'cock and bull' story.

Q: That wasn't true.
A: That is right. This whole thing was a pure fabrication except for the one name, Eltenton.

Then finally he administered the *coup de grâce*.

ROBB: Isn't it a fair statement today, Dr Oppenheimer, that according to your testimony now you told not one lie to Colonel Pash, but a whole fabrication and tissue of lies?
OPPENHEIMER: Right.

Even after this, Oppenheimer's ordeal that day was not yet over. He had to answer questions about his relationship with Jean Tatlock and in particular about his visit to her in June 1943 – his third year of marriage to Kitty. He was asked by Robb why he 'had' to see her. Oppenheimer replied that she 'was undergoing psychiatric treatment. She was extremely unhappy.'

ROBB: Did you find out why *she* had to see you?
OPPENHEIMER: Because she was still in love with me.

Then a little later.

ROBB: You spent the night with her, didn't you?
OPPENHEIMER: Yes.
ROBB: That is when you were working on a secret war project?
OPPENHEIMER: Yes.
ROBB: Did you think that consistent with good security?
OPPENHEIMER: It was as a matter of fact. Not a word – it was not good practice.

*Leslie Groves, then a businessman with Remington Rand, gave evidence on Oppenheimer's behalf during the hearing*

This blurred, defeated reply when earlier in the hearing he had answered the same line of questioning strongly and unrepentantly, showed how crushed Oppenheimer now was. Shortly after this exchange, the day came to an end.

I came home that night, after midnight – I'd been working – and my wife was still awake [says Robb] and I said 'I feel bad.' She said 'What's the matter?' 'I've just seen a man destroy himself on the witness stand.' That's the way Oppenheimer impressed me. You can't begin to feel the drama of the thing. Some people thought that Oppenheimer was going to commit suicide that night. I said 'Oh no, he won't' and he didn't, of course. Next morning, he was back just as cheerful as ever.

Fitted into that fourth day of the hearing was Major General Groves, now a businessman working for the Remington Rand Corporation.

He had already written to Oppenheimer on a previous occasion, stating that he would always be prepared to testify to the effect that he had cleared Oppenheimer after reviewing all the facts concerning his background, but he was in these troubled times in a difficult position. When interviewed by a member of Strauss's staff back in January, he had already said that he had cleared a number of people of dubious backgrounds for work on the bomb only 'in as much as his primary objective was to produce an atomic bomb in the shortest possible time'. He also quietly washed his hands of those cases by stating that 'since the Atomic Energy Act of 1946 had been passed, the AEC might desire to review those cases and make their own decisions and rulings concerning them'.

Yet, when he came to the stand he reaffirmed his decision to clear and appoint Oppenheimer and said that he would be 'amazed' if Oppenheimer would ever commit a disloyal act. As to Oppenheimer's refusal to reveal Chevalier's name to him, he shrugged that off as 'the typical American school boy attitude that there is something wicked about telling on a friend'. As far as Groves was concerned, he had named Eltenton and that was the main thing.

However, perhaps because Robb knew of the conversation about the Atomic Energy Act, he then asked Groves whether he would clear Oppenheimer today. Groves replied that, largely on the basis of Oppenheimer's pre-war associations, he 'would not clear Dr Oppenheimer today,' under his interpretation of the new security standards. Thus Groves had covered his back and the helpfulness of his testimony had been considerably blunted.

When Oppenheimer returned to the stand after Groves's departure, his bearing could not have been more different from the day before. He was his old confident and fluent self again, as can be seen in an exchange with Robb about Teller's and Lawrence's visits to Washington just before the 1949 GAC meeting. In a letter to Conant, he had referred to the fact that 'two experienced promoters have been at work'.

J. ROBERT OPPENHEIMER

ROBB: Would you agree, Doctor, that your references to Dr Lawrence and Dr Teller and their enthusiasm for the super bomb . . . are a little bit belittling?

OPPENHEIMER: Dr Lawrence came to Washington. He did not talk to the Commission. He went and talked to Congressmen and to members of the military establishment. I think that deserves some belittling.

ROBB: So you would agree that your reference to these men in this letter is belittling?

OPPENHEIMER: No, I pay my great respects to them as promoters. I don't think I did them justice.

ROBB: You used the word 'promoters' in an invidious sense, didn't you?

OPPENHEIMER: I promoted lots of things in my time.

ROBB: Doctor, would you answer my question? When you used the word 'promoter' you meant it to be in a slightly invidious sense, didn't you?

OPPENHEIMER: I have no idea.

ROBB: When you use the word now with reference to Lawrence and Teller, don't you intend it to be invidious?

OPPENHEIMER: No.

ROBB: You think that their work of promotion was admirable, is that right?

OPPENHEIMER: I think they did an admirable job of promotion.

This exchange is so neat, so quick that it leaves one wondering all the more about what had happened to Oppenheimer the afternoon before. The same thoughts may well have been going through the minds of the Board as they listened to him parry questions about the hydrogen bomb. Robb suggested that the witness had qualms about the bomb, and Oppenheimer responded sharply that he did not know of anyone who did not have qualms about it.

Shifting back, Robb again set a test for Oppenheimer's veracity. Commenting on the 'surprising unanimity' of the GAC about the H-Bomb at that October meeting, Robb asked Oppenheimer if everyone had expressed themselves. Yes, Oppenheimer replied, except Glenn Seaborg who had been in Sweden.

ROBB: So you didn't know how he felt about it?

OPPENHEIMER: We did not.

ROBB: You didn't know either how he felt about it. He was just not there.

OPPENHEIMER: He was in Sweden, and there was no communication with him. . . .

From the files in front of him, Robb produced a document.

ROBB: I am going to show you a letter taken from your files at Princeton . . . dated October 14th, 1949, signed Glenn Seaborg.

This time Oppenheimer saw the danger he was in.

OPPENHEIMER: I am going to say before I see that, that I had no recollection of it.

For the next few minutes he fought off yet another of Robb's carefully planned attacks. Normally he would have read out a letter from an absent member such as Seaborg, he said, but 'having no recollection of the Seaborg letter, I cannot say that I did this'. He was also able to point out that Seaborg had had later opportunities to express a view but had declined to do so. But Robb persisted in his attempts to make it seem that Oppenheimer had been lying over this issue.

ROBB: . . . didn't you tell the Joint Committee that Dr Seaborg had not expressed himself on this subject prior to the meeting of October 29, 1949?

OPPENHEIMER: I would have to see the transcript. I don't remember that question and the answer.

ROBB: If you did make that statement, it was not true, was it?

OPPENHEIMER: It is clear that we had an expression, not unequivocal, from Seaborg, before the meeting of October 29.

ROBB: Doctor, did you hear my question?

OPPENHEIMER: I heard it, but I have heard that kind of question too often.

ROBB: I am sure of that, Doctor, but would you answer it nevertheless?

Oppenheimer was becoming familiar with Robb's tactics and demanded to see the transcript of the Joint Committee. Garrison also asked to see the transcript, but was once again confronted by the curtain of secrecy which seemed to be being used by the Commission often at its own convenience. Information from a particular source would be available when Robb chose to use it, but unavailable when Garrison made a request.


That night, at the house of Randolph Paul in Georgetown, where the Oppenheimers were staying during the hearings, he and Kitty and his legal advisers sat down to talk about the progress of the case. On this occasion, they invited Joseph Volpe to join them. He had warned all along about ploys that the AEC counsel might use. Reluctant to become too closely involved in a case being directed by others, he nevertheless listened to their account of what had taken place during the first few days of the hearing.

Well Robert said to me, 'Joe, I would like to have these fellows describe to you what's going on in the hearing.' Well I don't think the others liked it very much, but finally they got around to telling me and honestly I was outraged. I was the one who had drawn up the procedures for these hearings when I was General Counsel and they were very definitely not meant to be an adversary procedure, and this one was. What's more, they told me that they were withholding documents which was utterly ridiculous. What were these documents? Information he already had except he didn't have the precise language. No this behaviour gave me great concern, and so after an hour or so, I finally said, 'Robert, tell them to shove it, leave it, don't go on with it because I don't think you can win.'

But Volpe's advice was, in the end, ignored.

Volpe was a fighter [recalls Garrison], and was so aroused by the evil that was taking place that he would have liked to have thrown the whole thing into the Courts somehow or other. . . . But in the temper of those days I don't think we would have got to first base in those courts.

So on the Friday of the first week, Oppenheimer took the stand for the last time. After about another hour's questioning by Robb, he was then questioned by the Board. Gordon Gray interrogated him for half an hour, but Thomas Morgan had no questions, and Ward Evans just one. At twelve-fifteen Oppenheimer was excused from the witness box that he had occupied for a total of more than twenty hours.

# CHAPTER 18 THE OTHER WITNESSES

A month or so before the hearings in Washington had opened, John Lansdale, one-time security adviser to General Groves and now a practising lawyer, had come to Washington to talk to Roger Robb about giving evidence at the hearing. According to Robb, at one point during their conversation, Lansdale was asked whether he would give Oppenheimer his security clearance. Landsale had replied that he would not.

Lansdale returned to Washington on the Thursday of the first week and that evening he met Robb to discuss the evidence he would give the following day. To Robb's surprise, he found that Lansdale, who earlier in the day had met with one of Oppenheimer's team, had now changed his stance and firmly held that he would now clear Oppenheimer just as he had done ten years earlier.

'So I said, "Jack, let me tell you this,"' recalls Robb, '"We have a memorandum of our first conversation. Now you're a lawyer and I'm a lawyer and if you say under oath that you'd be prepared to clear him today, then I'm going to impeach you. I give you that warning."'

The following day, Lansdale followed Oppenheimer to the stand as the first of the long parade of additional pro-Oppenheimer witnesses, and he seemed totally unperturbed either by Robb's threat or his style of questioning. When he calmly told the Board that the hearing was a manifestation of the current hysteria of the times, Robb followed with some aggressive questioning.

ROBB: You think this inquiry is a manifestation of hysteria?

LANSDALE: I think –

ROBB: Yes or no?

LANSDALE: I won't answer that question 'Yes' or 'No' . . . If you will let me continue, I will be glad to answer your question.

Robb backed off and Lansdale continued.

LANSDALE: I think that the fact that associations in 1940 are regarded with the same seriousness that similar associations would be regarded today is a manifestation of hysteria.

The crunch over his possible impeachment came at the end of his examination by Garrison, who asked him whether he would clear Dr Oppenheimer today.

LANSDALE: I will answer that, yes, based upon the same criteria and standards that we used then. I am making no attempt to interpret the present law. . . .

A minute or so later Roger Robb began his cross-examination with the following question:

ROBB: As I understand it, Mr Lansdale, you are not offering any opinion as to whether or not you would clear Dr Oppenheimer on the basis of presently existing criteria?

LANSDALE: That is a standard that is strange to me. I don't know what it is, if somebody would interpret it for me – isn't it getting pretty hypothetical?

No interpretation was forthcoming. Robb did not pursue him any further.

A luminous array of men came to Room 2022 over the next seven days to testify to the character and the loyalty of Robert Oppenheimer. There were the Nobel Laureates, Enrico Fermi, Isidor Rabi, and Hans Bethe; senior figures in government and scientific administration like James Conant (now US High Commissioner to Germany) and Vannevar Bush. Both Strauss's predecessors as chairmen of the AEC testified on Oppenheimer's behalf and also three former Commissioners.

As the days went by a pattern began to emerge in the examinations. Each witness would describe why he was convinced of Oppenheimer's loyalty. Then Robb, or perhaps Gray, would cite the Chevalier incident or some other Oppenheimer misdeed and ask how this affected the witness's feelings. More often than not the response would be that it did not, that times – or Oppenheimer – had changed.

However, within this broad framework of similarities, each witness brought some different slant to the case.

One of the first to appear was Hans Bethe who talked glowingly of Oppenheimer as the unifying force at Los Alamos, the man who was recognised by everyone as 'superior in judgement and superior in knowledge to all of us'. He told of how when he had to make the decision whether to join Teller in working on the Super, it was to Oppenheimer that he had turned for guidance. Bethe found the atmosphere of the hearing quite unreal, and described Robb as 'a real movie lawyer'. Robb did not even attempt to touch the central core of Bethe's faith in Oppenheimer but instead tried to reduce his standing and credibility by picking on a peripheral point.

*Hans Bethe, a pro-Oppenheimer witness. He recalled staying with the Oppenheimers in New Mexico in 1941 when Oppenheimer was said to have been hosting a Communist meeting in Berkeley*

ROBB: Doctor, how many divisions were there at Los Alamos?

BETHE: It changed somewhat in the course of time. As far as I could count the other day, there were seven, but that may have been eight or nine at some time.

ROBB: What division was Klaus Fuchs in?

BETHE: He was in my division.

ROBB: Thank you. That is all.

When James Conant came to the witness stand he lost no time in attacking the idea that Oppenheimer's opposition to the H-Bomb made him a security risk. If that were the case, Conant said, 'it would apply to me, because I opposed it – as strongly as anybody else'. But the edge was taken off his evidence, as it had been with other witnesses, by Robb's classic debunking technique.

ROBB: Of course, Doctor, you don't know what the testimony before this board has been?
CONANT: No, I don't.
ROBB: Nor do you know what the record or file before the board discloses?
CONANT: No. I only know what is in the letter of General Nichols.

However, another witness that same day who was not to be undercut by this technique was Isidor Rabi, a man whose friendship with Oppenheimer stretched back to their student days. First he made the point that what among security matters would be deemed 'horrifying' in 1954 would not in 1943 have merited anything more than 'throwing the man out of the house'.

Then he went on to make the point that, whatever Oppenheimer's behaviour, it should be judged against his contributions to the national interest, and here Rabi was at his most forceful.

There is a real, positive record . . . We have an H-Bomb and a whole series of [them]. What more do you want, mermaids? . . . This is just a tremendous achievement. If the end of that road is this kind of hearing, [I think it is] a pretty bad show.

Yet again Robb, using his customary technique, tried to imply that Rabi's judgement may be at fault because 'perhaps the board may be in possession of information which is not now available to you. . . .' Rabi's response threw into relief the obsessive probing of trivialities which had marked so much of the hearing so far.

'On the other hand,' he said, 'I am in possession of a long experience with this man, going back to 1929, which is twenty-five years, and there is a kind of seat of the pants feeling on which I myself lay great weight.'

But Robb persisted by trying to confine Rabi's opinion to the Chevalier incident only.

'I think that any incident in a man's life of something of that sort you have to take it in sum,' Rabi responded. 'That is what novels are about. There is a dramatic moment in the history of man, what made him act, what he did, and what sort of person he was. That is what you are really doing here. You are writing a man's life.'

The day on which Conant, Bethe and Rabi gave their evidence, 20 April, was the longest day in the hearing. The session ended at eight p.m. and the tight atmosphere of Room 2022 must have imposed a strain of its own, not dissimilar to those in group therapy, on the weary participants in the drama. It was turning into a bitter affair with little love lost between the two sides. Robb had taken a strong personal dislike to Oppenheimer. 'My feeling was that he was just a brain and as cold as a fish, and he had the iciest pair of blue eyes I ever saw.' He was also becoming more and more convinced of his guilt.

This dislike was mutual. On one occasion he and Oppenheimer were outside during a short recess when Oppenheimer developed a fit of coughing. Robb, who had had TB when he was younger, was solicitous but Oppenheimer turned on him, snapping out something Robb did not fully understand. The prosecutor walked away.

Those who knew Oppenheimer well were astonished at his resilience during the proceedings. Back in Princeton over the weekend breaks, he continued to deal with Institute business and with physics. However, they did notice a change in him. He seemed to be losing his self-confidence. Some of his close friends who knew what was going on even thought they saw the relish of a martyr in his predicament. But if that was the case, it certainly did not mean that he and his team had stopped fighting.

A man's life was at stake. It was like a murder trial and a murder trial in which the evidence was murky and half-known [Lloyd Garrison recalls]. We spent most evenings back at the Georgetown house. All we had the energy for was preparation, we were too weary to do much post-morteming.

Of course, Robert was in the most overwrought state imaginable – so was Kitty – but Robert even more so. He would pace his bedroom floor at night, so Randolph Paul told me, and he was just an anguished man. Then his anxieties were added to our own and it was a great torture really.

In the second week of the trial, another strange sequence of events must have added to the feeling of tension on Strauss's side. They are recounted in a report from Liaison Supervisor Bates, considered one of the most reliable of FBI sources. According to his report Lewis Strauss had told him that Stewart Alsop, one of the country's best known journalists and on friendly terms with Oppenheimer, had been to see Assistant Secretary of Defense, Seaton. Alsop had

told him that he had a hot tip that one of the Russian spies who had defected in Tokyo had heard that Oppenheimer was in continual contact with the Russians. . . . Strauss stated he then checked with the CIA regarding this information in Tokyo and was assured that there was nothing to it. . . . Strauss felt that this might be a plant to get the AEC to use such information in the hearings on Oppenheimer and then to expose it as completely false in the Press.

If nothing else this story illustrates Strauss's fears of a conspiracy but if it is true and Strauss's theory of a 'plant' is correct then it raises a whole series of questions. Did Oppenheimer know about the scheme? If he didn't then who had initiated Alsop's visit to Seaton and why? Was it an act of desperation on the part of Oppenheimer's supporters?

Unfortunately, Stewart Alsop is dead and his brother Joseph remembers nothing about it. Lloyd Garrison also remembers nothing about it.[1] So for the time being a specific report filed by a reliable agent must remain unexplained.

It was not Robb alone who was now causing problems. After more than a week of the hearing, it was possible to make an assessment of the attitude of the

[1] Roger Robb recalls the story of the Russian spy and the alleged information about Oppenheimer but nothing about Alsop's approach.

Board itself and again the prospect was bleak. After the initial fracas over the release of the charges to the press, Gray had remained fairly cool to Oppenheimer's counsel. On almost every procedural matter raised by Garrison, he found in Robb's favour. He also seemed to be playing the hearing according to the book and not interpreting the rules with any degree of freedom. An example of this arose during the evidence of a witness, Harry Winne, who had been closely allied with Oppenheimer on the Acheson-Lilienthal report. He read out to Winne some of the AEC's criteria for justifying a security ban, which included a reasonable belief that the individual or his spouse had 'held membership or joined any organisation which has been declared by the Attorney General to be totalitarian, Fascist, Communist, subversive. . . .'

In reply, Winne, an Oppenheimer ally, had to concede that there was proof that Oppenheimer had, to some extent, supported organisations later listed as subversive. Gray then said that the trouble with his criteria was that they did not confine this activity to actual members, and furthermore the inclusion of the word 'spouse' gummed things up still further. Yes, agreed Winne, for Oppenheimer had admitted that Kitty was a member of the Communist Party. However, Winne did add that none of this changed his opinion that his friend had been loyal but he then continued:

'You may, because of the wording of the law, be forced to make an adverse decision. I hope you will not, but you may be forced to.'

Even though the Board had instructions under the Act to exercise 'judgement', it certainly seemed that Gray had the 'wording of the law' very much in mind. As to the other members of the Board, they also seemed to be lining up against Oppenheimer. Morgan was certainly unsympathetic and Gray himself was to admit that at this stage in the proceedings Ward Evans had it in his mind to vote against Oppenheimer. In a restaurant one night he had to hush Evans for commenting that every time a subversive name came up it seemed to be Jewish.

However, the Board seemed already to have realised that the straightforward disloyalty claim was going to be untenable, so how then was Oppenheimer dangerous? Gray thought the answer might lie in the recurring theme of the defendant's 'arrogance of judgement'; his tendency to take his own line on vital issues time after time rather than to follow those whose duty it was to make the decisions.

But on the Friday of the second week this approach received a severe buffeting from another witness, Vannevar Bush, who minced no words in saying that he felt 'this board has made a mistake . . . a serious one'. The inclusion of Oppenheimer's opposition to the H-Bomb among the charges meant that they were

quite capable of being interpreted as placing a man on trial because he held opinions, which is quite contrary to the American system. . . . And as I move about I find discussed today very energetically, that here is a man who is being pilloried because he had strong opinions, and had the temerity to express them. If this country ever gets that near to the Russian system, we are certainly not in any condition to attempt to lead the free world toward the benefits of democracy. . . .

A few minutes later, he made the same point even more forcibly.

. . . If you want to try that case, you can try me. I have expressed strong opinions many times. They have been unpopular opinions at times. When a man is pilloried for doing that, this country is in a severe state.

Bush's statements affected Gray considerably. He commented, 'Whatever the outcome, this Board is going to be severely criticised.'

A little later, Gray sought out Robb to ask if there was any way of bringing the hearing to a close, but Robb told him that there was not.

So the witnesses kept coming and going. Charles Lauritsen, a scientist friend of Oppenheimer, had known him for more than twenty years, and said that he trusted Oppenheimer as he would his own son. Whereupon Robb rapidly had Lauritsen admit that he had not known that Frank Oppenheimer was a former Communist. Then Robert Bacher came to the witness stand, and like so many others before him, after testifying strongly in Oppenheimer's favour, had his evidence compromised by Robb. This time, Bacher had to concede that it was he who hired Philip Morrison, once a suspected Communist, for the Manhattan Project.

Then on 27 April, as the hearing neared its end, a part of the proceedings began which was without precedent in any of the AEC's regulations or previous hearings – the presentation of 'the government's case' through witnesses called by a 'representative of the government.' In so many ways, this hearing had become more and more a trial for treason rather than a simple inquiry.

The first of these witnesses was a chemistry professor from Berkeley, Wendell Latimer, whose main qualification as a witness seemed to be his dislike of Oppenheimer. Certainly he had never been close to him, professionally or socially, but that had not prevented him from advancing a case against Oppenheimer based on his hypnotic power.

It is just astounding the influence he has upon a group [Latimer said]. He is a man of tremendous sincerity and his ability to convince people depends so much upon this sincerity. . . . A whole series of events involved the things that started happening immediately after he left Los Alamos. Many of our boys came back from it pacifist. I judged that was due very largely to his influence, this tremendous influence he had over these young men.

Latimer's evidence was shown time and again to be based on hearsay and not on direct experience. Yet even though, up to this point in the hearing, Gordon Gray had always asked a question of a witness, on this occasion, in spite of the loose nature of Latimer's evidence, he had none.

On the following day, two more 'government' witnesses took the stand. The first was Major General Roscoe Wilson, of the Air Force, who objected to the

*Air Force General Roscoe Wilson, one of the witnesses called in the presentation of the 'government's case'*

'pattern' of Oppenheimer's judgements because he believed a nuclear strike force was the 'greater deterrent to further Russian aggression'. The next witness was Kenneth Pitzer, director of research for the AEC, who began by making the statement that he was not appearing voluntarily but, 'only at the very specific and urgent request of the General Manager'. He then went on to charge that Oppenheimer's lack of enthusiasm had affected recruitment for the H-Bomb programme. '. . . The program would not have had certain difficulties that it did have if he had enthusiastically urged individuals to participate in the program. . . .' In other words, Oppenheimer's sin was not opposition but lack of enthusiasm. This charge seemed so far removed from those made in the Borden letter that had started these proceedings.

Then at four p.m. that afternoon, a third witness made his appearance at the stand. Sitting at the chair just in front of Oppenheimer, Edward Teller was sworn in to begin what many regard as the most potent of all the thousands of words of testimony given at this hearing.

Edward Teller was by now a figure of considerable importance in the scientific world. He had already attracted the tag 'Father of the H-Bomb' and he had been director of his own establishment, the Livermore Laboratories. Whatever he said was bound to have considerable influence.

As we have already seen, Teller had been under pressure from both sides to testify, but he had decided to testify as a 'government' witness in answer to a request from the effective appellate judge in this case, General Manager Nichols. Nevertheless, six days before he was due to appear he was still wrestling with his conscience as to his proper role in the hearing. His thoughts were in all probability clouded by the years of frustration and pent-up emotion and he felt the strong need to talk to someone in the hope of clarifying them. An AEC liaison officer, Chester Heslep, who went to Livermore found that Teller wanted to talk about nothing else but the 'Oppenheimer case'. Heslep sent a memo of the conversation to Strauss and that memo provides a valuable insight into the resentment felt by Teller towards a man of rival power and opposite persuasion. Here are some of the points from the memo:

2 Since the case is being heard on a security basis, Teller wonders if some way can be found to 'deepen the charges' to include a documentation of the 'consistently bad advice' that Oppenheimer has given, going all the way back to the end of the war in 1945. . . .

4 Teller said that 'only about one per cent or less' of the scientists know of the real situation and that Oppie is so powerful 'politically' in scientific circles that it will be hard to 'unfrock him in his own church'. (This last phrase is mine [wrote Heslep] and he agrees it is apt.)

5 Teller talked at length about the 'Oppie machine' running through many names, some of which he listed as 'Oppie men' and others as not being on his team but under his influence. He says the effort to make Conant head of the National Academy of

Sciences is typical of the operation of the 'Oppie machine'. He adds that there is no organised faction among the scientists opposing the 'Oppie men'.

6 Teller feels deeply that this 'unfrocking' must be done or else – regardless of the outcome of the current hearing – scientists may lose their enthusiasm for the program.

It is a memo that gets behind the statements which have been carefully honed by Teller over the years to rationalise his actions. His jealousy, his feeling of impotence as an outsider facing a man of great personal magnetism and considerable intellect are all there. These were the emotions he sought to control as he journeyed towards Washington for his appointment of 28 April.

'Actually, when I left for Washington I was prepared for the question that was going to be asked of me,' Teller has recalled, 'namely: *Do I consider Oppenheimer a security risk?* And I was prepared to answer "no" to that question.'

However, when Teller flew into Washington the day before his scheduled appearance at the hearing, he found a note waiting for him from Roger Robb requesting a meeting. At first Teller hesitated: 'I considered it not quite right. But considering that Oppenheimer had asked me to do the same thing, I felt that I could not say no to Robb.'

Would someone who, only days before, had allegedly stated that Oppenheimer must be unfrocked, be so coy about seeing the Commission's counsel? Also Teller had already met Robb to talk about the case. What was different about this meeting in Washington?

Anyway, with whatever intent, the two men did meet and sure enough Robb did want to know how Teller would answer the crucial question.

I told him [Teller remembers] that I did not consider Oppenheimer a security risk. Whereupon, Robb showed me part of the testimony, showing that Oppenheimer had lied to a security person; that he admitted so lying, but that he could not now be prosecuted for what was a criminal offence because the statute of limitations had taken effect.

When Robb showed this to me and gave me this argument, I said I guess that I cannot simply say that Oppenheimer is not a security risk. So in retrospect I am quite unhappy about this event.

Had Oppenheimer not asked me to talk to *his* lawyer, I would not have listened to Robb. I would have gotten into less hot water, personally. On the other hand, you may say that this brought out more of the actual facts.

Teller does seem concerned to justify this conversation with Robb. Why then, if he was so conscious of being manoeuvred by Robb, did he not refuse to read the material Robb offered him? Surely it was clear what Robb was trying to do?

So Edward Teller came to the witness stand having been presented with selected material from the hearing.

ROBB: Dr Teller, may I ask you at the outset, are you appearing as a witness here today because you want to be here?

TELLER: I appear because I have been asked to and because I consider it my duty upon request to say what I think in the matter. I would have preferred not to appear.

ROBB: I believe, sir, that you stated to me some time ago that anything you had to say you wished to say in the presence of Dr Oppenheimer?

TELLER: That is correct.

Very quickly Robb's questioning got to the heart of the matter.

ROBB: To simplify the issues here, let me ask you this question: Is it your intention in anything that you are about to testify to, to suggest that Dr Oppenheimer is disloyal to the United States?

TELLER: I do not want to suggest anything of the kind. I know Oppenheimer as an intellectually most alert and very complicated person, and I think it would be presumptuous and wrong on my part if I would try in any way to analyse his motives. But I have always assumed, and I now assume, that he is loyal to the United States. I believe this, and I shall believe it until I see very conclusive proof to the opposite.

ROBB: Now a question which is a corollary to that. Do you or do you not believe that Dr Oppenheimer is a security risk?

TELLER: In a great number of instances, I have seen Dr Oppenheimer act – I understood that Dr Oppenheimer acted – in a way which for me was exceedingly hard to understand, and his actions frankly appeared to me confused and complicated. To this extent I feel I would like to see the vital interests of this country in hands which I understand better and therefore trust more.

In this very limited sense I would like to express a feeling that I would feel personally more secure if public matters would rest in other hands.

These were the first of the remarks that Teller made during this hearing which would come back to haunt him over the years. His testimony was to continue for another hour, first under direct examination by Robb and then under an atypically short cross-examination by Garrison's colleague Sam Silverman. It was very close to six p.m. when Gordon Gray took up the questioning.

GRAY: Do you feel that it would endanger the common defense and security to grant clearance to Dr Oppenheimer?

TELLER: I believe that Dr Oppenheimer's character is such that he would not knowingly and willingly do anything that is designed to endanger the safety of this country. To the extent, therefore, that your question is directed toward intent, I would say I do not see any reason to deny clearance.

Then came the *coup de grâce*.

If it is a question of wisdom and judgement, as demonstrated by actions since 1945, then I would say one would be wiser not to grant clearance.

Many people regard this statement of Teller's as critically damaging to Oppenheimer's cause, but they were also to inflict great hurt to Teller himself. It was these same statements which caused the sense of outrage amongst his fellow scientists and caused Teller to be ostracised for years to come.

At six-ten p.m. Edward Teller was excused from the witness chair. As he left the room, he paused before the frail man seated on the couch and held out his hand. 'I'm sorry', he said.

'After what you've just said,' Oppenheimer replied, taking Teller's outstretched hand, 'I don't know what you mean.'

Teller then turned and walked with his uneven gait out of the hearing room.

*John J. McCloy, a pro-Oppenheimer witness who in 1954 was President of the Chase National Bank. At the time of this 1951 meeting with Eisenhower he had been US High Commissioner to Germany*

The next day, Roger Robb's presentation of the government's case was interrupted by the testimony of another of Oppenheimer's witnesses, John J. McCloy. McCloy was now Chairman of the Board of the Chase National Bank, but had been Stimson's Assistant Secretary of War during World War II, when he met Oppenheimer and came to admire him. When asked by Garrison whether he felt Oppenheimer was a 'security risk' he said – as part of a lengthy reply –

I don't know just exactly what you mean by security risk. I know that I am a security risk and I think every individual is a security risk. You can always talk in your sleep . . . In other words, you can't be too conventional about it or you run into a security problem the other way. We are only secure if we have the best brains and best reach of mind in this field. . . .

Immediately Robb took over from Garrison and in a classic piece of cross-examination eroded the effectiveness of McCloy's evidence. Robb addressed McCloy about banking.

ROBB: . . . Suppose you had a branch bank manager and a friend of his came to him one day and said, 'I have some friends and contacts who are thinking about coming to your bank to rob it. I would like to talk to you about maybe leaving the vault open some night so that they could do it,' and your branch manager rejected the suggestion. Would you expect that branch manager to report the incident?

MCCLOY: Yes.

ROBB: If he didn't report it, would you be disturbed about it?

MCCLOY: Yes.

ROBB: Let us go a little bit further. Supposing the branch bank manager waited 6 or 8 months to report it, would you be rather concerned about why he had not done it before?

MCCLOY: Yes.

ROBB: Suppose when he did report, he said this friend of mine, a good friend of mine, I am sure he was innocent, and therefore I won't tell you who he is. Would you be concerned about that? Would you urge him to tell you?

MCCLOY: I would certainly urge him to tell me for the security of the bank.

And so McCloy went on, innocently damning the man he had come to support, through his answers to Robb's carefully constructed analogy of the Chevalier incident. It was a masterly piece of cross-examination which, years later, Robb was pleased to see being used as a textbook example in law schools.

After McCloy came the remainder of the government witnesses. David

Griggs, the former Chief Scientist of the Air Force, took much the same line as Air Force General Wilson in expressing concern about Oppenheimer's 'pattern of activities'. He was followed to the witness stand by Luis Alvarez, professor of physics at Berkeley. Originally, he had expected to testify along with Ernest Lawrence against Oppenheimer, but both men had been subjected to considerable pressure from other physicists not to do so. In particular, Lawrence was told that any unfavourable testimony on his part would simply be discounted due to their personal differences over recent years. So, somewhat conveniently, Lawrence had become ill, cancelling his plans to testify. Alvarez did the same, only too pleased to 'get off the hot seat' but within hours he received a personal plea from Lewis Strauss to come to the hearing. 'How are you going to look at yourself in the mirror,' Alvarez recalls Strauss saying, 'if you back out on an important responsibility such as this?'

Alvarez came to Washington and testified for nearly a whole day about his difficulties back in 1949 in promoting the H-Bomb. Finally it was the Board's turn to ask questions and for the first time Ward Evans' questions seemed to take a pro-Oppenheimer tone. 'The main thing we have gotten out of you', he said, 'is that you have tried to show that Dr Oppenheimer was opposed to the development of the super weapon. Is that true?' Alvarez agreed and Evans then asked, 'What does that mean in your mind – anything?'

ALVAREZ: By itself it means absolutely nothing because I have many other friends in the scientific world who feel precisely this way. The point I was trying to bring out was that every time I have found a person who felt this way, I have seen Dr Oppenheimer's influence on that person's mind. I don't think there is anything wrong with this . . . I just point out the facts as I see them.

EVANS: It doesn't mean that he was disloyal?

ALVAREZ: Absolutely not, sir.

Next on the witness stand came Boris Pash who corroborated the evidence already available from the taped interviews, and then late on Friday came Robb's final government witness, William Borden. Borden, the man whose letter had catalysed these proceedings, had had to be subpoenaed to appear. Now for the first time Oppenheimer was to see both the letter of charges and the man who had written them.

There was a tussle between Garrison and the Board as to whether the letter should be read into the record – a pointless exercise since the Board had always had it in their possession. Garrison was overruled and Borden began reciting to the Board his 'exhaustively considered opinion' that 'more probably than not' Oppenheimer 'is an agent of the Soviet Union . . . [who had] been functioning as an espionage agent . . . under a Soviet directive in influencing United States policy.'

When Borden finished reading, Gray dismissed outright this central conclusion, saying there was 'no evidence' to support Oppenheimer's link with the Soviet Union. Robb asked Borden only a few questions and after the weekend's recess, Garrison decided not to cross-examine Borden at all. On the

Monday morning of the fourth and final week of the hearing, Borden left the stand, his charges apparently dismissed by Oppenheimer's judges. It was clear that Borden had only been a catalyst in bringing about the hearing because it continued fuelled by all manner of half-truths, political neuroses and personal enmities.

Now the Board called Oppenheimer back to the stand for further questioning. It was the Chevalier incident which was obviously concerning them and in particular the discrepancy between the versions Oppenheimer told to Pash and Lansdale in 1943 and the later versions that Oppenheimer had recounted. Why had he invented the 'cock and bull story' for Pash and Lansdale, a version which was more injurious to both him and Chevalier?

Or to put the question in another way [continued Gray] I ask you whether it is not a fair inference from your testimony that your story to Pash and Lansdale as far as it went was a true story, and that the fabrication may have been with respect to the current version.

No [said Oppenheimer, referring to what he had told Pash and Lansdale], it was a false story. It is not easy to say that. Now when you ask for a more persuasive argument as to why I did this than that I was an idiot, I am going to have more trouble being understandable.

I think I was impelled by two or three concerns at that time. One was the feeling that I must get across the fact that if there was, as Lansdale indicated, trouble at the Radiation Laboratory, Eltenton was the guy that might very well be involved and it was serious. Whether I embroidered the story in order to underline the seriousness or whether I embroidered it to make it more tolerable, that I would not tell the simple facts, namely Chevalier had talked to me about it, I don't know.

He then went on to say that he realised now that he should have reported the incident immediately and 'completely accurately, but that it was a matter of conflict for me . . . I may add one or two things. Chevalier was a friend of mine.'

This conflict of loyalties between friendship on the one hand and the nation's security on the other was an issue fundamental to the hearing. Should Oppenheimer have felt himself able to judge between these two choices? It was a question which seemed certainly to concern Chairman Gray greatly and he asked him whether today he 'had a friend in whom you had the highest degree of confidence as to his loyalty to this country' but who was known to have been a member of the Communist Party 'whether again you would say, well, it depends on the individual?'

To this Oppenheimer replied that 'it would not be up to me to determine whether his disengagement from the Communist Party was genuine. I would think that at this time investigation would be called for.' It was a very correct answer, but would it be enough to dispel any of the doubts about his 'rehabilitation' since 1943 that the Board still had?

Three more witnesses came to the stand, including Kitty, before the proceedings wound down to their conclusion on Thursday 6 May 1954. At nine-thirty that morning, Oppenheimer took the stand for the last time, called by Garrison to rebut the testimony against him. He was challenged once again by Robb on certain of the all-too-familiar general issues current during the hearing but soon his questions came to an end. As he was about to leave the stand for the last time he said he wished to make a comment. 'I am grateful to and I hope properly appreciative', he said, 'of the patience and consideration that the Board has shown me during this part of the proceedings'.

With this he left the stand, his part in the proceedings over. It was left to Garrison the following day to make a summation to the Board, which he did finely, extemporaneously, using only the shortest of notes to help him. When he had finished, mutual courtesies were exchanged and then Gray said, 'We now conclude this phase of the hearing'.

# THE VERDICT

## CHAPTER 19

After four weeks in Room 2022 listening to the Oppenheimer case, everyone involved needed some respite and the Board members took ten days to return home and gather their thoughts. The first thing that Gordon Gray did was to dictate a memorandum for history, in which he said the proceedings had been as fair as circumstances permitted. He was uneasy about some of Robb's tactics, but he felt that no damage had been done because everything pertinent had entered the record. He overlooked the psychological effect on Oppenheimer and his counsel of those tactics.

Then on 17 May, the members of the Board made their way back to Washington. Gray and Morgan travelled on the same plane and on comparing notes found that they had reached very much the same conclusions. Neither of them could find a basis for offering Oppenheimer security clearance. Thus they arrived in Washington convinced that the Board would reach a unanimous decision. Evans had always shocked them with his anti-Oppenheimer views but when Gray and Morgan arrived at the Commission work room they were amazed to find him already there working on what he said would be a recommendation to restore Oppenheimer's 'Q' rating. They suspected that Evans had been 'got at' back home in Chicago, but Evans furiously denied this. Whatever had occurred to transform his views, he was now absolutely unshakable in his support of Oppenheimer. News of Evans's change of heart got back to Strauss at the AEC and, according to an FBI report, Strauss and Robb decided to take some action.

At 12.20 p.m. Roger Robb called [wrote the author of the report, C. E. Hennrich]. He recalled that he had been acquainted with me several years ago and said he wants to be sure that the Director [Hoover] knows that he thinks it extremely important that the Director discuss this matter with the Board; that the Board wants the discussion on an informal basis, not as a witness; and that the Board would not ask for the Director's evaluation. Robb said that he feels it will be a tragedy if the decision of the Board goes the wrong way and that he considers this to be a matter of extreme urgency. He pointed out that the Board wants to issue its decision tomorrow, May 21, but they feel they cannot finish their deliberations until they talk with the Director.

At 12.40 p.m., Agent Bates advised that Strauss had stated that he would not insist on personally seeing the Director himself, but that he very strongly felt that Robb should see the Director regarding this matter and that he, of course, would be glad to see the Director, if possible. Addendum by Belmont – May 20, 1954.

At 12.30 p.m., Commissioner Strauss called Belmont to advise that he had just returned from the White House where he had been attending the National Security Council meeting. He said that the Oppenheimer Hearing Board is in the last stages of its considerations and that things are 'touch and go'. He said a slight tip of the balance would cause the Board to commit a serious error.

Commissioner Strauss said that he felt most urgently that the three members of the Board, namely Gordon Gray, Thomas H. Morgan, and Dr Ward Evans, together with counsel Roger Robb, should see the Director. He stated that he understood the Director was out of town but that the Board members and Mr Robb would be glad to go to the Director's location for the express purpose of talking to him . . .

At the end C. E. Hennrich added his own observations.

This all boils down, it seems to me, to a situation where Strauss and Robb, who want the Board to make a finding that Oppenheimer is a security risk, are doubtful that the Board will so find at this point. Therefore they would encourage a meeting between the Board and the Director for the purpose of having the Director influence the Board. It appears that Strauss wants Robb to see the Director in advance to brief him on the thinking of the Board. It is my feeling that the Director should not see the Board, but that the Bureau's position should be that the Board has held a hearing during which witnesses appeared and testimony was given and the Bureau furnished the full results of its investigation.

Alongside this last sentence in the margin are three lines linking it to a sentence written round the page, presumably by Hoover himself. It begins, 'This is what I intend to do. . . .'

As the report and, in particular, Hennrich's observation, imply improper behaviour and even illegality the report was shown to Roger Robb.

When he saw it for the first time when I met him in September 1978, his reaction was one of surprise. 'Well I thought I had a good memory but damned if I remember this,' he said.

Then after considering the twenty-five-year-old report in full, an opportunity Oppenheimer could well have welcomed with some of the documents produced at the hearing, he offered his considered opinion on the report.

1. I specifically and categorically deny that I ever encouraged a meeting between the Board and the Director for the purpose of having the Director influence the Board. I deny that I did anything improper. I also deny that I ever told Hennrich that I considered 'this to be a matter of extreme urgency' because unless the Board talked to Mr Hoover it might decide in favour of Oppenheimer . . . this statement by Hennrich, and others in his memorandum to the same effect, simply do not make sense. At the time Hennrich says I talked to him I knew the Board's decision was adverse to Oppenheimer.

2. I have no knowledge whatsoever of any conversation between Admiral Strauss and Mr Belmont, as reported in the 'Addendum by Belmont' in the Hennrich memorandum. I never heard of any such conversation, had nothing to do with it if it occurred, and any implication to the contrary is unwarranted.

Robb's own theory of what might have occurred was arrived at after discussion with a number of parties involved directly or indirectly and included Bates, his fellow counsel Art Rolander, and Gordon Gray. He believes he may have 'explored the possibility of arranging for Mr Hoover's appearance if the Board decided it wanted to hear him, but that is as far as it went.'

Certainly for a group of politically experienced men to put any store by Hoover's intercession with the Board does seem doubtful, but the report is specific, and it is impossible absolutely to confirm or deny it. Whatever the truth behind it, Robb very soon decided in his capacity as counsel to the Board to act directly with them.

I thought it would be a tragedy if the Board went the other way. No doubt about that at all after the hearing . . . and I didn't want 'Doc' Evans's opinion to be too vulnerable. If it was, it would look as though he was just a plant on the Board, do you follow me, it would look as though we put a nincompoop on the Board.

So Robb worked with Evans on his dissenting notice and paradoxically Robb's professionalism contributed greatly to produce a document which was to be praised for its 'jabbing directness and its conciseness in showing up the charges against Oppenheimer'.

The Board's findings were ready on 27 May. The majority report found no less than twenty out of the original twenty-four charges either 'true' or 'substantially true', and in certain instances, such as its disapproval of Oppenheimer's help to David Bohm in getting a teaching post, even went beyond the listed charges.

As to the significance of the charges, the Board considered the single charge concerning the H-Bomb separately and the other twenty-three that concerned Oppenheimer's leftist connections all together.

After considering these 'earlier involvements' it found in them 'no indication of disloyalty'. Indeed its conclusion was 'that Dr Oppenheimer is a loyal citizen'.

As to the single H-Bomb charge, it was here that Evans parted company with Morgan and Gray. They all agreed that any implication of disloyalty or of 'attachment to the Soviet Union' which might be inferred from his resistance to the H-Bomb was 'not supported by any material which the Board has seen'. However, Gray and Morgan then went on to say that this was outweighed by 'their conclusion that, whatever the motive, the security interests of the United States' had been 'affected'.

Thus a man employed and used as a consultant was being condemned not for any motives he might have had but for the effect of his genuinely held opinions. As Isidor Rabi had said in his testimony, '. . . the suspension of the clearance of Dr Oppenheimer . . . should not have been done. In other words, there he was; he is a consultant, and if you don't want to consult the guy, you don't consult him, period.'

Next in their findings, Morgan and Gray make the most extraordinary statement: 'It must be said, that Dr Oppenheimer seems to have had a high degree of discretion, reflecting an unusual ability to keep to himself vital secrets.'

Given this, how could they still consider him a security risk?

The answer they found in Oppenheimer's 'tendency to be coerced, or at least influenced in conduct, over a period of years.' They then cited two examples, both involving intercessions by Dr Ed Condon. The first was where he was persuaded to intercede with the draft Board not to draft Lomanitz back in 1943. The second was his recantation of damaging remarks made about another left-wing ex-student of his, Bernard Peters. That was all. Two incidents in a twenty-year period.

Then they moved on to the Chevalier incident where they felt that Oppenheimer had 'repeatedly exercised an arrogance of his own judgement'. Furthermore they had not been convinced that he had been 'rehabilitated' in recent years. His visit to Chevalier in Paris the previous December demonstrated that. They could have talked about old times or just the weather, it would have made no difference. 'It is not important to determine that Dr Oppenheimer discussed with Chevalier matters of concern to the security of the United States,' the Board stated. Thus even though they had credited him with an 'unusual ability to keep to himself vital secrets' they held that the mere act of 'association with him [Chevalier – a known Communist] . . . is not the kind of thing that our security system permits. . .'.

Finally came their recommendation. Although he was 'a loyal citizen' this was their verdict.

We have . . . been unable to arrive at the conclusion that it would be clearly consistent with the security interests of the United States to reinstate Dr Oppenheimer's clearance, and, therefore, do not so recommend.

They then stated that 'an alternative recommendation would have been possible [one in Oppenheimer's favour] if we were allowed to exercise mature practical judgement without rigid circumscription of regulations and criteria established for us.'

They seemed to have overlooked completely a phrase in the AEC's *Criteria for Determining Eligibility for Personal Security Clearance*:

'The decision as to security clearance is an overall common-sense judgement.'

Such were the views and recommendations of Messrs Morgan and Gray, the Board. There followed the 'Minority Report of Dr Ward V. Evans' – shaped with the calculated assistance of Roger Robb. It was indeed a 'jabbingly direct' document.

'Most of the derogatory information was in the hands of the Commission when Dr Oppenheimer was cleared in 1947,' said Evans. He was cleared then because he continued to do a good job. 'Now when the job is done, we are asked to investigate him for practically the same derogatory information. . . . To damn him now and ruin his career and his service, I cannot do it.'

As to his interviews with Pash and Lansdale, he had 'in one place in his testimony said that he had told a tissue of lies. What he had said was not a tissue of lies, there was one lie.' Bearing in mind the way Robb had worked to extract that admission from Oppenheimer in the hearing, it is intriguing to think of him assisting in the phrasing of this succinct rebuttal.

In the remaining points in his dissent, Evans examined certain of Oppenheimer's actions.

In recent years he went to see Chevalier in Paris. I don't like this but I cannot condemn him on this ground. I don't like his about face in the matter of Dr Peters, but I don't think it subversive or disloyal.

[Oppenheimer] did not hinder the development of the H-Bomb, and there is absolutely nothing in his evidence to show that he did. . . . If his opposition to the H-Bomb caused any people not to work on it, it was because of his intellectual prominence and influence over scientific people and not because of any subversive tendencies.

He ended with a strong personal statement. 'I personally think that our failure to clear Dr Oppenheimer will be a black mark on the escutcheon of our country.'

Two weeks later, General Nichols, the AEC General Manager, passed on to the Commissioners the Gray Board's findings, together with his own unfavourable recommendations in which he had elevated Oppenheimer's two versions of the Chevalier incident to 'criminal *** dishonest *** conduct'.[1] It was also his assertion that Oppenheimer's original story on the Chevalier incident was the factual one; the revised version, the lie.

In those intervening weeks, a running battle to gain some advantage in the arena of public opinion was developing. On 1 June Garrison had sent a copy of the Gray Board's findings along with his own letter of refutation to the press. The following Sunday, the continuously nervous Strauss called in 'Scottie' Reston for an 'exclusive' on the Oppenheimer case.

During the following week, both sides made available more and more documents, but that Friday an accident of sorts played right into Strauss's hands. AEC Commissioner Eugene Zuckert left secret documents relating to the hearing findings on the train taking him out to Connecticut for the weekend. It could have fallen into anyone's possession.

An emergency meeting was called by Strauss for that Saturday night. At that meeting Strauss stated that the Gray Board was now obviously compromised and that it was essential that the entire transcript be made available to the press as soon as possible. Even though the offending secret documents turned up that night in the lost-and-found department of Boston's South Station, this decision was still upheld by four votes to one at another meeting of the Commissioners on the Monday. This was in spite of Gordon Gray's promise to each witness that the AEC would 'not take the initiative' in publishing the hearing.

The reason for Strauss's move seems to have been the success of

[1] These asterisks appear in the original published document. They normally denote material censored for security reasons.

*The AEC Commissioners who voted to deny Oppenheimer his security clearance. They are (l to r) Thomas Murray, Eugene Zuckert, Joseph Campbell, and the Chairman, Lewis Strauss*

Oppenheimer's camp in getting his point of view across to the press during the previous week. Also, Strauss had seen the internal revolution he had been expecting for months now fast becoming a reality. Just before the weekend, 158 scientists at Los Alamos had protested at the Board's treatment of Oppenheimer. It was possible that their protest might turn into a strike. Therefore on 15 June the transcript of the hearing was made public.

Throughout the four weeks of the hearing the AEC's Commissioners had followed the event closely through the daily transcripts. Now the findings and General Nichols' opinion were before them awaiting their judgement.

Those punters assessing the chances for Oppenheimer saw some hope in the political complexion of the Commission. Three were Democrats, who might have less of a vested interest than the two Republicans in the present campaign to rid the government of Communists. Only one of them, however, was a scientist – Henry De Wolf Smyth. Smyth was a professor of physics at Princeton who, after the war had produced the Smyth Report – an unclassified account of the building of the Atomic Bomb. He had known Oppenheimer for more than ten years but did not particularly like him. He was one of those who thought Oppenheimer was a poseur, a player with language and a player of one-upmanship games. These feelings, however, were not of the kind that should have affected his judgement in an issue as important as the one he was now being called upon to judge.

The Commissioners had to produce their decision speedily – by the end of June. It was then that Oppenheimer's consultancy ran out and paradoxically not only ended his involvement with the Commission's affairs anyway but also rendered its report invalid. To help him absorb the immense amount of material available, Smyth managed to recruit two aides from within the AEC. One of them, Philip Farley, had been working for Nichols and when Smyth had requested his services, Nichols had made it very clear what would happen to Farley's career if he chose to take on this assignment. Farley took the assignment nonetheless.

Smyth and his two assistants had to wade through a stack of investigative reports and the Gray Board transcript itself which was nearly four feet high. At the end of it there was no doubt where the sympathies of all three men lay – with a vote to clear Oppenheimer.

However, at a meeting of the Commissioners on 22 June, Smyth was shocked and depressed to find that he alone amongst the Commissioners intended to vote to reinstate the scientist's clearance. Thinking back, Smyth did not dismiss the possibility of Strauss having bribed some of his fellow commissioners. He even began seriously to wonder whether certain oblique offers of jobs Strauss had made, and several lunches that he had treated him to, were not aimed at buying his vote as well. Certainly he felt very much under threat as he and the two AEC men worked to produce a draft of his minority opinion.

But then he found that the text of the majority report kept changing and each time he was forced to rewrite his own opinion. On the final attempt he was given less than twelve hours to produce his modification – twelve hours that meant working through the night. As the three men worked away, they could see a lone car parked out in the street, its occupants watching the house. Such was the atmosphere of threat and suspicion under which Henry Smyth produced his minority report. At one point, in the early morning hours, Smyth turned to his assistants. 'You know it's funny I should be going to all this trouble for Oppenheimer,' he said, 'I don't even like the guy much'.

At four p.m. the following afternoon, 29 June, the Commissioners' opinions were handed to the press. There was less than thirty-six hours to go before Oppenheimer's contract with the AEC expired. The opinions had an all too familiar ring about them. Commissioner Strauss and his two colleagues, Murray and Zuckert, found against Oppenheimer because of his fundamental character defects (he lied) and because of his associations (Chevalier). One other Commissioner, Thomas Murray, produced an opinion which was fervid in its hatred and fear of 'the Communist conspiracy' and he came to the firm conclusion that Oppenheimer was actually disloyal. Smyth was the lone voice in Oppenheimer's favour.

The only question being determined by the Atomic Energy Commission [Smyth wrote] is whether there is a possibility that Dr Oppenheimer will intentionally or unintentionally reveal secret information to persons who should not have it. To me, that is what is meant within our security system by the term security risk. . . . In my opinion, the most important evidence in this regard is the fact that there is no indication in the entire record that Dr Oppenheimer has ever divulged any secret information. . . . For much of the last eleven years, he has been under actual surveillance ... This professional review of [Oppenheimer's] actions has been supplemented by enthusiastic amateur help from powerful personal enemies.

The point was made but the battle was lost. Oppenheimer did not regain his 'Q' clearance. Later in Princeton, Oppenheimer thanked Smyth for his vote.

'I must admit I find it hard to get over the whole thing', Smyth said. 'I never expect to get over it', Oppenheimer replied.


On 30 June, 1954, the day after the AEC's decision appeared in the press, Kitty and Oppenheimer met with Lloyd Garrison.

It was decided to prepare a detailed critique of the AEC verdict for publication at some later date, but that was all that was left for them to do.

He never went out of his way to thank us at all although we were doing all this without fee and at vast personal cost [says Garrison]. I sometimes think that he may well have thought that I wasn't adequate for the occasion. Never a word of that was suggested to me, but he might well have felt that.

As Garrison has described it, 'our professional relationship with Robert dwindled to its melancholy end.'

Elsewhere a victorious Lewis Strauss, much encouraged by a press reaction largely favourable to the AEC decision, went one stage further in his personal fight with Oppenheimer.

On 7 July, Strauss told Liaison Agent Charlie Bates that he had met with the Chairman of the Trustees at the Institute for Advanced Study at Princeton, who had stated

that he desired to call a meeting of the Board of Trustees for some time in July and if Oppenheimer would not submit his resignation, it would be requested. Strauss discussed the matter further with the Chairman of the Board and it was decided that this meeting should be put off until early fall, since, if Oppenheimer were requested to resign now, it would appear that this was a direct result of a personal vindictiveness on the part of Strauss. Strauss commented that of the 13 members of the Board of Trustees, 8 of them would vote to oust Oppenheimer from his position at the Institute.

In the same report, Strauss told Bates about a recent meeting he had had with Lord Cherwell, the Chairman of Britain's Atomic Energy Authority, when he visited the USA. There had been a report that Oppenheimer might be offered a post at a British university and Strauss had warned Cherwell that this could quite possibly lead to another Pontecorvo case. 'As a result,' the report went on, 'he [Lord Cherwell] told Strauss that he would look into the matter and make sure that no such invitation was extended to Oppenheimer.'

Not satisfied with having helped to ruin Oppenheimer's political career, Strauss was now doing all he could to destroy his academic career. It is very difficult to see any reason for his actions other than personal vindictiveness.

In mid-July, Robert and Kitty set off for a holiday in the Virgin Islands, but before he left, Oppenheimer made quite sure that Hoover knew of his plans

*Oppenheimer on holiday with his family*

and that he would be sailing in and around the 'US Virgin Islands'. It seems that Oppenheimer might almost have been taunting Hoover, but if that was the case then he would have been surprised to know that the FBI had been concerned about the possibility of his defecting since before the hearing. At one time they even considered removing his passport.

But while Oppenheimer was on his sailing holiday, the FBI got hold of an alarming rumour, which prompted Hoover to send an urgent request for help to the CIA. According to his report to the director of the CIA, an informant working for the Soviets in Paris had reported 'that the Soviet secret service has established contact with Dr J. Robert Oppenheimer in order to arrange Oppenheimer's defection to the Soviets. The Soviet informant did not know Oppenheimer's intentions concerning this matter, nor did he know to what extent Oppenheimer was aware of the purpose of the contact that was reportedly made with him.'

Hoover was obviously very concerned that Oppenheimer's exact where-abouts were not known in the Virgin Islands and asked the CIA to give the matter their 'urgent attention'. Nearly a month later in late August, the FBI

received information from a second French source, this time from an agent in the French Atomic Energy Commission which seemed to confirm the Soviet intention to have Oppenheimer defect.

According to our informant [the report reads], the agent reports that 'Operation Oppenheimer' has been scheduled for September 1954. According to the plan Oppenheimer will first travel to England, from England he will travel to France, and while in France he will vanish into Soviet hands. According to our informant the agent furnished no information as to the manner in which Oppenheimer will be 'spirited' out of France and behind the 'Iron Curtain'.

Two days later, however, 27 August, Oppenheimer returned from his holiday in the Virgin Islands. When he and his family flew into New York, a team of FBI agents were waiting for him and he was immediately taken into a side room to be questioned. The cue for the interrogation was a short piece in a newspaper column which leaked that a scientist holidaying in the Virgin

J. ROBERT OPPENHEIMER

Islands had been approached by the Russians.

He [Oppenheimer] stated there was absolutely no truth in it if the scientist in question was supposed to be he [the FBI interview team reported]. He categorically stated he had not been offered sanctuary by representatives of any country. He said that while he thought the Russians were damn fools, he didn't think they were foolish enough to approach him with such an offer. He stated that if such ever did happen, he would notify the FBI.

Whereupon he was followed by another team of agents as his chauffeur-driven station wagon took him down the New Jersey turnpike to Princeton. Within days his phone was tapped and he was under regular physical surveillance yet again. But there was nothing more reported about 'Operation Oppenheimer'. It could be that the timely intervention by the FBI had scotched any plans there were in their infancy, or it could be that the whole matter had been a wild goose chase. Whichever is true, Oppenheimer remained safely in Princeton, preparing for the forthcoming academic year.

# CHAPTER 20  THE FINAL YEARS

It was Edward Teller who remarked that Oppenheimer had a martyr complex. Perhaps this was a less than charitable remark by an anxious man but certainly there was a remarkable confluence of circumstance and talent to produce that image which later grew into a legend. His soft reflective voice, the tall gaunt figure crowned with the cropped iron grey hair, meant that physically he was ideally suited to the part. His case history was rich in the ingredients necessary for the construction of a legend and Oppenheimer himself seemed happy to adapt to the role.

An indication of how he impressed people in those years comes from the author John Mason Brown who creates a vivid picture of him in his book *Through those Men*:

*Oppenheimer after the hearing. It had noticeably aged him*

The power of his personality is the stronger because of the fragility of his person. When he speaks he seems to grow, since the eagerness of his mind so affirms itself that the smallness of his body is forgotten. His tiny hands and fingers are bird-like and as he talks, when not gesturing with his horn-rimmed glasses, he emphasises his leanness by being apt to encircle his right elbow or forearm with his left hand, or stroke his scrawny gobbler neck with it.

As to the impact of the hearing, Brown wrote:

. . . the hearing abides in the Oppenheimer home as a permanent resident. In Kitty's blood it continues to boil, an understandable source of indignation. Oppenheimer has tried to put it behind him, explaining in a phrase large in spirit and Biblical phrasing, 'I cannot sit with anger'.

When Brown put it to him that the hearing had been like a dry crucifixion, Oppenheimer had smiled 'the unhappiest of smiles and said, "You know, it wasn't so very dry. I can still feel the warm blood on my hands."'

Certainly for some years he suffered personally from his censure.

As much as anything [said one friend], he was hurt by a sudden realisation that there were people who he had failed to charm, who actively disliked him. I think he had this feeling of being irresistible if he wanted and he actually discovered that there were quite a lot of people who had resisted him quite well.

As immediate reminders of his rejection, he found that an invitation to chair a session in high energy physics at the University of Washington, Seattle, was cancelled. Haakon Chevalier wrote in hurt tones of his friend's duplicity.

Now I learn that eleven years ago [he wrote], according to your own admission, you wove an elaborate fabric of lies about me of the most gravely compromising nature. . . .

During all those years that story, without my knowing it, has hounded me, plagued and blocked me and played untold havoc with my career and my life.

Apart from occasional formal letters between them, this letter marked the end of their friendship. In the ensuing years the embittered Chevalier was to write both a factual and fictional account based on their relationship.

But if certain private relationships were permanently damaged the public storm soon blew over and Strauss was not successful in his quest for Oppenheimer's resignation. With his re-election as Director of the Institute of Advanced Studies at Princeton, in October 1954, the FBI at last felt it politic to withdraw its full-time surveillance of him. At the same time, the Princeton authorities decided to establish a guest house at the Institute for the use of Oppenheimer's visitors and this seemed as much as anything to presage his future for the next ten years. He was to become a much-travelled and much-visited celebrity, almost, it seems, a landmark on the map of intellectual tourism; a person whom everyone wanted to meet and to have spoken with.

Staying at Princeton, it was inevitable that Oppenheimer would have to come to terms with Strauss and, just after his reappointment as director, Strauss appeared in Oppenheimer's office and had himself announced. Oppenheimer emerged from his inner office, hand outstretched. 'Lewis . . .' he said as if greeting a much-missed colleague. 'Robert . . .' Strauss beamed back. An onlooker in the room who witnessed this reunion thought that if a match were lit the whole place would have exploded.

Now that the call no longer went out from Washington for his services, he had more time to spend on his administrative duties at the Institute and again found that there were those who were not totally taken in by his air of martyrdom. In particular Oppenheimer found himself in dispute with Deane Montgomery, one of the mathematicians on the staff who felt that Oppenheimer favoured physics and philosophy over maths and practical science. People remember shouting matches between the two men.

'I want the best men in the world,' Montgomery demanded.

'I understand this, but we must consider how they will fit in here harmoniously,' replied Oppenheimer.

The argument mounted with Oppenheimer resorting to the strong language he was prone to use when aroused. Montgomery retorted with a barbed reference to Oppenheimer's house, Olden Manor, as 'Bourbon Manor' and Oppenheimer accused him of being arrogant and a gossip.

But the mathematician had a case. Oppenheimer did favour physics. He had brought a strong team of his old students with him from California after the war and had built up the department on that basis. In 1957, two of this team, the Chinese Lee and Yang, were to win the Nobel Prize for their work in quantum mechanics. Oppenheimer admitted that he took a pride just in watching these two walk the grounds of the Institute. Montgomery also had a

*Olden Manor, the Oppenheimers' home at Princeton*

point when he referred to the Oppenheimer home as 'Bourbon Manor'. Both Kitty and Oppenheimer had drunk heavily while at Los Alamos, and the tensions of the past few years had taken their inevitable toll.

Through two FBI reports – of uncertain reliability – it is possible to catch a glimpse of the misery that Oppenheimer had been going through. In early 1955, an informant in the Virgin Islands where the Oppenheimers were again on holiday reported that 'Oppenheimer is drinking very heavily, in fact – to the point of making himself a nuisance.'

Three months later, on 27 May, another report from an agent in the FBI's Newark office reported that 'through confidential sources he had determined that Oppenheimer had returned to Princeton and, under doctor's orders, had been put to bed at home with orders to stay in bed until Tuesday, 31 May. It was indicated that Oppenheimer was approaching nervous exhaustion'.

But Kitty was the one who had been worst affected, as in her case emotional stresses had been compounded by a diseased pancreas which caused her considerable pain and needed continual treatment with drugs. She had continued with her old way of life; she would sit with groups of friends in the late afternoon and evening solemnly drinking.

'I can remember a typical evening at that house,' recalls her sister-in-law Jackie Oppenheimer. 'You would sit in the kitchen, just gossiping and drinking with not a thing to eat. Then about ten o'clock Kitty would throw some eggs and chilli into a pan and, with all that drink, that's all you had.'

Others who went to dinner at the house remember Kitty starting the evening as an agreeable hostess, then slowly as time went by her behaviour and her manners would lapse. Oppenheimer would do all he could to overlook this. 'He knew of Kitty's traits,' said Frank, 'but was unwilling to admit them – again perhaps because he couldn't admit failure.'

The miseries of the years in the early fifties had communicated themselves to the Oppenheimers' two children. Peter had been devoted to his father and at the height of the hearing had chalked on the blackboard in his room:

The American Government is unfair to Acuse [sic] Certain People that I know of being unfair to them. Since this is true, I think that Certain People, and may I say, only Certain People in the US government, should go to HELL.

Yours truly
Certain People

After the hearing, friends describe him as seeming to resent any intrusion on his father's life, any reminder of his banishment from government. He tried to spend as much time as he could with his father though Oppenheimer was still very much an absentee parent, who found it difficult to relate to his children. Still there were Sunday poker games with the family, and occasionally Oppenheimer would relax to watch Perry Mason on television. By the mid-fifties, however, Peter had grown into a painfully shy teenager, and much to his father's distress was not particularly bright at school. He had been sent away to school, to the Quakers' George School in Pennsylvania – because in

Oppenheimer's view Quakers were honourable – but in 1958 things came to a head when Peter failed to gain a place at Princeton. Oppenheimer reacted by refusing to take Peter along with the rest of the family on a two-month European lecture tour. In April, Oppenheimer, Kitty and Toni set off for Paris where Oppenheimer was to be an exchange professor in physics at the Sorbonne, and then to go on to give lectures in Israel, Greece and Belgium. Before the summer term had ended, Peter had come home from George School, vowing that he would never return. A short time afterwards, he set off on a journey west across the country, eventually arriving at Frank's ranch in Colorado where he found a sympathetic ear to his plight.

*Oppenheimer with Kitty and Toni at Orly Airport in 1958 at the beginning of their European tour*

From then on, father and son saw much less of each other. The schism was made worse by the fact that Kitty and Peter had not got on well for years – it was inevitable that Oppenheimer would side with Kitty in any dispute. However, their separation was painful to both Peter and Oppenheimer and on more than one occasion he cut short a holiday at his cottage in the Virgin Islands because he was 'homesick for Peter'.

Increasingly Oppenheimer took to the road, accepting invitations to speak on wide-ranging themes at colleges, at dinners and in foreign countries. Even the University of Washington apologised for cancelling his visit in 1954 and asked him back for the International Congress of Theoretical Physics. The French awarded him the Legion of Honour. Marlene Dietrich called him an outstanding man of his time. One cannot help feeling, however, that, after the unique experience of Los Alamos and his attempts to implement his ideals through the exercise of real power, his forays into well-meaning but loosely conceived meetings and organisations aimed at furthering international understanding in some way must ultimately have been a saddening experience.

In 1960 an invitation came with a difference. He was asked to go to Japan, to Tokyo, by the Japanese Committee for Intellectual Interchange. He was advised not to go for fear of the kind of reception he might get, but he went nevertheless.

At the airport he was met by a clutch of reporters who very quickly homed in on the issue of the bomb. Was he sorry now he made it?

'I do not regret that I had something to do with the technical success of the atomic bomb,' he replied. 'It isn't that I don't feel bad,' he added, 'it is that I don't feel worse tonight than I did last night.'

With the arrival of the Kennedy administration in Washington, Oppenheimer's exile was to ease greatly. The new men in the administration, the liberal intellectuals such as Arthur Schlesinger Jr, McGeorge Bundy and Dean Rusk had, in the past, all learned from him. To them he had been something of a champion.

There were moves made to have him reinstated but they had eventually come to nothing. Then in 1962, at a White House dinner given for Nobel Laureates, Oppenheimer was asked as a guest. During it, he was approached by Glenn Seaborg, by now Chairman of the AEC, and asked whether he would submit to another security hearing, to clear his name. 'Not on your life', Oppenheimer is said to have replied.

So his friends in government had to think of other ways of helping his rehabilitation. One possibility seemed to lie in the annual award given by the AEC, named after Enrico Fermi who had died of cancer shortly after the 1954 hearing. The normal practice was for the AEC to canvass the opinions of a number of scientists for nominations and early in 1963 this is what they did. One person they canvassed was the previous year's winner, Edward Teller, who saw it as a wonderful opportunity to end his differences with Oppenheimer and ease the difficulties of the past ten years. He was one of those who voted for Oppenheimer as the next recipient of the award. Oppenheimer's nomination was approved unanimously by the General Advisory Committee of the AEC, then by the Commission, and in April the White House announced the 1963 award would go to Oppenheimer.

Oppenheimer himself was delighted. He issued an immediate statement. 'Most of us look to the good opinion of our colleagues, and to the goodwill and the confidence of our Government. I am no exception.'

Some reporters pressed him to say more, but he resisted. 'Look, this isn't the day for me to go shooting my mouth off,' he said to one. 'I don't want to hurt the guys who worked on this.'

There was initially some doubt as to who would present the award. The President had performed the ceremony for both Teller and Hans Bethe, but would he do so for the controversial Oppenheimer? Already there had been some critical reaction to the announcement among Republicans in the Congress. But on 22 November, it was announced that Kennedy would make the presentation himself in little over a week's time. That afternoon, President Kennedy was assassinated in Dallas.

Early the following week, it was announced that Lyndon Johnson would still make the presentation and on the date already fixed, 2 December – twenty-one years to the day after Fermi's pile had gone critical in Chicago. It was also ten years, all but one day, since President Eisenhower had placed a 'blank wall' round Oppenheimer, pending the security hearing.

The presentation was made in the Cabinet Room of the White House in the presence of a number of relatives and old friends. Johnson began by making a short speech. 'One of President Kennedy's most important acts,' he said, 'was to sign this award.' Then 'on behalf of the people of the United States' he presented Oppenheimer with the citation, the medal, and a cheque for $50,000.

For a few moments, Oppenheimer stood, silently reflecting on the situation

Oppenheimer receiving the Fermi Award from President Johnson on 2 December 1963. It was seen by many as an act of rehabilitation but practically nothing had changed. Oppenheimer still did not have security clearance

and the medal and then, turning to Johnson, he said, 'I think it is just possible, Mr President, that it has taken some charity and some courage for you to make this award today. That would seem to me a good augury for all our futures.'

After the ceremony, there was a reception and there the two adversaries, Oppenheimer and Teller, were asked to pose in a handshake of reconciliation. The two men seemed to find little difficulty in obliging, but Kitty's face as she looks on tells another story.

Many people were to comment on the rehabilitation that this award represented, but practically speaking nothing had changed. Robert Oppenheimer was still considered unworthy of being trusted with his country's secrets.

For Oppenheimer the return from exile had a mellowing effect. Those around him saw his arrogance dissolve to be replaced by an irony about himself, and much greater humility and gentleness. Peter, his son, noticed a greater kindness and after their years of alienation they became closer again. One symptom of change he noticed was that his father no longer upstaged people in conversation.

Resigned to the fact that he would no longer achieve power, Oppenheimer tried to work towards a more peaceful world through other means. In this he enlisted the help of Agnes Meyer, the wealthy widow of the one-time owner of the *Washington Post*. He wanted to bring together groups of the world's most notable intellectuals to discuss what the pre-conditions were for a more

OPPOSITE *After the presentation of the Fermi Award at the White House, the two long-time rivals, Oppenheimer and Teller, posed for cameramen in a gesture of reconciliation. In the background is Glenn Seaborg*

THE FINAL YEARS

*Oppenheimer with Nehru at Princeton in 1958. Kitty is seen in the background*

peaceful civilisation and Mrs Meyer was only too happy to loan her home at Mount Kisco, New York, for such a purpose. So in the summer of 1964, the two arranged the first Mount Kisco meeting. The participants were a catholic mixture, including George Kistiakowsky, now himself a government adviser, Dr Morris Carstairs, the Scottish anthropologist, the Swiss philosopher, Miss Jeanne Hirsch and the poet, Robert Lowell.

In the early sessions of the meeting, the participants were encouraged to talk about themselves as frankly as possible, before moving on to judge society generally. It was an attempt by Oppenheimer, the scientist, to assess this particular group, as an instrument of analysis. To encourage the others, he was as open about himself as he had ever been to any but his closest friends.

Up to now [he said] and even more in the days of my almost infinitely prolonged adolescence, I hardly took any action, hardly did anything, or failed to do anything, whether it was a paper on physics, or a lecture, or how I read a book, how I talked to a friend, how I loved, that did not arouse in me a very great sense of revulsion and of wrong.

It turned out to be impossible ... for me to live with anybody else, without understanding that what I saw was only one part of the truth ... and in an attempt to break out and be a reasonable man, I had to realise that my own worries about what I did were valid and were important, but that they were not the whole story, that there must be a complementary way of looking at them, because other people did not see them as I did. And I needed what they saw, needed them.

In the end the meeting, like so many of its kind, was inconclusive, providing a better analysis of existing ills than it did solutions for the future. Oppenheimer's own theme for future meetings was indicative. 'We most of all should try to be experts on the worst among ourselves,' he said at one meeting. Spoken with the conviction and style that Oppenheimer would have given it, it must have sounded like a fundamental truth. Left to stand on its own on the printed page it leads to more uncharitable thoughts about the gap between such finely tuned phrases and any practical action, or about the gap between self-analysis and self-improvement. But no one could deny the good intentions those meetings represented and it must have been encouraging to Oppenheimer to see more planned for the future.

That same year, Oppenheimer returned to Los Alamos – to give a memorial address on Niels Bohr, the physicist, who had died two years previously and who had been one of Oppenheimer's mentors. The auditorium was jammed to the doors when Norris Bradbury, Oppenheimer's successor as director, introduced him as 'Mr Los Alamos', and added that Oppenheimer had built Los Alamos by the sheer force of personality and character. His subsequent sentence was drowned by applause which rippled from the front row, gathered to a deafening roar and a standing ovation. It was a sentimental homecoming, matched only by his return to Berkeley the same year where a crowd of twelve and a half thousand again gave him a rousing ovation. For Oppenheimer these were both deeply affecting moments.

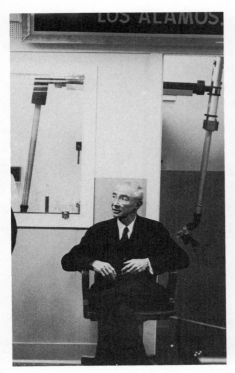

That visit to Los Alamos was to be his last, as his health was failing badly. A bout of pneumonia weakened him further and in 1965 he had to give up the directorship of the Institute, accepting instead Einstein's old post as senior professor of theoretical physics.

That, too, he had to give up after a short time as, in 1966, it was diagnosed that he had throat cancer. Radiation therapy was started on the small lump in his throat, and continued for months. He gave up smoking, taking instead to sucking sugary throat lozenges to ease his sore throat. These in turn exacerbated the problems with his teeth which, due to years of neglect, were in a poor state. Even though the dental treatment he received was extensive he always refused an anaesthetic.

By June he could walk only with the help of a stick and a leg brace, but he still attended a commencement ceremony at Princeton to receive an honorary degree. In the citation he was described as 'physicist and sailor, philosopher and horseman, linguist and cook, lover of fine wine and better poetry.'

In an interview with a magazine reporter, he told an anecdote. It was about a general, who was reviewing his troops after a bitter battle. He stopped in front of one soldier to ask him what he had done during the fighting. 'The soldier,' said Oppenheimer laughing, 'replied "I survived".'

As the year wore on his health deteriorated rapidly. In replies to queries from friends, he was objectively clinical. In October he wrote, 'my cancer is spreading rapidly; thus I am being radiated further, this time with electrons from a betatron.' In November, 'I am much less able to speak and eat now.'

LEFT *Oppenheimer on a return visit to Los Alamos in 1958*

ABOVE *Oppenheimer with his brother Frank (r) at a physics conference in Berkeley in 1966*

THE FINAL YEARS 279

And in mid-February 1967, he wrote, 'I am in some pain . . . my hearing and my speech are very poor.'

A few days later, on the evening of Saturday, 18 February, at the age of sixty-two, Robert Oppenheimer died.

The funeral on 25 February, a bitterly cold day, was attended by people whose associations with Oppenheimer stretched back through every phase of his life.

There was Isidor Rabi, who had remained close to him since their student days in Europe in the twenties – one of the few men who could really tell Oppenheimer what he thought. From his pre-war days in Berkeley there was Robert Serber, who, for years, had been Oppenheimer's right-hand man and confidant. And from his Los Alamos years there was General Leslie Groves, who had flown in a specially chartered plane to attend the service. John Lansdale, the wartime security officer who had supported Oppenheimer at the hearing, flew in from Cleveland to pay his last respects.

The addresses were delivered by George Kennan, Hans Bethe and Henry De Wolf Smyth. The Juillard String Quartet performed two movements from Beethoven's Quartet in C sharp Minor and after that, Kitty and Frank received guests in the Institute library.

Then Oppenheimer's ashes were flown to the Virgin Islands and there they were scattered on the sea.

OPPOSITE *Oppenheimer receiving an honorary degree at Princeton in 1966. He already showed the ravages of his final illness*

# CHAPTER 21 **PERSPECTIVE**

Oppenheimer once commented that he wished that he had been paid a fraction of the money that had been spent on keeping him under surveillance because it would have made him an extremely rich man.

Few people can have been subject to surveillance in such depth and over such a period of time. From 1942 to 1955, with the exception of one or two short spells, Oppenheimer was followed, his phone was tapped, his mail was opened, and his offices and homes were bugged. At various times during that thirteen-year period, alarm bells were sounded and the accumulated evidence was then thoroughly reassessed. On each occasion, it was decided to allow him to continue. Indeed, after the final exhaustive investigation of the Gray Board, it was concluded that, despite the 'most serious view' they took of Oppenheimer's 'earlier involvements', it found in them 'no indication of disloyalty'.

Now that many of the security reports on which the Board based this judgement are available, there are no grounds whatever for disputing this conclusion. All that emerges is the strong possibility that Oppenheimer was more deeply involved in Communist Party activities before the War than he himself was ever prepared to admit. In conversations reported between Communists such as Adelson and Pinsky, they refer to him and to past meetings in such a way that it does suggest that he was more than some kind of dilettante hanger-on. This is backed up by the articles he allegedly wrote for the series *Reports to our Colleagues*. Written in 1940, after both the Soviet–Nazi pact and the Soviet invasion of Finland, these articles are defending the Communist Party. However, they are fighting to preserve the liberalising role of the Party rather than defending its links with the Soviet Union. In effect, they are saying 'stay with the Party in spite of Russia, not because of it'. At the same time there is Haakon Chevalier's assertion that Oppenheimer was a member of a Communist cell.

However there is no evidence that his connections with the party survived beyond the early months of 1942. Indeed, while the conversations reported by the FBI between Steve Nelson and other Communists in October 1942 indicate their interest in Oppenheimer, they also make it clear that Oppenheimer himself was by then inactive. Nevertheless, the security officers with responsibility for the Project took clues such as these seriously and kept Oppenheimer under strict surveillance. Given the immense difficulty in screening for possible security risks, it is entirely reasonable that they should have responded in this way but once surveillance had begun one would have expected more concrete evidence to emerge if Oppenheimer had been a genuine risk. But it did not. Pash and de Silva continued to make allegations which were based largely on circumstantial evidence except that is for Oppenheimer's visit to Jean Tatlock and his tardy and incomplete reporting of the 'Chevalier incident'. These incidents, in particular the 'Chevalier incident', sparked off renewed speculation and led de Silva to propose that Oppenheimer 'was playing a key part in the attempts of the Soviet Union to secure, by espionage, highly secret information which is vital to the security of the United States'. Yet no evidence of such espionage was forthcoming from the CIC (Counter-Intelligence Corps) agents who were shadowing Oppenheimer throughout this period. Indeed once he had extracted Chevalier's name from him, Groves was content to allow Oppenheimer to continue with his work. Thus after assessing all the evidence against him the Gray Board commented 'that Dr Oppenheimer seems to have had a high degree of discretion reflecting an unusual ability to keep to himself vital secrets.'

But surely this is to all intents and purposes a definition of the good security risk? As Commissioner Henry Smyth wrote in his lone dissenting opinion on the case: 'The security [system] . . . is a necessary means to an end. Its sole purpose, apart from the prevention of sabotage, is to protect secrets. If a man protects the secrets he has in his hands and in his head, he has shown essential regard for the security system.'

Yet when the Gray Board came to the issue of the H-bomb, which initially had only been introduced as a test of Oppenheimer's veracity, they looked beyond Henry Smyth's essentially practical definition.

We cannot dismiss the matter of Dr Oppenheimer's relationship to the development of the hydrogen bomb, simply with the finding that his conduct was not motivated by disloyalty, because it is our conclusion that, whatever the motivation, the security interests of the United States were affected.

We believe that, had Dr Oppenheimer given his enthusiastic support to the program, a concerted effort would have been initiated at an earlier date.

In effect the Board was making a political assessment of Oppenheimer's negative attitude towards a particular weapons strategy, which by inference they supported. They were then censuring him because of his effectiveness in making his opinions felt.

In doing so they took the crucial step of making a political evaluation of Oppenheimer's influence on policy rather than considering him as a practical security risk. It was a step fraught with danger as was pointed out by an old colleague of Oppenheimer's in a speech he gave at a meeting of scientists while the hearing was still in progress.

I do not imply that Oppenheimer's advice is always right and should be heeded [Sam Goudsmit said on 30 April 1954], but if advisers, whose strong convictions are occasionally not shared by the administration are called disloyal, differences of opinion, which form the basic strength of democratic rule, would soon be replaced by totalitarian conformity.

In other words, once disloyalty becomes a matter of holding certain opinions rather than carrying out actual acts of espionage, then the whole question of security becomes just another arena in which political feuds can be fought out. There is no doubt that this is what happened in the Oppenheimer case and this is what made it such a travesty of justice. There was no reason why the very real political battle over arms strategy in which Oppenheimer was embroiled should not have been fought out through the normal political channels. Oppenheimer was an appointed consultant. His contract was so near expiring that the Commissioners had to rush through their decision before he passed from their jurisdiction. As a consultant or as chairman of an *advisory* committee he was there to be used as required. As Isidor Rabi put it so pithily during the hearing, 'Here you have a guy who is a consultant. If you don't like the advice he gives, don't consult him. Period.'

But, however much one believes in the infinite capacity of the democratic system to contain and eventually resolve differences of opinion, the maintenance of a security system to preserve a nation's constitution and political ideals and policies is a political act. It is inevitable that those ideals and policies will become the criteria which will be used by security officers in judging a security risk. Take for example the case of Klaus Fuchs. He did attract the attention of security officers in Britain in 1941, before he ever became involved in the Manhattan Project. However, those officers chose to discount a report from the German consul in Bristol that Fuchs had strong left-wing connections. Firstly they thought the consul was a tainted source, but also they believed that Fuchs was likely only to betray secrets to the Russians not to the Germans who were seen as the country's main enemy. In the United States, however, Russia was seen as the much more significant threat from very early on and it was against this background that Oppenheimer and other left-wingers were to be assessed.

It is crucial therefore to keep a country's basic security criteria under continual review. To ask two vital questions: firstly, in order to avoid the system becoming self-perpetuating and self-justifying – is security cost-effective?; secondly, given the State's political value-judgements – security against what?

For example, there are few statistics of any value on the effectiveness of a security system, but there are some which relate to the countrywide Truman loyalty programme which ran between 1947 and 1952. In that period, 4,756,705 individuals were screened. Of that number, only five hundred and sixty were either dismissed or refused employment, and how many of this one-hundredth of one per cent were real risks is not known. Yet in spite of programmes such as these costing billions of dollars, at least eleven individuals who passed a vigilant screening process turned out to be spies.

Further, much of the secret information these security procedures are reputedly designed to protect is less 'keepable' than anyone would imagine. Certainly there is a hard core of strategic information (such as the strength and deployment of a nation's forces) which would be valuable to an enemy, but much of the scientific information regarded as secret will eventually be rediscovered by other people. Oppenheimer was well aware of this when, in 1943, during his interview with Boris Pash, he said, 'My view about this whole damn thing, of course, is that the information we are working on is probably known to all the governments that care to find out. . . .'

So this leads to the next question – security against what? If many of the secrets are not 'keepable' anyway and the system protecting them is expensive and by no means foolproof, then what is being protected? The answer often given is the 'free' world – against Communism. But is this really so?

Before the Second World War, security systems were rudimentary. Governments and armed forces worked on the basic premise that people were trustworthy. Since then, catalysed in large measure by the arms race between the super powers, security systems have blossomed. They have provided a structure for institutionalising suspicion between nations and created cynicism and mistrust between individuals. They are intended to protect the 'free' world against Communism, but instead they can be seen as assisting in the rapid convergence of the two political systems. In 1951, Alan Barth in his book *Loyalty of Free Men* described an 'authoritarian society'.

Any American hearing of a foreign country in which the police were authorised to search out the private lives of law-abiding citizens, in which a government official was authorised to proscribe lawful associations, in which administrative tribunals were authorised to condemn individuals by star-chamber proceedings on the basis of anonymous testimony, for beliefs and associations entailing no criminal conduct, would conclude without hesitation that the country was one in which tyranny prevailed.

In such a country was Oppenheimer 'tried'. His private life was investigated. He belonged to organisations which were then 'proscribed' as unlawful. He was subjected to an 'administrative tribunal' which 'condemned' him 'on the basis of anonymous testimony.' And all in the name of security.

But America is only one of the countries of the 'free' world which conforms to this description of an authoritarian society and this is why the case of J. Robert Oppenheimer is no isolated incident of justice miscarried. It stands as a warning of where our mistrust, not only in others but in ourselves, will lead.

# CHAPTER 22 **POSTSCRIPT**

*Dr Edward Teller*

In the summer of 1954, a few weeks after the AEC's judgement had been made public and the Gray transcript published, Edward and Mici Teller arrived at Los Alamos for a scientific conference. It was the kind of meeting where the scientific meat is sandwiched between ample opportunities for reunions, discussion and socialising. The first of these social events was in the dining room of the central building and as the Tellers were about to sit down Edward saw an old colleague from his wartime Los Alamos days, Bob Christie. Impulsively, Teller left his table and with great bonhomie went over to Christie, hand outstretched. Christie, in what he has described as a 'spontaneous reaction of that moment', looked down at the outstretched hand and turned away.

The effect was as if Teller had been punched. He staggered back to his table to rejoin Mici, trying as hard as he could to sustain his composure, but the shock was too great. He and Mici abruptly left the dinner and returned to their room where Teller broke down and wept.

The ostracising of Edward Teller by his fellow scientists for his part in Oppenheimer's hearing did not end at Los Alamos. Over the next decade, as he travelled round the country, he could never be sure of the reception he would receive.

If a person leaves his country, leaves his continent, leaves his relatives, leaves his friends [Teller has said], the only people he knows are his professional colleagues. If more than ninety per cent of these then come around to consider him an enemy, an outcast, it is bound to have an effect. The truth is it had a profound effect. It affected me, it affected Mici, it even affected her health.

In many ways, no one was more painfully altered by the Oppenheimer case than Edward Teller.

In 1959, five years after he had sat in judgement over Oppenheimer, Lewis Strauss himself was being judged. The US Senate was considering his nomination to be Secretary of Commerce. Normally such nominations went through virtually unchallenged, but Strauss was being confronted by two ex-Los Alamos scientists for abusing his power at the AEC. They cited the Oppenheimer case and two others in which Strauss had used the AEC security programme as a means of dealing with employees who had disagreed with him.

These normally brief hearings went on for a month and Strauss just scraped home with a nine votes to eight verdict in his favour. However, at midnight on 18 June 1959, a full vote of the Senate·resulted in a forty-nine to forty-six vote against Strauss. He was never to become Secretary of Commerce and indeed was not to hold public office again.

Many of the other people caught up in the events surrounding Robert Oppenheimer were as much victims of the times and of their own actions as he was, though their involvement with him did serve to focus attention on them.

Following his 'resignation' from the University of Minnesota in 1949, Oppenheimer's brother Frank sought refuge in Colorado, where he spent several years as a sheep farmer. Throughout the 1950s, he was not secure even here from the activities of the FBI. Periodically they would call at local stores and visit neighbours, to ask about the Oppenheimers' activities. Did they have a radio? Was Frank doing any physics experiments up at the ranch? For almost ten years, this periodic scrutiny continued, then, with the changing political climate in the late fifties, it came to an end.

After seven years of exile, Frank found his way back into teaching again, at the high school in a small township in Colorado. Only in 1959 was he invited to join the department of physics at the University of Colorado, and started to teach physics at college level again.

Some years ago, he and his wife, Jackie, helped to establish a new kind of science museum, the Exploratorium in San Francisco, where a new generation can discover the excitement of science through participation and experimentation. It was here that I interviewed them in September 1978.

What happened to Rossi Lomanitz after his appearance before the House Un-American Activities Committee in 1949 is typical of what occurred to so many of Oppenheimer's students from the 1930s who had strong left-wing sympathies.

The day following his appearance before the Committee, he and Fisk University in Nashville, Tennessee, parted company, and he was to begin his ten years of exile from the establishment.

His ensuing occupations were to include: tarring roofs for the Clint Cook Roofing Company; loading barley bags for the Arrow Bag Company; trimming trees for the Asplundh Tree Expert Company; and bottling hair oil for the Rossman Products Company.

All the time he was dogged by the FBI, who, time and again, turned employers and neighbours against him. He and his wife, Mary, lived in a shack which he had built himself and which was described by one person as a 'hovel on the edge of a swamp' and for four years he continued to pick up what labouring jobs he could.

There is a telling letter from the Conoco oil company in Ponca City to which he had applied for a job and who then wrote to Oppenheimer for a reference. It illustrates the double bind Lomanitz was now in.

Provided . . . his only weakness has been an outspoken belief in the freedom of speech, then because of the position in which he has placed himself [his state of poverty] I am doubtful of the man's ability to do effective work.

Whatever the nature of Oppenheimer's reply, the Conoco manager remained unconvinced and yet another job eluded a physicist who, at twenty-one, had been a group head at the Radiation Laboratory.

Eventually, he moved closer to the University of Oklahoma and took up private tutoring. Then in 1959, he obtained a consultancy with General Electric and a year later he had accepted a college teaching post. After more than ten years, Lomanitz had been accepted back into his profession, but the time he had lost, the most fruitful years of a scientist's life, could never be made up.

For David Bohm, for Bernard Peters, and to a lesser extent, for many others of those past students of Oppenheimer, it was a similar story, of wasted years, exile and disrupted careers.

All of this occurred in the name of security. No doubt the alleged activities of some left-wing individuals tainted that whole group at the Radiation Laboratory at least as far as the security officers were concerned. But how many should have been found guilty for his actions? One of the witnesses before the Gray Board, the banker John J. McCloy, voiced an opinion which raises questions about the whole approach to security.

'We are only secure,' he said, 'if we have the best brains and the best reach of mind in this [nuclear] field.'

The dividing line between what was done in the name of security in the United States in those years, and what was done in exiling talent in the name of anti-semitism in Nazi Germany, is indeed a thin one.


What happened to Oppenheimer's immediate family – Kitty, Peter and Toni?

In her last years, Kitty became a close friend of Robert Serber. There were even rumours that they might marry, but it never came to anything. The two of them were on holiday together in the Virgin Islands in 1972 when Kitty was taken suddenly ill with a recurrence of her abdominal complaint. Within a short time she was dead.

Toni married and divorced. In 1977 after a particularly unhappy affair, she took her own life.

Peter lives with his wife and children on the Perro Caliente ranch among the New Mexico mountains. For a time he worked as a photographer but, in recent years, he has worked as a one-man building contractor. He shuns journalists and will not talk about his parents.

**BIBLIOGRAPHY**
**ACKNOWLEDGEMENTS**
**PICTURE CREDITS**
**INDEX**

# BIBLIOGRAPHY

Blumberg, Stanley A., *Energy and Conflict: The Life and Times of Edward Teller*, G. P. Putnam's Sons, 1976

Brode, Bernice, *Tales of Los Alamos*, published in the bi-weekly *LASL Community News*, Los Alamos, New Mexico, 2 June–22 September 1960

Brown, John Mason, *Through these Men*, Hamish Hamilton, 1956

Chevalier, Haakon, *The Story of a Friendship*, André Deutsch, 1966

Compton, Arthur Holly, *Atomic Quest*, Oxford University Press, 1956

Davis, Nuel Pharr, *Lawrence and Oppenheimer*, Simon and Schuster, 1968; Jonathan Cape, 1969

Frisch, Otto, *What little I remember*, Cambridge University Press, 1979

Groueff, Stephane, *Manhattan Project*, Collins, 1967

Groves, Leslie R., *Now It Can Be Told: the Story of the Manhattan Project*, André Deutsch, 1963

Hewlett, Richard G. and Anderson, Oscar Jr., *The New World, a History of the Atomic Energy Commission, Vols I & II 1939–1946*, Pennsylvania State University Press, 1962

Irving, David, *The Virus House. Germany's Atomic Research and Allied Counter-measures*, William Kimber, 1967

Jette, Eleanor, *Inside Box 1663*, Los Alamos N.M., Los Alamos Historical Society, 1967

Jungk, Robert, *Brighter than a Thousand Suns*, Harcourt Brace Jovanovich, Inc, 1958

Kimball Smith, Alice and Weiner, Charles (Ed.), *Robert Oppenheimer, Letters and Recollections*, Harvard University Press, 1980

Kunetka, James W., *City of Fire. Los Alamos and the Birth of the Atomic Age 1943–1945*, Prentice Hall Inc, 1978

Lamont, Lansing, *Day of Trinity*, Atheneum, 1965

Lifton, Robert Jay, *Death in Life. The Survivors of Hiroshima*, Weidenfeld and Nicolson, 1967

Michelmore, Peter, *The Swift Years*, Dodd, Mead and Company, 1969

Oppenheimer, J. Robert, *Science and the Common Understanding*, BBC Reith Lecture, 1953, Oxford University Press, 1954

Sherwin, Martin J., *A World Destroyed. The Atomic Bomb and the Grand Alliance*, Vintage Books Random House, 1977

Stern, Phillip M. (in collaboration with Harold P. Green), *The Oppenheimer Case: Security on Trial*, Harper & Row, 1969

US Atomic Energy Commission, *In the Matter of J. Robert Oppenheimer, Transcript of Hearing before Personnel Security Board and Texts of Principal Documents and Letters*, MIT Press, 1971

Wilson, Jane (Ed.), *All in Our Time*, The Bulletin of the Atomic Scientists, 1975

# ACKNOWLEDGEMENTS

This book has its origins in the research for the BBC Television series *Oppenheimer*, and in the course of that research I interviewed very nearly fifty of Oppenheimer's former colleagues and friends who gave freely of their time and advice. The insights and reminiscences they provided were invaluable and in particular I am grateful to the following whose interviews are quoted in the book and who, in many cases, also advised on sections of the manuscript: Dr Kenneth Bainbridge, Mrs Priscilla Duffield, Lloyd Garrison, Professor Harold Green, Professor George Kistiakowsky, General Kenneth D. Nichols, Dr and Mrs Frank Oppenheimer, Professor Isidor Rabi, Judge Roger Robb, Professor Edward Teller, Joseph Volpe and Professor Robert Wilson.

During the early stages of research I was greatly assisted by Barbara Mulkin of the public relations office at Los Alamos and I am indebted to her and her colleagues for their help – particularly with the illustrations.

I am also indebted to Dr James Tuck, Dr Robert Serber and Mrs Ulla Frisch who provided photographs from their personal collections and Colonel Boris Pash who provided photographs from his book *The Alsos Mission*: also to Dr W. G. Marley and Professor John Charap for help on the technical aspects of the manuscript.

As a result of the Freedom of Information Act, we have had access to the FBI files on Robert Oppenheimer and I am especially grateful to Caroline Davidson for the expert way she systematically analysed the vast quantity of material contained in those files and also in the files of Oppenheimer's correspondence held in the Library of Congress.

The burden of finding the many illustrations for this book fell upon Katharine Everett and I owe her a particular debt of thanks for the way she has single-handedly assembled such a complete photographic record to complement the text.

My writing of this book has been paralleled by the production of the television series and I have benefited a great deal from the dialogue with the production team. In particular I am indebted to Peter Prince who wrote the series and with whom I researched and discussed so much of the subject matter.

Last, but not least, I am grateful to Rena Butterwick and to Pamela King for their secretarial assistance and to Victoria Huxley and Charles Elton of BBC Publications for the sympathetic way they have edited and presented the manuscript.

# PICTURE CREDITS

# INDEX

Italic figures at end of entries refer to captions to illustrations

298